2025年度版

鹿児島県の
英語科

過 去 問

協同教育研究会 編

協同出版

本書には，鹿児島県の教員採用試験の過去問題
を収録しています。各問題ごとに，以下のように5
段階表記で，難易度，頻出度を示しています。

難 易 度

非常に難しい　☆☆☆☆☆
やや難しい　　☆☆☆☆
普通の難易度　☆☆☆
やや易しい　　☆☆
非常に易しい　☆

頻 出 度

◎　　　ほとんど出題されない
◎◎　　あまり出題されない
◎◎◎　普通の頻出度
◎◎◎◎　よく出題される
◎◎◎◎◎　非常によく出題される

※本書の過去問題における資料，法令文等の取り扱いについて
　本書の過去問題で使用されている資料や法令文の表記や基準は，出題さ
れた当時の内容に準拠しているため，解答・解説も当時のものを使用して
います。ご了承ください。

はじめに～「過去問」シリーズ利用に際して～

　教育を取り巻く環境は変化しつつあり，日本の公教育そのものも，教員免許更新制の廃止やGIGAスクール構想の実現などの改革が進められています。また，現行の学習指導要領では「主体的・対話的で深い学び」を実現するため，指導方法や指導体制の工夫改善により，「個に応じた指導」の充実を図るとともに，コンピュータや情報通信ネットワーク等の情報手段を活用するために必要な環境を整えることが示されています。

　一方で，いじめや体罰，不登校，暴力行為など，教育現場の問題もあいかわらず取り沙汰されており，教員に求められるスキルは，今後さらに高いものになっていくことが予想されます。

　本書の基本構成としては，出題傾向と対策，過去5年間の出題傾向分析表，過去問題，解答および解説を掲載しています。各自治体や教科によって掲載年数をはじめ，「チェックテスト」や「問題演習」を掲載するなど，内容が異なります。

　また原則的には一般受験を対象としております。特別選考等については対応していない場合があります。なお，実際に配布された問題の順番や構成を，編集の都合上，変更している場合があります。あらかじめご了承ください。

　最後に，この「過去問」シリーズは，「参考書」シリーズとの併用を前提に編集されております。参考書で要点整理を行い，過去問で実力試しを行う，セットでの活用をおすすめいたします。

　みなさまが，この書籍を徹底的に活用し，教員採用試験の合格を勝ち取って，教壇に立っていただければ，それはわたくしたちにとって最上の喜びです。

協同教育研究会

C O N T E N T S

第1部 鹿児島県の英語科
　　　　出題傾向分析 ⋯⋯⋯⋯⋯**3**

第2部 鹿児島県の
　　　　教員採用試験実施問題 ⋯⋯⋯⋯⋯**7**

第1部

鹿児島県の
英語科
出題傾向分析

鹿児島県の英語科　傾向と対策

　近年出題されているのは，リスニング問題，文法・語法問題，英作文問題，読解問題であり，すべて中高共通問題になった。配点は大問1から順に，30点，20点，40点，55点，55点。計200点満点である。読解問題と英作文問題の配点が高いので，重点的に学習する必要がある。

　リスニング問題は全10問で，Part1とPart2の各5問ずつである。Part1はダイアローグ，Part2はモノローグである。放送は一度のみであり，質問も問題用紙には印刷されていない。受験の際には解答を選択して直ちに次の問題に集中する切り替えが重要となるであろう。問題用紙には4つの選択肢が印刷されているため，事前に目を通して放送文や質問文の内容を予想し，解答に必要な情報に注意して内容を聞くようにしたい。対策としては，日頃からニュースや映画等で英語を聞く機会を増やし，単語を正確に聞き取る力，読まれるリズムやセンテンス，区切りで意味をつかむ力をつけておくこと，実用英語検定向けのCD教材やTOEIC対策教材などを利用して，問題形式に慣れておくことが有効だろう。

　文法・語法問題は空所補充形式で出題されている。内容は語彙に関するものが多い。英語教育や言語学に関する専門用語の問題も出題される。過去にはスキャニングと呼ばれる読み方の定義を問う問題が出題された。過去問題を解いて問題形式に慣れておくとともに，語彙や文法を復習し，英語教育を中心に基礎的な知識をストックしておくことが必要である。

　英作文問題は，自由英作文の形式で出題されている。内容は，歴史上の人物や教育者の言葉などを題材にして考えを述べるものや，学習指導要領に関して考えを述べるものもある。学習指導要領の内容をよく理解し，我が国の英語教育の方向性等を把握しておくことが必要である。今年度は外国語を学ぶ意義について80語程度で書く問題であった。教育についての自分なりの意見をしっかり持ち，多様なテーマについて語るべき言葉やポイントとなる定型的な表現を持っていることも必要である。

日頃から様々な話題について語数制限を意識しながら，自分の意見をまとめておき，事前に何度も書いて学習しておくことを勧めたい。参考までに，採点基準として①内容・論の展開の適切さ(24点)，②語彙・文法の適切さ(10点)，分量(6点)と示されている。

　読解問題は長文総合読解問題の形式で出題されている。これまでは，英語教育に関するトピックが出題されていたことが多かったが，近年は幅広いトピックの英文が出題されるようになってきた。一般的な教育や英語教育だけに限らず，様々なトピックの英文を普段から読む習慣をつけておくとよいだろう。設問は空欄補充や下線部の箇所について日本語で記述させるものが多く出題されている。解説にあるように，本文の該当箇所を日本語訳すれば解答できる問題や，空欄や下線部の近くに解答のポイントがある問題が中心で，全体的に素直な問題が出題されている。しかし，設問数が多いことから，全ての問題に正答するには，英文のほとんどの箇所を正確に理解できるようにしておくことが求められている。また，本文の内容に関連させて，教育や指導に関する自分の考えを英語で述べる問題が英作文とは別に出題されることもある。日頃から教職についての自分の意見や工夫を頭の中でまとめる，英語教育に関する最新情報を収集する，学習指導要領の配慮事項をまとめるなどして，30語から100語程度の範囲で英文をまとめる学習をしておき，試験場では，時間を有効に使うようにしておこう。

過去5年間の出題傾向分析

●：中学　▲：高校　◎：中高共通

分類	設問形式	2020年度	2021年度	2022年度	2023年度	2024年度
リスニング	内容把握	●	◎	◎	◎	◎
発音・アクセント	発音					
	アクセント					
	文強勢					
文法・語法	空所補充	●	◎	◎	◎	◎
	正誤判断					
	一致語句					
	連立完成					
	その他					
会話文	短文会話					
	長文会話					
文章読解	空所補充	●	◎●▲	◎	◎●▲	◎
	内容一致文	●				
	内容一致語句	●	▲	▲		◎
	内容記述	●	◎●▲	◎	◎●▲	◎
	英文和訳					
	英問英答			●	▲	
	その他	●	◎●▲	◎	◎●▲	◎
英作文	整序					
	和文英訳					
	自由英作	●	◎	◎	◎	◎
	その他					
学習指導要領						

第2部

鹿児島県の
教員採用試験
実施問題

2024年度　実施問題

【中高共通】

【1】聞き取りテスト

　このテストには，[Part 1]と[Part 2]があります。英語はそれぞれ一度ずつ読まれます。設問ごとの間隔は約8秒です。それでは始めます。

[Part 1]　1～5の対話とその対話に関する質問を聞き，答として最も適切なものを次のア～エの中からそれぞれ一つ選び，記号で答えよ。対話と質問はそれぞれ一度放送される。

1　W : Excuse me. How much is this jacket?

　　M : It's 100 dollars, but we are having a sale today. If you have a membership card, you will get a 10% discount. If you don't, you will get a 5% discount.

　　W : Ah, I have one!! I'm lucky. I can get 10% off!!

　　Question (M) : How much will the woman pay for the jacket?

　　ア　$90　　イ　$95　　ウ　$100　　エ　$105

2　(phone ringing)

　　W : Hello, this is IBP Hotel. How can I help you?

　　M : I'd like to reserve a single room for this weekend.

　　W : OK. How many nights are you going to stay?

　　M : Just Saturday night.

　　W : OK. Just a minute, please. (pause) We have only one room for smoking. Will that be OK?

　　M : Hmm... I have no other choice but to stay.

　　Question (W) : What will the man do next?

　　ア　Find a non-smoking room.　　イ　Cancel the reserved room.
　　ウ　Book the smoking room.　　エ　Call another hotel.

8

3 W : Hey, look at this credit card bill. We're spending too much on subscriptions.

M : Wow! It's about 10,000 yen a month! I just realize that!

W : Don't you think they cost a lot? Why don't we cancel some of them?

M : Yes, let's.

Question (W) : How did the man respond to the woman's suggestion?

ア   He agreed to it.

イ   He disagreed to it.

ウ   He changed the subject.

エ   He didn't understand what she meant.

4 M : I know you're interested in Japanese history like me.

W : Yes, John. I like watching weekly drama series about Japanese history.

M : So, how about visiting Aichi Prefecture in August? Aichi is a prefecture full of history.

W : That's a great idea!! I want to visit Okazaki Castle, because *Tokugawa Ieyasu* was born there. Also, we can go to some other historical spots like Atsuta Shrine.

M : I see. Well, if we have time, let's enjoy some delicious local food such as *misokatsu*.

W : Sounds good. I can't wait!!

Question (M) : What is the main purpose of their visiting Aichi?

ア   To attend events at a shrine.

イ   To watch weekly drama series.

ウ   To eat local food.

エ   To enjoy some historical sites.

5　W : Hey, you look tired.

M : I am. Driving makes me exhausted.

W : Really? Why is that?

M : Traffic has been bad lately. It's been taking me twice as long to go to work.

W : Ugh, that's frustrating. Have you tried taking a different route?

M : Yeah, but it doesn't seem to make any difference.

W : Maybe you can use public transportation.

Question (W) : Why is the man tired?

ア　Because he is in trouble at work.

イ　Because he has a hard time commuting.

ウ　Because he gets on a crowded train.

エ　Because he takes another way to his office.

[Part 2]　6〜10の英文とその英文に関する質問を聞き，答として最も適切なものを次のア〜エの中からそれぞれ一つ選び，記号で答えよ。英文と質問はそれぞれ一度ずつ放送される。

6　A newspaper says that since the outbreak of the new coronavirus, sales of spices and seasonings made with garlic have increased in Japan. This is partly because of the perceived health benefits of garlic, as well as the fact that people are less concerned about the smell after eating. In fact, some consumers even say that they spend more time at home these days and don't mind the garlic smell while wearing masks. According to some data, sales of garlic spices and seasonings in 2022 reached around 8.7 billion yen, which is 1.3 times higher than before the COVID-19 pandemic.

Question (M) : What is the main topic of this passage?

ア　The reason for the increase in sales of garlic spices and seasonings.

イ　The impact of the COVID-19 pandemic on health conditions.

ウ　The types of garlic spices and seasonings that are popular.

エ　The amount of money spent on garlic spices and seasonings.

7　A major Japanese conveyor-belt sushi chain has announced that it plans to produce "sustainable aviation fuel" (SAF) from the cooking oil used in its restaurants. SAF is a type of jet fuel that can be made from sustainable sources. The sushi chain is working with a company that recycles waste cooking oil, and they aim to start supplying domestic airlines with the product by 2025. This is the first time a major restaurant chain in Japan has undertaken such an initiative on a national scale.

Question (W) : Which is true about this passage?

ア　The restaurant chain plans to make fuel for airplanes from waste oil.

イ　The restaurant chain is competing with a waste cooking oil recycling firm.

ウ　It is usual for international airlines to make use of SAF for their flight.

エ　It is common practice for major Japanese restaurant chains to produce SAF.

8　According to a new study, listening to music or playing an instrument can delay cognitive decline as we age. The researchers followed over 100 retired people who had never practiced music before. They were enrolled in piano and music awareness training for six months, which resulted in an increase in working memory performance by 6% in the piano playing group.

Question (M) : What is the main topic of this passage?

ア　Senior citizens can enjoy their jobs by performing music.

イ　Senior citizens have difficulty in playing musical instruments.

ウ　Music has turned out to be irrelevant to cognitive impairment.

エ　Music can slow down the decline in cognitive function.

9　A UK supermarket is removing best-before dates from nearly 500 fresh food products in an effort to reduce food waste. The supermarket is removing the dates on packaged fruits and vegetables, including lettuce, cucumbers and peppers, to encourage customers to use their own judgement about when the food has gone bad. According to the retailer, this movement is expected to cut food waste by preventing people from throwing away products that we can still eat.

Question (W) : Which would be the best title for this passage?

ア　Removal of fresh food products

イ　Popularity of fresh food products

ウ　Recycling of food waste

エ　Effort against food waste

10　An invasive species is a creature that is not native or indigenous to a particular area. Invasive species can cause significant economic and environmental harm to the new area. Some species are intentionally introduced to a new area as a form of pest control, but this can lead to unexpected results. For example, in 1949, five cats were brought to Marion Island in the southern Indian Ocean, to control the mouse population. However, by 1977, about 3,400 cats were living on the island, endangering the local bird population.

Question (M) : Which is NOT mentioned in this passage?

ア　The definition of invasive species.

イ　The benefits of controlling invasive species population.

ウ　The unintended consequences of introducing invasive species.

エ　The example of cats being introduced to an island.

以上で聞き取りテストを終わります。次の問題に進みなさい。

(☆☆○○○○)

【2】次の各文の(　　)に入る最も適切なものを以下のア〜エの中からそれぞれ一つ選び，記号で答えよ。

1　He can speak English well, because he is (　　) online learning to talk with foreigners.

　　ア　making fun of　　イ　running short of　　ウ　coming out of

　　エ　taking advantage of

2　I tried to solve this question, but I couldn't. It was (　　) me.

　　ア　beside　　イ　before　　ウ　beyond　　エ　behind

3　It is important for teachers to guide students in a long-term (　　) for their future.

　　ア　perspective　　イ　habitat　　ウ　opponent　　エ　experiment

4　(　　) the lottery then, I could travel around the world now.

　　ア　If I won　　イ　Had I won　　ウ　I had won

　　エ　Should I win

5　(　　) is the method of teaching English as a foreign language to non-native English speakers.

　　ア　CEFR　　イ　TESL　　ウ　CLIL　　エ　TEFL

（☆☆☆○○○）

【3】コミュニケーションにおいて人工知能(AI)の活用が進む中，外国語を学ぶ意義について，あなたの考えを80語程度の英語で書け。なお，使用した語数を記入すること。

（☆☆☆☆○○○）

【4】次の英文を読んで，以下の問に答えよ。

　　Children are heartily encouraged to read in their early years of school. However, once students have mastered this skill and they move from learning to read, to reading to learn, the role of pleasure in the activity can be forgotten.

　　If reading is just seen as a tool for learning, the will to read may not be fostered in young people. Recreational book reading involves (　A　) reading for pleasure, and research suggests that students in Australia and internationally are reading less over time.

Regular recreational book reading is one of the easiest ways for a student to (　B　) developing their literacy skills. The ability to read fluently is by no means the end of development of literacy skills.

Reading for pleasure has been associated with a range of benefits, including achievement across a range of literacy outcomes, with literacy levels linked to advantages for academic and vocational prospects. Regular recreational reading also offers benefits for cognitive stamina and resistance to cognitive decline, the development of empathy and even achievement in other subjects, including mathematics.

While much of the discussion around reading is concerned with skill acquisition, which usually (but not always) occurs during the early years of schooling, there is little focus on ①will acquisition, where students who have developed the skill to read continue to choose to do so.

Students with the skill to read, but without this will, are considered to be aliterate. They exclude themselves from ②the range of benefits conferred by regular reading, perhaps without ever understanding the consequences of their recreational choices.

The West Australian Study in Adolescent Book Reading (WASABR) examined adolescent attitudes to reading and how often they do it, as well as how teachers, schools and parents can contribute to supporting it. The WASABR found that the most common reason for (　C　) reading was related to (　D　) for other recreational activities; the more time spent playing video games and watching TV, the less time spent reading for pleasure.

③Teachers and parents may cool off in encouragement once students have demonstrated that they can read. Research suggests that adolescent aliteracy may be inadvertently perpetuated by withdrawn encouragement from both

14

parents and teachers.

Parents may assume that once the skill of reading has been acquired, their job is complete. They may assume the role of encouraging further literacy development lies with the school.

Teachers may struggle to find time to encourage reading within the demands of a crowded curriculum, which focuses on reading skill, without recognizing the role that reading for pleasure plays in fostering reading skills. The WASABR study sought to provide insight into how teachers and parents can successfully continue to encourage recreational book reading into the teen years.

問1 本文中の(A)に入る最も適切な語を次のア～エの中から一つ選び，記号で答えよ。

 ア necessary イ compulsory ウ voluntary エ intensive

問2 本文中の(B)には英語1語が入る。その語を本文中から抜き出して書け。

問3 下線部①の内容を本文に即して30字程度の日本語で書け。

問4 下線部②について，その例として本文で挙げられているものを次のア～エの中から一つ選び，記号で答えよ。

 ア To understand other people's feelings

 イ To prevent the cognitive decline in other people

 ウ To develop physical strength

 エ To focus on and succeed in one specific subject

問5 本文中の(C)，(D)に入る語の組み合わせとして最も適切なものを次のア～エの中から一つ選び，記号で答えよ。

 ア C：fluent   D：dislike

 イ C：fluent   D：preference

 ウ C：infrequent   D：preference

 エ C：infrequent   D：dislike

問6 下線部③の理由を本文に即して85字程度の日本語で書け。

問7 次の問に対するあなたの考えを，(例)に示されている内容のほか

に三つ英語で書け。

As a teacher, what can you do to encourage students' regular recreational reading in school?

(例)・Show my interest in reading

　　・Teach strategies for choosing books

(☆☆☆☆◎◎◎)

【5】次の英文を読んで，以下の問に答えよ。

Westford, Mass. A group of about 40 sixth graders at Stony Brook School here has been trying to figure out when and where the next earthquake will hit outside of North America. The students researched continental plates and convection currents; they practiced graphing earthquake magnitudes; they looked at case studies in China, Japan and Nepal and considered how people adapt to earthquakes; and, ultimately, they had to write about why they expect the next earthquake to hit when and where they say it will, proving their hypothesis with a well-reasoned argument and evidence.

①This single assignment asks students to master four core disciplines; science, math, history and language arts standards. They are needed for the course for these sixth graders. Their school schedules don't make distinctions among the four core subjects, which are co-taught by two teachers in an (　A　), project-based environment.

Academically, last year's sixth graders performed just as well as their peers on the state math test and placed into advanced math at just about the same rate—②two big concerns for Westford parents. In English language arts, they did even better than their peers, growing more over the course of the year than students in the school's traditional classrooms. Christopher Chew, Stony Brook's principal, believes that's because the project-based assignments constantly require students to support their arguments with evidence, and because the interdisciplinary, collaborative nature of the work demands critical thinking skills. "There is direct instruction that takes place, but the

16

work is being driven by the students' passion and their ability to collaborate with each other," Chew said. "Their ability to communicate has been profound, and the families and the students are quick to reflect that."

The middle school has about 600 students and fewer than 80 are on the sixth and seventh grade project-based learning teams. All of them chose to take part in so Chew hasn't faced any ③pushback from families who don't want to make the shift — and there are plenty who don't. That's fine with Chew. He believes that some students will do better in the project-based learning classroom and others will need the traditional environment. And he says he's confident students will get a good education no matter what classroom they end up in. Still, students and teachers have noticed the differences that project-based learning inspires. "I like that we are expected to do more (B) and take things into our own hands," Meghan Gardner, a seventh grader, said. While some parents didn't want their kids on the project-based learning teams because they feared the experience wouldn't be academically rigorous enough, Meghan feels she may have learned more this year than she would have in a (C) classroom. She thinks she learns better when she's having fun, and also when she has more control over the learning process. "You're learning it more deeply because you're actually the one finding information," she said. "It's not looking in a textbook that just gives it to you."

Teachers say they see this deeper learning. Jennifer Masterson, the sixth-grade math and science teacher, said students get excited when they are given choices about what to research for their projects and how to present their learning. Because the projects all have real-world connections, there are natural audiences beyond the school building for the final products, which makes students take their work more seriously. A driven student will turn in high-quality work for a teacher to grade, but Masterson says that same student will go above and beyond when the work is being sent to outside researchers, community members or organizations around the world. Masterson has been

17

teaching for more than 10 years and says she would not go back to a traditional math-only or science-only classroom. She delights in the heights her students reach now.

An important factor in Stony Brook's success with project-based learning is Chew's support of flexibility. He trusts his teachers' grasp of the standards their students have to learn and he gives them room in the school schedule to design projects that require hours of uninterrupted work time. Teachers can focus more on science on certain days or with certain projects, knowing a later project will focus more on math or language arts standards.

Teachers and administrators are keeping a close eye on student performance, Chew said, carefully making sure students don't face any academic disadvantages of project-based learning. But as the second year of the program is coming to an end, Amity Baldwin, the seventh-grade humanities teacher, sees a lot of positives.

Baldwin, who has taught seventh-grade language arts and social studies for 14 years, believes her students have a stronger grasp of the material they learn. And their understanding goes beyond memorizing facts. "They really are interconnecting the disciplines but also connecting it to the outside world," Baldwin said. "And that's the point."

問1　下線部①を説明した次の日本文の[　あ　]，[　い　]に適切な日本語を書け。

　　地震に関する研究や解析を行い，[　あ　]について仮説を立て，[　い　]という課題。

問2　本文中の（　Ａ　）には英語1語が入る。その語を本文中から抜き出して書け。

問3　下線部②の内容を本文に即して70字程度の日本語で書け。

問4　本文中での下線部③の意味に最も近いものを次のア～エの中から一つ選び，記号で答えよ。

　　ア　agreement　　イ　protection　　ウ　arrangement
　　エ　resistance

18

問5　本文中の(B)，(C)に入る最も適切な語を次のア～ウの中からそれぞれ一つ選び，記号で答えよ。

B：ア　independently　　イ　limitedly　　ウ　passively
C：ア　collaborative　　イ　global　　ウ　traditional

問6　次の問に対する答えを75字程度の日本語で書け。

What does Stony Brook's principal do to make project-based learning succeed?

問7　次は本文を読んだ教師とALTの対話である。(1)，(2)に入る最も適切な語を以下のア～カの中からそれぞれ一つ選び，記号で答えよ。

Teacher : This article is interesting, because it illustrates how project-based learning (1) students' engagement and understanding.

ALT 　　: Yeah. Teachers in this article speak confidently about the teaching method in which students learn by actively engaging in (2).

ア　reality　　イ　separates　　ウ　behavior　　エ　lowers
オ　nature　　カ　boosts

(☆☆☆☆◎◎◎)

解答・解説

【中高共通】

【1】Part 1　1　ア　　2　ウ　　3　ア　　4　エ　　5　イ
　　　Part 2　6　ア　　7　ア　　8　エ　　9　エ　　10　イ

〈解説〉Part1は，男女間で2，3回やり取りされる日常会話を聞いて質問に答えるもの。質問は「男性は次に何をするか」，「男性は女性の提案にどのように応じるだろうか」などから成る。Part2は，100語程度の英文から成るパッセージを聞いて質問に答えるもの。「メインのトピ

ックは何か」や「内容について正しいものを選択せよ」という質問か
ら成る。どちらも選択肢が印刷されているので，話題を予測しながら
問題に臨むこと。特に難しい内容ではないが，放送は1度のみなので
聞き逃さないこと。

【2】1　エ　　2　ウ　　3　ア　　4　イ　　5　エ
〈解説〉1　「外国人と話すためにオンライン学習を活用しているので，彼
は上手に英語を話すことができる」。take advantage of～「～をうまく
利用する」。　2　「私はこの問題を解こうとしたが，できなかった。
それは私の理解を超えていた」。beyond me「理解不能で」。　3　「教師
は生徒の将来を長期的な視点で指導することが重要だ」。perspective
「見通し」。　4　「あのとき宝くじが当たっていたら，今頃は世界中を
旅していただろうに」。仮定法のIfの省略。後ろのSVに倒置が起こる。
If節は仮定法過去完了，主節は仮定法過去。　5　「TEFLとは英語を母
国語としない人々に外国語として英語を教える方法である」。
　ア　CEFR(Common European Framework of Reference for Languages)は
「外国語の学習・教授・評価のためのヨーロッパ言語共通参照枠」の
こと。外国語の運用能力を同一基準で評価する国際標準である。
　イ　TESL(Teaching English as a Second Language)は，「第2言語としての
英語教授法」で，英語圏の国で留学生や移民など英語を母語としない
人々に英語を教えること。　ウ　CLIL(Content and Language Integrated
Learning)は「内容言語統合型学習」のことで，言語と教科内容を同時
に教えることを目的とした指導法のこと。

【3】In human communication, it is essential to tell our ideas and feelings in
our own words. Although we can communicate through the use of AI
technology such as translation apps, I believe that relationships get stronger
through communicating with others without AI. This is because real
communication consists of not only words but also facial expressions, tones
of voice, gestures, etc., which enables us to understand each other better.

Therefore, learning foreign languages is still meaningful in the AI era. (80 words)

〈解説〉採点基準は，①内容・論の展開の適切さ(24点)，②語彙・文法の適切さ(10点)，③分量(6点)となっている。解答例の文意は次の通り。「人間のコミュニケーションでは，自分の考えや感情を自分の言葉で伝えることが不可欠だ。翻訳アプリなどのAI技術を使ってもコミュニケーションはとれるが，AIを介さずに他者とコミュニケーションをとることで人間関係はより強固なものになると思う。なぜなら本当のコミュニケーションは言葉だけでなく，表情や声のトーン，ジェスチャーなどで構成され，それがお互いをより深く理解することを可能にするからだ。したがって，外国語を学ぶことは，AIの時代になっても意味があるのだ」。

【4】問1　ウ　　問2　continue / encourage　　問3　読む技能を身に付けた生徒が読み続けようとする意志を持つこと。(30字)　　問4　ア　問5　ウ　　問6　読む技能の習得後，親は自分たちの役割は終わり，それ以上は学校の役割だと考えるが，教師は読む技能に焦点を置いた過密なカリキュラムの中で，読むことを勧める時間を持てないから。(85字)　　問7　・Talk about books in class　　・Find out what books students are interested in　　・Take students to the library

〈解説〉問1　recreational book reading「娯楽の読書」についての説明となるようにする。「自発的な楽しみのための読書が含まれる」。
問2　日常的な娯楽の読書は，生徒が読み書きの能力発達を(　)する最も簡単な方法のひとつである」。第5段落と第10段落からcontinue「継続する」，第10段落からencourage「奨励する」を抜き出す。
問3　where以下を訳出する。下線部を含む文意は「読書をめぐる議論の多くは，通常(必ずしもそうとは限らないが)学校教育の初期に起こる技能の習得に関するものであるが，読む技能を身につけた生徒がそれを選択し続けるという意志の取得(will acquisition)にはあまり焦点が当てられていない」。　問4　下線部は「日常的な読書によってもたら

されるさまざまな恩恵」。第4段落2文目参照。the development of empathy「感情移入の発達，人の気持ちを思いやれること」からア「他人の感情を理解する」が正しい。　問5　WASABR(West Australian Study in Adolescent Book Reading)の調査結果が述べられている部分。第7段落最終文「ビデオゲームやテレビ視聴に費やす時間が長いほど，楽しみのための読書に費やす時間は少なくなる」から，「WASABRによると，読書頻度が低い最も一般的な理由は，他の娯楽活動への嗜好と関連していたことがわかった」となる。infrequent「めったに起こらない，めずらしい」，preference「好み，優先傾向」。　問6　下線部の文意は「教師や親は(生徒が読めることを示すと)励ましの手を緩めることがある」。親については第9段落「親は読書の技能が身につけば，自分の仕事は終わったと思い込んでいるかもしれない」，教師については第10段落「教師は，多忙なカリキュラムの中で読書を奨励する時間を確保するのに苦労しているかもしれない」参照。　問7　設問は「教師として学校での日常的な娯楽の読書を奨励するために何ができるか」。解答例では「授業で本について話す，生徒が興味のある本を探す，生徒を図書室に連れていく」ことを挙げている。

【5】問1　あ　次の地震が発生する時期と場所　い　論文を書き実証する(論文で論証する)　　問2　interdisciplinary　　問3　課題解決型学習に取り組む児童が，州一斉の数学のテストで同級生と同様の成績を収めたことと，同級生とほとんど同じ速さで高等数学に移行できたこと。(70字)　　問4　エ　　問5　B　ア　　C　ウ　　問6　生徒が学習すべき水準を教師が把握していると信じて，学校のスケジュールの中で，何時間も集中して取り組む必要のある課題を計画する余地を教師に与えている。(74字)　　問7　1　カ　　2　ア
〈解説〉問1　第1段落後半参照。「最終的に生徒たちは，きちんとした論拠とエビデンスで自分たちの仮説を証明しながら，なぜ，次の地震はいつ，どこで発生すると予想するのかを書かなければならなかった」とある。　問2　空所を含む文意は「彼らの学校の授業計画では4教科

(科学，数学，歴史，国語)が区別されておらず，この4教科は，分野を超えたプロジェクトベースの環境で，2人の教師により共同で教えられている」。第3段落から，interdisciplinary「多分野にまたがる」を抜き出す。　問3　下線部の意味は「Westfordの保護者にとっての2つの大きな関心事」。ハイフン前の英文を訳出する。分野を超えたプロジェクトベースの環境で学習した生徒たちの学業結果がどうだったか述べられている。　問4　pushback「反発，抵抗」。　問5　B　この学校で学ぶ第7学年(日本における中学校1年に相当)のMeghan Gardnerのセリフを完成させる。「私はもっと自主的に，自分たちの好きなようにすることが求められているのが好きだ」。independently「自主的に，自由に」。　C　子どもにプロジェクトベースの学習をさせたがらない保護者もいるが，Meghanはプロジェクトベースの学習について，「従来の授業で学ぶよりも多くのことを学べたかもしれないと感じている」。traditional「従来の，伝統的な」。　問6　Stony Brook校の校長はプロジェクトベースの学習を成功させるために何をしているか」。第6段落冒頭に，校長が教師を柔軟にサポートしていることが述べられている。続く2文目に例示されている具体的なサポート法を簡潔にまとめればよい。　問7　教師「この記事はプロジェクトベースの学習がいかに生徒の意欲と理解を高めるかを示しており，興味深い」となる。boost「高める，後押しをする」。ALT「この記事の教師たちは，生徒が現実のことに積極的に関わることで学ぶ教授法について，自信を持って語っている」となる。reality「現実，事実」。

2023年度　実施問題

【中高共通】

【１】聞き取りテスト

　このテストには[Part 1]と[Part 2]があります。英語はそれぞれ一度ずつ読まれます。設問ごとの間隔は約8秒です。それでは始めます。

[Part 1]　1～5の対話とその対話に関する質問を聞き，答として最も適切なものを次のア～エの中からそれぞれ一つ選び，記号で答えよ。対話と質問はそれぞれ一度ずつ放送される。

1　W：Come in, Mr. Williams. Take a seat. What happened?

　　M：When I was on a ladder painting my house, I lost my grip and fell. Now my ankle is twisted, and it hurts.

　　W：Well, it doesn't appear to be broken. It's probably just a sprain. I'll write you a prescription to ease the pain. You should be fine in a week or so.

　　M：Thank you. That was very helpful.

　　W：Take care.

　　Question(M) : What is the woman's occupation?

　　ア　Pharmacist　　イ　Receptionist　　ウ　Painter　　エ　Surgeon

2　M：Mom, we've already bought our'clothes. Let's go to the next place.

　　W：Wait a minute. Dad wanted something for himself, didn't he?

　　M：He did. He said he wanted new socks.

　　W：Okay, I'll get them. Can you go stand in line at the cashier again?

　　M：OK, I will.

　　Question(W) : What is the mother expected to do after this conversation?

　　ア　Ask her husband what he wants.

イ　Get socks for her husband.

ウ　Head to the next shop immediately.

エ　Wait in line at the checkout.

3　W : This pizza looks delicious! Can I have some? Oh no! I dropped it! It was so hot! I really wanted it.

　　M : Don't worry about it. There's the five-second rule!

　　W : What does that mean?

　　M : It is said that when you drop food like cookies, bacteria won't stick to it within 5 seconds.

　　W : But I'm afraid I might have a stomachache, and unlike cookies, pizza has a sticky surface.

　　Question(M) : What is the woman most likely to do after this conversation?

　　ア　Wait for five seconds.

　　イ　Exchange the pizza for cookies.

　　ウ　Pick up the pizza and eat it.

　　エ　Avoid eating the pizza.

4　M : Good job, Momoko! Your performance was much better than usual.

　　W : Thank you, but my hands didn't move smoothly, even though I practiced a lot.

　　M : You've only been playing the piano for eight months. The more experience you have on the stage, the better you will play.

　　W : I see, but my goal is to be able to play without making mistakes like you.

　　Question(M) : What can you understand about the woman from this conversation?

　　ア　She was not satisfied with her performance.

　　イ　She had enough stage experience.

ウ　She played the piano better than the man.

エ　She was not as nervous as she had expected.

5　M : My daughter wants to go to law school, but I just don't have the means to send her to a decent university at the moment.

　　W : Why doesn't she apply for a scholarship? She fits the profile for a recipient, doesn't she?

　　M : I've investigated that avenue. Even a good grant will only partially cover the cost. She'll probably have to work while being a student.

　　W : Your daughter needs to understand this as well.

　　Question(M) : What obstacle does the man's daughter face?

ア　Tuition is very expensive.

イ　She is not eligible for a scholarship.

ウ　Her diploma is not acceptable.

エ　She has been rejected by the law school.

[Part 2]　6～10の英文とその英文に関する質問を聞き，答として最も適切なものを次のア～エの中からそれぞれ一つ選び，記号で答えよ。英文と質問はそれぞれ一度ずつ放送される。

6　This year marks 11 years since the Kyushu Shinkansen line fully opened between Hakata Station and Kagoshima Chuo Station. Many people say that the time it takes to travel between them has been greatly reduced. Some students are able to take the Shinkansen to school without living in a dormitory. Some workers are able to commute between Kumamoto and Kagoshima without moving residences. Couples who live far away from each other, hoping to getting married, are able to meet more frequently. Young people in Kagoshima can go to a concert in Fukuoka and come back in the same day. The bullet train helps us lead happier lives.

　　Question(W): Which of the following is NOT mentioned?

ア　Some students do not have to leave their dormitories.

イ　Some workers can commute to their offices from their houses.

ウ　Couples do not have to give up on their relationship.

エ　Young people can take a day trip to a different prefecture.

7　We can see many colorful tulips in spring. There are two ways of growing tulips. One way is to grow tulips from seeds. This produces flowers of different colors, stem heights, and leaf sizes. It takes about five years to bloom. The other way is to grow tulips from bulbs, which are made under the ground. They produce flowers of the same color and shape as their ancestors. It takes about half a year to bloom. Tulip producers prefer to grow tulips using the latter method because they can anticipate their colors, shapes and sizes. Besides, they can spend less time growing popular tulips for consumers.

Question(M) : Which is NOT true about this passage?

ア　Tulip seeds produce flowers in various colors.

イ　It takes more time to grow tulips from seeds than from bulbs.

ウ　Tulip producers like tulips grown from seeds.

エ　Tulip bulbs bloom flowers of the same colors as their parents.

8　Human beings make and use a lot of plastic. But much of it is not recycled and is discarded as garbage. In fact, the plastic problem has a big influence on our lives. So, we are under great pressure to invent effective ways to increase recycling. Currently, technologies of converting plastic waste into other things are being developed. For example, they can convert the waste into raw material for new plastics, or fuel for running machinery. Recycling all plastic waste may be difficult, but we should make every effort to achieve this goal.

Question(W): Which is the best title for the passage?

ア　The discovery of a new type of plastic

イ　Technological advances in recycling plastic

ウ　How to reduce the amount of plastic use

エ　The importance of giving up the use of plastic

9　The Broadcasting Ethics and Program Improvement Organization of Japan (BPO) expressed its concerns on variety shows that include punishment games and surprise plans, stating, "There is a risk that young people will imitate those who make pain the object of their laughter. One such program broadcasts the state of a comedian left in a hole for six hours while guests in the studio watch and laugh. Even if the punishment is actually approved by the performers, young viewers may not understand that." The committee urged the program producers to be considerate because making a fool of people in pain could be a model for allowing audiences to watch bullying scenes.

Question (M): What is the main message of this passage?

ア　BPO should ban any TV programs about violence.

イ　Laughing at a person's suffering can lead to bullying.

ウ　Young viewers should be more considerate of comedians.

エ　To make people embarrassed is an important element of laughter.

10　According to the National Police Agency, first-graders were most frequently involved in traffic accidents during a five-year period beginning in 2017. Nationwide, 2,522 elementary school students were killed or seriously injured in traffic accidents while walking, 55 of whom died. Most accidents involving first-graders occurred while crossing the street, resulting in the deaths of 14 first-graders. It is important to teach students not to cross the street immediately after the light turns green, and also to check their surroundings carefully.

Question (W) : Which is true about this passage?

ア　In 2017, 55 first-grade students lost their lives while walking across

28

the street.

イ　Children should not start crossing the street as soon as the signal turns green.

ウ　Teaching elementary school students how to cross the street quickly is important.

エ　The number of elementary school children who were killed in traffic accidents was the highest in 2017.

以上で聞き取りテストを終わります。次の問題に進みなさい。

(☆☆☆○○○○○)

【2】次の各文の(　　)に入る最も適切なものを以下のア〜エの中からそれぞれ一つ選び，記号で答えよ。

1　She tried to (　　) her lack of sleep by taking a nap during the day because she didn't set enough sleep.

ア　catch up with　　イ　do away with　　ウ　make up for

エ　go in for

2　Many students had difficulty understanding the sentences, so the teacher tried to (　　) them by using simpler words.

ア　persuade　　イ　paraphrase　　ウ　revive　　エ　divide

3　A: Olivia has been looking for a new apartment for three months, but she hasn't found what she really likes.

B: I'm not surprised. She is very (　　) about where she lives.

ア　ignorant　　イ　optimistic　　ウ　furious　　エ　particular

4　Fossil fuels do not support (　　) very well because they are limited resources that eventually run out.

ア　singularity　　イ　sustainability　　ウ　conformity

エ　temporality

5　(　　) is an approach to learning that emphasizes the students role in the learning process. Rather than the teacher telling students what they need to

29

know, students are encouraged to explore the material, ask questions, and share ideas.

ア　Inquiry-based learning　　イ　Computer-based learning
ウ　Task-based learning　　　エ　Subject-based learning

(☆☆☆☆○○○○)

【3】英語教員として，生徒の「話すこと(やりとり)」の能力を育成するために，授業においてどのような言語活動を行うべきか，80語程度の英語で説明せよ。なお，使用した語数を記入すること。

(☆☆☆☆○○○○)

【4】次の英文を読んで，以下の問に答えよ。

In the middle of a recent Thursday dinner, my 13-year-old daughter, Sasha, had ①a question for my wife and me: Can I skip school tomorrow?

This seemed pretty understandable to me. Middle-schoolers in New York City — and elsewhere — have had it rough the last few years, caught between the pandemic, their fast-changing bodies and emotions, and their parents' unchanging ambitions and expectations. As eighth grade draws to a close, Sasha has handled those pressures well. I could see why she would want a break.

Still, obviously, the answer was no. You can't skip school, my wife, Jean, and I told her. You just can't. Not allowed.

But I offered Sasha a bit of unsolicited advice, too: ②Next time you want to skip school don't tell your parents. Just go. Browse vintage stores, eat your favorite snack, lie on your back in Prospect Park and stare at the clouds. Isn't that the point of skipping school, after all? To hell with permission! That's being a teenager — carving out a private life for yourself under the pressure of the authority figures who surround you.

But when I look at the broader cultural landscape, ③I feel isolated in my permissiveness. Parents — or at least the parents who seem to win media attention ― are freaking out over everything their kids see, read and do. Recently there were the parents who hated "Turning Red," the Disney Pixar movie about a 13-year-old Chinese Canadian girl who rebels against her perfectionist mother, crushing on boys, lying about her club activities and (worst of all) listening to terrible pop music. Those parents complained that the film promoted bad values and that its portrayal of puberty and metaphorical menstruation was just too mature for an impressionable audience.

What's at play here are ④<u>two fundamentally different conceptions of parents' duty to their children</u>, with the same ultimate goal: Do you offer your kids broad exposure to the world, in all its beauty and foulness, and hope they make good decisions? Or do you try to protect them from ideas and activities that you see as dangerous or immoral ― and also hope they make good decisions? Obviously, both approaches involve a leap of faith. And it's impossible to adhere entirely to either philosophy.

I understand the desire to persuade your children to think and live as you do. I mean, who wants his or her children to reject the values, tastes and beliefs they've been brought up in? To pick up ideas, frameworks and plans that we disagree with or even find morally repugnant? I'm surely hoping that Sasha and her 9-year-old sister, Sandy, (A) my footsteps, in one way or another. Ideally, they'll grow up to be globe-trotters who love spicy food, subtly funky fashion and making new friends like me. But as long as they don't end up greedy, selfish or the leader of a fascist personality cult, Jean and I will be (B).

To me, the more hands-off approach is also the more realistic one. It acknowledges that our children are, in some basic sense, beyond our reach: not precious innocents to be culturally cocooned, but thinking, feeling, increasingly independent human beings who are busy making up their own minds. I won't dictate their preferences: I want them to navigate this huge, messy planet on their own, when they're old enough to ― and be ready for things not to go their way.

　Will Sasha skip school? I hope so ─ and I hope not. But if she does, she shouldn't tell me. At least not for another decade. Then we can laugh about it over cocktails.

問1　次の英文が，下線部①に対する筆者の対応となるように，（　a　），（　b　）に適切な英語1語をそれぞれ書け。

　　　When Sasha asked the writer and his wife if she could skip school the next day, they wouldn't (　a　) her do it, although he (　b　) her feelings quite well.

問2　下線部②のように筆者が述べた理由を本文に即して70字程度の日本語で書け。

問3　下線部③の説明として最も適切なものを次のア～エの中から一つ選び，記号で答えよ。

　ア　He tries to force his children to obey his instructions.

　イ　He does not have the right to scold his children.

　ウ　Other parents try to exclude him from their groups.

　エ　Other parents do not want their kids to act freely.

問4　下絲部④の内容を本文に即して70字程度の日本語で書け。

問5　本文中の（　A　），（　B　）に入る語の組み合わせとして最も適切なものを次のア～エの中から一つ選び，記号で答えよ。

　ア　A：avoid　　　B：satisfied

　イ　A：avoid　　　B：disappointed

　ウ　A：follow　　　B：satisfied

　エ　A：follow　　　B：disappointed

問6　次の英文が，筆者の子育て観をまとめたものとなるように，（　a　），（　b　）に適切な英語1語をそれぞれ書け。

　　　His kids are individuals whom he cannot (　a　). He wants them to take (　b　) for determining their own lives.

問7　次の質問に対するあなたの考えを50語程度の英語で書け。ただし，「I think (　　　) is the most important thing.」の空所に，英語を記

32

入して始めること。なお，使用した語数を記入すること(与えられ
た英文は語数に含めない)。

What do *you* think is the most important thing for children to live in this
complicated world?

(☆☆☆☆◎◎◎)

【中学校】

【 1 】次の英文を読んで，以下の問に答えよ。

On Christmas Eve, in the small American town of Bedford Falls, ①<u>George
Bailey is about to take his own life</u>. Bailey, the head of a small savings and
loan association, an upstanding man with a wife and four children, is facing
bankruptcy because his uncle has gambled away all his money. He's standing
on a bridge, about to jump into the river. In the nick of time, an old man falls
into the water and cries for help. Bailey saves him, and the old man tells
Bailey, "I'm an angel." Naturally Bailey doesn't believe him. Instead, he
wishes he'd never been born. The angel grants his wish, transforming Bedford
Falls into the miserable place it would have been if George Bailey had never
existed. When he wakes up again on Christmas Eve, ②<u>George Bailey has
been liberated from his depression</u>. Overjoyed that he's still alive, he runs
down the main street of the snowy town, laughing and shouting "Merry
Christmas! Merry Christmas!"

This tragicomedy, *It's a Wonderful Life*, has since become a Christmas
classic. Less familiar, however, is the strategy the angel uses in the film,
which is called *mental subtraction*. Let's do a quick demonstration. First,
think about how generally happy you are with your life, on a scale from 0
(deeply unhappy) to 10 (ecstatic). Write down your answer.

Close your eyes. Imagine you cannot use your right arm. How does it feel?
How much more difficult is your life? What about eating? Hugging someone?
Now imagine you cannot use your left arm too. No picking anything up, no
touching, no caressing. How does it feel? Finally, imagine you cannot see.

You can still hear, but you'll be unable to see another landscape, never see the faces of your partner, your children, or your friends. Take at least two minutes to "feel" through the situations before reading on.

How happy are you now, after the exercise, with your life? If you're anything like most people, your perception of your own happiness has just skyrocketed. 　　　③　　　 That's the dramatic effect of *mental subtraction.*

Of course, you don't have to pretend you can't use your arms to boost your sense of wellbeing. Just think about how you would feel if you were standing on the edge of a cliff or lying on your deathbed. 　　　④　　　

You may also feel that "gratitude" is a very appropriate emotion given all the lucky coincidences in our lives. There's scarcely a single self-help book that doesn't encourage its readers to reflect on the positives in their lives every night and feel grateful. But there is ⑤a problem with gratitude—habituation. The human brain reacts violently to change but adapts rapidly. This is an advantage when disaster strikes—our grief at being abandoned or injured will fade more swiftly than we think, thanks to habituation. Unfortunately, however, the effects of habituation are not limited to disasters. Six months after we win millions on the lottery, for instance, the effect on our happiness will have disappeared. Because most of the positive aspects of our lives didn't just crop up today but are of long standing, habituation has negated the joy we originally felt about them. Gratitude is an explicit attempt to fight this process by deliberately naming the positive things we have. Sadly, however, we grow accustomed to this tactic too. People who make a mental "gratitude" checklist each evening find it weakens the effect on their wellbeing compared to people who do it less frequently.

Now the good news; *mental subtraction* brings none of these disadvantages. Several studies have shown that *mental subtraction* increases (　⑥A　) significantly more markedly than simply focusing on the (　⑥B　).

Say you're an Olympic athlete and you win a medal. Although you might think silver would make you happier than bronze, a survey of medalists in the 1992 Olympic Games revealed that silver medalists were less happy than bronze medalists. Why? Because silver medalists measured themselves against gold, while bronze medalists measured themselves against ⑦runners-up. However, with *mental subtraction*, you're always comparing yourself against non-medalists — and of course you can substitute "non-medalists" with whatever you like.

All in all, *mental subtraction* is an effective way of tricking your brain into valuing the positive aspects of your life more highly. Since it makes you happy, it also (⑧A) to the *good life*. Instead of thinking about the things you don't yet have, consider how much you'd (⑧B) the things you do have if you didn't have them any longer.

問1 下線部①のような状況になっている理由を本文に即して30字程度の日本語で書け。

問2 下線部②の状況を説明した次の日本文の[あ], [い]に適切な日本語を入れよ。

> ジョージは, [あ]を天使によって見せられ, [い]と気づいたから。

問3 本文中の ③ に入る最も適切なものを次のア〜ウの中から一つ選び, 記号で答えよ。

ア It feels like a ball released from deep underwater.

イ It feels like a stone rolling from the top of a mountain.

ウ It feels like chocolate melting in a warmed bowl.

問4 本文中の ④ に入る最も適切なものを次のア〜ウの中から一つ選び, 記号で答えよ。

ア It is important to think about the past as well as your current situation.

イ It is crucial not to think in the abstract but to really feel the situation.

ウ It is essential to consider ways to overcome the inconveniences in your life.

問5　下線部⑤の内容を説明した次の日本文の[　あ　]～[　う　]にそれぞれ10字程度の日本語を入れよ。

> 感謝における問題点は，脳が[　あ　]にも慣れてしまい，さらに[　い　]という感謝の試み自体にも慣れが生じてしまう。その結果，感謝の念を頻繁に抱こうとする人は，そうでない人よりも[　う　]傾向がある。

問6　本文中の(　⑥A　)，(　⑥B　)に入る最も適切なものを次のア～ウの中からそれぞれ一つ選び，記号で答えよ。

⑥A：ア　happiness　　　イ　wealth　　　ウ　concentration

⑥B：ア　belongings　　　イ　results　　　ウ　positives

問7　下線部⑦と文脈上同じ意味を表す表現を本文中から抜き出せ。

問8　本文中の(　⑧A　)，(　⑧B　)に適切な英語1語をそれぞれ書け。

(☆☆☆◎◎◎)

【高等学校】

【 1 】 Read the following text, and answer the questions.

There is a term: 'KGOY' or 'kids getting older younger', meaning children are more savvy than previous generations. Yet, though many worry that kids may seem to be growing up too quickly, there's also evidence that they could, in fact, be maturing more slowly.

To understand how we measure growing up, it's important to think about what most people mean by "childhood" and "adulthood", (　①A　) In most countries, people are considered adults from the age of 18, but this varies. (　①B　) Definitions of childhood have also varied historically: in the 19th Century, it was common for children under the age of 10 to work, and the idea of being a "teenager" didn't exist until the 1940s. (　①C　)

How, then, do we understand the idea of growing up more quickly — and is it really the case? ②"The basic stages of children's development aren't changing," says Shelley Pasnik, senior vice president of the Center for Children and Technology. "The external world is constantly shifting, but children's cognitive and emotional milestones stay the same."

"What has changed is kids' exposure to information," says Pasnik. Children are now constantly getting what Pasnik calls "media-delivered ideas" — content aimed at adults and viewed mostly over the Internet — much sooner than previous generations.

"There is increased exposure to violent or sexual content at a younger age, which causes a desensitization, because children's brains aren't fully developed," says Dr. Willough Jenkins, a director of psychiatry at Rady Children's Hospital, San Diego. "Part of the exposure is to other people, too. Children can communicate with strangers without supervision, which leads to an increased risk of cyberbullying or adult conversations that they are not equipped to handle."

All of this, says Pasnik, can lead to children confronting adult realities before they are developmentally ready to do so — something that is often interpreted as 'growing up too quickly' . Jenkins is quick to point out, however, that ③technology is neither bad nor good, and that there's plenty of scaremongering around youth's increased access to social media. It's an often cited anecdote that in previous generations parents worried about their children watching TV, and now social media has become the new societal ill for people to fear.

In fact, exposure to content not available to previous generations enables children to independently seek knowledge and to think critically, due to their access to a wider range of sources. For children in remote areas, the ability to find more knowledge and social connections outside their immediate family can be invaluable.

④Technology is far from the only social force affecting how children develop, and at what pace. Over the past few decades, parenting has become more intensive in the US and many other countries, and children today can expect more structured play, extracurricular activities and parental supervision than previous generations.

Today, in an age of low birth-rates and high life-expectancies, children tend to be closer to their parents and grow up in a safer environment, and thus can mature more (⑤A). This means that they aren't pushed towards independence in the same way that children growing up in a fast maturation environment — what previous generations experienced — might be.

The pandemic also seems to be exacerbating this trend. Children stayed at home instead of traveling to attend university and were furloughed from the jobs that offered a first taste of independence. By most traditional measures they were unable to grow up at the rate that ⑥children just a few years ahead of them had done — yet by other measures they were exposed to uncomfortable truths and social responsibilities such as mask-wearing that forced them to confront the adult world more (⑤B).

Viewed one way, children really are growing up more slowly, seemingly kept young by a socially distanced and digital world where their parents are their closest real-life companions. Viewed another way, children are simply showing how it looks to mature in today's world. A broader view of life outside a hometown and local friendship circles given by technology, or an ability to navigate an online world, is just as valid a set of milestones and markers of growing up as drinking, driving, and moving out of the family home.

⑦Getting 'older' might seem more complicated these days, but kids don't know the difference, just as their parents didn't know a life without the Internet of television or telephones — or whatever it was their parents worried was making them grow up too fast or slow.

Q1　Put the following sentences (ア ～ ウ) in the most appropriate blanks from (①A) to (①C).

　ア　Before then, adolescents were simply seen to transition straight from childhood to adulthood.

　イ　Excluding biological measures such as when children hit puberty, our understanding of childhood is largely a social construction.

ウ　In Japan, you are legally a child until you are 18, while in other countries such as Iran, individuals as young as nine years old can be treated as adults in law.

Q2　As for underlined part ②, why does Pasnik say so? Tell the reason <u>in about 40 Japanese letters</u>.

Q3　As for underlined part ③, why is technology not always bad? Tell the reason <u>in about 60 Japanese letters</u>.

Q4　As for underlined part ④, what are the different social forces that affect children's growth speed? Explain <u>in detail in Japanese</u>.

Q5　As for blanks (　⑤A　) and (　⑤B　), fill them with the most appropriate words from the text above.

Q6　As for underlined part ⑥, what were the two specific things that they were able to do? Answer <u>in Japanese</u>.

Q7　The following statement explains the content of underlined part ⑦. Choose the most appropriate words for blanks (　a　)〜(　c　) from the word list (ア〜カ) below.

　There are many factors that (　a　) the rate at which children mature. Our understanding of when childhood ends and adulthood begins is (　b　). Society is not static but constantly evolving. What childhood looks and feels like depends on the times we live in. Ultimately whether one generation grows faster or slower is a matter of (　c　).

ア　identical　　イ　perspective　　ウ　influence

エ　disinterested　　オ　subjective　　カ　maintain

(☆☆☆☆◎◎◎)

39

解答・解説

【中高共通】

【１】Part 1　1　エ　　2　イ　　3　エ　　4　ア　　5　ア

　　　Part 2　6　ア　　7　ウ　　8　イ　　9　イ　　10　イ

〈解説〉Part 1　1　女性の2つ目の発話に着目する。男性のけがに対する見解を示した上で，処方箋を書くと言っている。　　2　男性の2つ目と女性の2つ目の発話に着目する。息子が，父は新しい靴下を欲しがっていたと言っている。それを受けて，母親は靴下を取ってくると答えている。　　3　女性の1つ目の発話と男性の2つ目の発話，そして女性の3つ目の発話に着目する。まず，女性はピザをもらおうとしたところ落としてしまった。それを受けて男性はいわゆる5秒ルールについて説明し，5秒以内なら細菌などが付着しないので大丈夫だと伝える。しかし，女性はおなかをこわすかもしれないと懸念している。

4　女性の1つ目または2つ目のいずれかの発話に着目する。女性の発話の前に男性が女性のことをほめているが，女性は自分の演奏に満足していない返事をしている。　　5　男性の2つ目の発話に着目する。男性の娘はロースクールに進学を希望しているが，よい奨学金をもらえたとしても費用が足りず，働きながら学んでもらわないといけない可能性が高いと述べている。　　Part 2　6　3文目に着目すると，学生寮に住まなくても九州新幹線で学生が通学できると述べられている。

7　9文目に着目すると，チューリップの色，形そして大きさがわかるので，生産者は球根から生産する方を好むと述べられている。

8　5文目と6文目に着目すると，プラスチックごみを原料に転換するための技術が発展途中であること，そしてその具体例が述べられている。　　9　最後の文に着目すると，苦しんでいる人を馬鹿にすることは視聴者にいじめの場面を見せることになるため，BPOが番組プロデューサーに配慮を求めたと述べられている。　　10　最後の文に着目すると，信号が青になった直後に横断するのではなく，周りの状況を確

認するように子どもたちに教えることが重要だと述べられている。

【2】1　ウ　　2　イ　　3　エ　　4　イ　　5　ア
〈解説〉1　空欄を含んだ英文は「十分な睡眠をとれていないので，彼女は日中に昼寝をして睡眠不足を補おうとした」の意である。make up for〜は「〜を補う」の意味である。　2　空欄を含んだ英文は「多くの生徒がその文章を理解するのが難しかったので，教師はより易しい言葉に言い換えようとした」の意である。paraphraseは「言い換える」の意味である。　3　空欄を含んだ英文は「彼女はどこに住むかにとてもこだわる」の意である。particular about「〜に好みがやかましくて，気難しくて」の意味である。その前のAの発話で，Oliviaは新しいアパートを3カ月間も探しているが，気に入ったものが見つからないと述べていることに着目するとよい。　4　空欄を含んだ英文は「いずれはなくなる限られた資源であるため，化石燃料は持続可能性を支えるものではない」の意である。sustainabilityは「持続可能性」の意味である。　5　空欄を含んだ英文は「探究学習は学習過程における生徒の役割を重視する学習アプローチである」の意である。inquiry-based learningは「探究学習」の意味である。

【3】 "Think-Pair-Share" is a good speaking activity in class. In this activity, students think about then discuss the pros and cons of a familial social topic, such as mandatory volunteering. First, students think individually and then share their opinions in English in pairs. Lastly, they share their ideas in groups or with the whole class. After the activity, teachers can provide necessary expressions or feedback on common errors. This is a good activity because it will enable them to communicate more smoothly. (81 words)
〈解説〉「話すこと(やりとり)」の能力を育成するための言語活動としては，解答例にあるように，ペアやグループまたはクラス全員で生徒同士がやりとりをするような活動の具体例を説明すると書きやすいだろう。Think-Pair-Shareでは，「自分で思考する→ペアでの対話活動→シ

ェアリング」というプロセスを経る。まず話す内容を自分で構成し，対話し，グループでの議論へ展開していく。解答例はやや高度な内容である。別解として，対象とする学年や生徒に応じて，やりとりに必要な能力を育成するための基礎的な言語活動なども考えられるだろう。採点基準は「①内容・論の展開の適切さ(24点)」，「②語彙・文法の適切さ(10点)」，「③分量(6点)」となっており，①の配点が高いが，②と③でも得点の4割を占めるため，内容面だけでなく形式面にも留意したい。

【4】問1　a　let　　b　understood　　問2　自分を取り囲む権威的な人々のプレッシャーのもとで，私的な生活を自分自身で作り出すのが十代というものであり，許可など全く必要ないと考えていたから。(72字)　　問3　エ　　問4　自分の子どもに美しいものや汚いもの全てが存在する世界に広く触れさせるという考えと，自分が危険で非道徳だとみなすことから子どもを守るという考え。(71字)　　問5　ウ

問6　a　control　　b　responsibility　　問7　*I think* <u>*critical thinking*</u> *is the most important thing.*　The ability to think critically will protect children from people with ill intentions and help children lead happier lives. Children today live in a world where information floods in from everywhere. If they cannot decide whether it is true or not by themselves, they could be easily deceived. (48 words)

〈解説〉問1　第2パラグラフの1文目と第3パラグラフの1文目に着目する。学校を休みたいと言ったSashaに対して，父である筆者はSashaの考えを非常に理解できると述べている一方で，許可をしなかったのである。問2　下線部では，学校を休みたいときは両親に何も言わずにただ好きに出かければよいと述べられているが，筆者は両親に許可を取ることが不要であると考えている。To hell with permission!「許可なんかくそくらえだ」に着目し，これ以降を和訳しながらまとめればよい。問3　下線部では，筆者が自身の寛容さの中で孤立しているように感じているとあり，他の親とは異なる考え方を持っていることがわかる。

下線部を含んだ文の直後の文に，少なくともメディアの注目を集めるような親は子どもたちの一挙手一投足に敏感になっていると述べられており，ここの言い換えになっているエが適切。　問4　下線部では，子どもに対する親の責任として根本的に異なる2つの考え方があると述べられており，この直後にある2つの疑問文を和訳しながらまとめればよい。2つ目の文がOrで始まっていることもヒントになるだろう。問5　空欄Aについては，このパラグラフの1文目で筆者が，親が子どもたちに自分たちと同じように考えて生きていくように説得したいという願いはよくわかると述べている。そのため，自分の娘たちに自分の歩んだ道をたどってほしいという意味になるfollowが適切である。また，空欄Bについては，空欄を含んだ文の直前の節で，「娘たちが貪欲であったり，自己中心的であったり，もしくは独裁者の性質をもつ狂信的教団のリーダーなどにならない限りは」とあるため，「満足する」を意味するsatisfiedが適切である。　問6　第8パラグラフに着目すると，子どもたちは親が制御するのでもなければ，ただ保護される存在でもなく，自分自身で判断しながら生きていく自立した存在であると述べられている。従って，空欄を含んだ文は「子どもたちは彼が制御できないものである。彼は子どもたちに，自分の人生を決める責任を取ってほしいと考えている」の意になる。　問7　設問は「あなたは，この複雑な世界に暮らすうえで子どもたちに最も必要なものは何だと思うか」。自分自身の考えを書くことが求められているため，英文に書かれている内容に固執する必要はない。解答例では，クリティカルシンキングの重要性について述べている。採点基準は「①内容・論の展開の適切さ(8点)」，「②語彙・文法の適切さ(4点)」，「③分量(3点)」となっている。語彙・文法の適切さおよび分量で得点の5割弱を占めている。内容面だけでなく形式面にも留意すること。

【中学校】

【1】問1　おじがギャンブルで全財産を使い果たし，破産しそうだったから。(30字)　問2　あ　自分が存在しない悲惨な世界　い　今，自分が生きているだけで十分だ　問3　ア　問4　イ　問5　あ　悪いことにも良いこと　い　その慣れに抵抗しよう　う　幸福感が薄れてしまう　問6　⑥A　ア　⑥B　ウ　問7　non-medalists　問8　⑧A　contributes／leads　⑧B　miss

〈解説〉問1　下線部の直後にある文に着目する。Baileyは小さな貯蓄貸付組合の代表を務めているが，叔父がギャンブルでお金を使い果たしてしまったために破産の危機に直面することになり，自殺を考えているのである。　問2　下線部の前後の文に着目する。Baileyは老人の姿の天使を助けて自分が生まれてこなかった世界を望んだところ，天使はその願いを叶えてBaileyがいない世界に変えた。しかし，Baileyはクリスマスイブに再び目を覚ますと，自身がまだ生きていることに喜んで町を走り回ったとある。　問3　空欄部の直前にある文に着目すると，あなたの幸福に関する認識が急上昇したとある。この箇所の言い換えになっているア「水中深くから放たれたボールのようである」が適切である。　問4　空欄部の前にある文に着目すると，幸福感を高めるためには，腕を失ったふりをしなくても，崖の端に立っていたり，死の床に横たわっていたりする状況でどのように感じるかを考えてみるとよいと述べられている。この箇所の言い換えになっているイ「抽象的に考えるのではなく，その状況を感じることが重要である」が適切である。　問5　下線部の後に続く3文で，人間の脳は変化に激しく反応するが，すぐに適応するとあり，それは悪いことだけでなく良いことでも同様であると述べられている。また，同パラグラフの後ろから3文目以降にあるように，感謝は前向きなことを意図的に列挙して強調することによって良いことへの慣れに抵抗することができるが，その試み自体にも慣れが生じてしまい，結果として，感謝のチェックリストを作るような人は幸福感の影響が小さくなることがわかると述べられている。　問6　空欄部を含んだ文の前にある文に着目すると，

44

心の引き算は慣れという短所がないと述べられている。心の引き算は所有しているものがなかったことを想像することによって，それを所有している価値を確認することで幸福感を得ることができる。従って，ただ何かしら良いことだけに焦点を当てるよりも，心の引き算をする方がより幸福感を感じることができるのである。　問7　下線部を含んだ文とその前にある文に着目すると，ある調査では銀メダリストは銅メダリストよりも幸福感が低かったとある。銀メダリストは金メダリストと比較する一方で，銅メダリストは上位の銀メダリストではなく，自身より下位のメダルを逃した選手(runners-up「次点者，入賞者」)と比較したと考えるとよい。　問8　空欄を含んだ第9パラグラフはこの英文全体のまとめになっていることに着目する。問6の解説でも書いた通り，心の引き算は既に所有しているものがなかったことを想像することで，所有しているものの価値を認識する考え方であり，幸せな人生に貢献すると述べられている。

【高等学校】

【1】問1　①A　イ　　①B　ウ　　①C　ア　　問2　外の世界は絶えず変化しているが，子どもたちの認知や感情に関する指標は同じままだから。(42字)　　問3　テクノロジーのおかげで，広い範囲の情報源にアクセスできるため，子どもたちは自主的に知識を求め，批判的思考を身につけられるから。(63字)　　問4　より熱心な子育てや，念入りに構成された遊びや課外活動，親の監督など。

問5　⑤A　slowly　　⑤B　quickly　　問6　・家にいないで，大学に出席するために出かけること。　　・自立の経験を最初に提供してくれる，仕事(アルバイト)をすること。　　問7　a　ウ　　b　オ　　c　イ

〈解説〉問1　それぞれの空欄の直前に着目する。まず，①Aについては，ほとんどの人が「子ども時代」と「大人時代」をどのように捉えているかを考えることが重要であると述べられている。従って，私たちの子ども時代に対する理解は社会の構成によるとするイが適切。次に，

①Bについては，ほとんどの国では18歳からが大人と見なされているが国によって異なると述べられている。従って，日本もほとんどの国と同様に18歳までは法律的に子どもであるが，イランなどでは9歳でも法律上大人になるというウが適切。最後に①Cについては，1940年代まではティーンエイジャーという考えはなかったとあり，それ以前は，思春期は，単に子ども時代から大人時代へのまっすぐな推移であると考えられていたというアが適切。　問2　設問にあるように下線部はPasnikの発話であるので，引用符がついているその次の文The external world…を訳しながらまとめればよい。　問3　下線部では技術自体は良いものでも悪いものでもないと書かれているが，設問では技術の良い面を書くことが求められている。下線部の直後には技術の悪い面の例が書かれており，良い面は第7パラグラフに書かれている。1文目を訳しながらまとめればよい。　問4　設問は「子どもたちの成長速度に影響を及ぼす社会的な力とは何か」。下線部の直後にある文Over the past few decades,…を訳しながらまとめればよい。　問5　まず，⑤Aについては，空欄の直後にある文に着目すると，現代の子どもたちは早く成長する環境にいた前の世代とは同じようには自立が進まないとあるため，より成長が遅いという意味になるslowlyが適切。また，⑤Bについては，空欄の前の文に着目すると，コロナ禍の子どもたちはコロナ禍より前の子どもたちと同じようには成長できていなかった一方で，不快な真実やマスクの着用といった社会的責任を負わされるなどの大人の世界により早く直面することになったのである。

問6　下線部を含んだ文の前にある文に着目する。コロナ禍によって子どもたちができなくなったことが述べられているので，ここをコロナ禍以前の子どもたちができたこととしてまとめればよい。

問7　まず，空欄aについては，関係代名詞のthatの直後なので，ここには動詞が入ることが推測できるため選択肢はウとカに絞られる。あとはこの英文で子どもたちの成長速度が時代や環境で変化していることが述べられていることを踏まえれば，「子どもたちが成長する速度に影響する要因がたくさんある」の意になるinfluenceが適切。次に，

空欄bについては，子ども時代と大人時代の捉え方に関するものである。問1の解説にあるように，その境界線は絶対的なものではなく，時代や国によって異なることから，「主観的」を意味するsubjectiveが適切。最後に，空欄cについては，第11パラグラフに着目する。見方や指標によって子どもたちの成長の速度というのは一定ではないということから，「究極的にはある世代の成長が早いかどうかは見方の問題である」の意になるperspectiveが適切。

2022年度　実施問題

【中高共通】

【１】聞き取りテスト

　このテストには[Part 1]と[Part 2]があります。それぞれの指示に従いなさい。

[Part 1]　1～5の対話とその対話に関する質問を聞き，答として最も適切なものをア～エの中からそれぞれ一つ選び，記号で答えよ。対話と質問はそれぞれ一度ずつ放送される。

1　W : Oh, you're watching the basketball game between Japan and America, Steve.

　　M : Yes. It's so exciting.

　　W : Who's winning?

　　M : Japan is ahead for now. They were losing in the first quarter, but they caught up with America in the second quarter.

　　Question (W) : What is happening in the game?

　　ア　Japan is leading.　　　　　イ　America is ahead.

　　ウ　Japan is calling a time-out.　エ　The players are warming up.

2　M : Austen, thank you for listening to my presentation. How was it?

　　W : It was great, James. I don't think you need to revise it. By the way, can you share the file with me? I've got to go now, but I want to check the references again.

　　M : Sure, I'll email it to you. What's your address?

　　W : My email address is austen, small letters, a, u, s, t, e, n, 6413(sixty-four thirteen)@ABC.com. Thanks. See you tomorrow!

Question (M) : What is the woman's email address?

ア   austen6430@ABC.com   イ   austin6413@ABC.com

ウ   austen6413@ABC.com   エ   austin6430@ABC.com

3   M : You are busy preparing for tomorrow's presentation, right? Shall I
        buy something for dinner?

    W : You're so sweet. But let's have the leftovers from breakfast in the
        fridge.

    M : OK. I'll check. Is there anything else I can do?

    W : Can you do the laundry?

    M : Sure. I'll do it right away.

Question (W): What is the man most likely to do after the conversation?

ア   Go to the supermarket   イ   Cook something for dinner

ウ   Wash the dishes   エ   Wash clothes

4   M : What are you doing, Cathy?

    W : I'm trying to set a password for this website, but I can't.

    M : Let me see... Oh, your password should be between 6 to 10 digits in
        length and contain both capital and small letters, and also numbers.

    W : Really? I didn't know that. I'll try again.

Question (M):   Which password can be set for the website?

ア   K1234   イ   kevinABC

ウ   KEVIN   エ   Kevin123

5   W : Hi, James. I like your new tie. It looks good on you!

    M : Thanks. I had been looking for a tie that would match my suit. I really
        like the color. Most importantly, I got this on sale. It was 70% off.

    W : No way! How lucky are you?

    M : Yes! I decided to buy it immediately.

Question (W) : Why did the man buy the tie?

ア　He really liked the shape of the tie.

イ　He was able to get it cheaper.

ウ　The woman complimented him on it.

エ　The woman thought he was lucky.

[Part 2]　1〜4の英文とその英文に関する質問を聞き，答として最も適切なものをア〜エの中からそれぞれ一つ選び，記号で答えよ。ただし，1〜3については質問が一つ，4については質問が二つある。英文と質問はそれぞれ一度ずつ放送される。

1　The modern Olympic Games, which started in Athens in 1896, were first held in Asia more than half a century ago in 1964. The games were held in Tokyo, where 93 countries participated and medals in 20 events and 163 disciplines were awarded. As the games were broadcast on TV, the final volleyball match between Japan and the Soviet Union achieved the highest audience rating of 85％. The Japanese government declared October 10, the day of the opening ceremony of the Summer Games, as a national holiday to remember this historical event.

Question (M):　What is the theme of this passage?

ア　The first modern Olympic Games in Asia

イ　The description of 1896 Summer Games

ウ　The rise of Japan at the Olympic Games

エ　The popularity of the final volleyball match

2　Nowadays, a café is a place to drink coffee, chat and read, but in the beginning it served as a "literary salon." Le Procope, the first café in Paris, was initially a social gathering place for nobles and artists rather than a place for the general public to relax. As such, it was first used as a theatrical café where theater people gathered. Later, in the latter half of the 18th century, the café, Le Procope, became a literary salon for poets and

50

writers, and then a political salon. Toward the end of the 18th century, revolutionaries gathered there to have a heated discussion, and it became the starting point of the French Revolution.

Question(W) : Which is true about "Le Procope"?

ア　It was the most popular café in Paris.

イ　It was built in a theater in the 18th century.

ウ　The café was named after a famous novelist.

エ　The gatherings there led to the French Revolution.

3　Welcome and thank you so much for shopping at ABC shopping center. May we have your attention, please? Please do not walk while using your smartphone or mobile phone in the store. It is dangerous and may cause you to bump into other customers. If you wish to use your smartphone or mobile phone, please be careful not to obstruct other customers as they shop or pass by. Also please don't let small children play and run around the sales areas, escalators and stairways. We ask for your understanding and cooperation. Thank you.

Question(M) : What is the purpose of the announcement?

ア　To advertise a campaign for smartphones

イ　To tell customers about their business hours

ウ　To inform customers of the rules they must follow

エ　To stimulate customers' purchasing intentions

4　W : This passage will be followed by two questions. Choose the best answer to each question.

　　M : Remote work is a form of work in which employees work at home or at other locations away from the office. The number of companies introducing remote work as part of their work style reforms is increasing every year, because it is easier to balance work with childcare and nursing care. The difference between telecommuting and remote work is the place of work. While remote work covers "any place other than the office," telecommuting only covers the "home." Remote work is considered to be a good match for knowledgeable workers who create intellectual products that add value to companies and society through their specialized knowledge, such as system engineers, designers, writers, salespeople, and customer service representatives. On the other hand, it is difficult to work remotely in industries such as manufacturing, construction, agriculture, fishing, and hospitality, where you need a specific location or equipment to do your job.

Question (W) : No. 1　Why are more companies introducing remote work?

　ア　Companies don't have to pay for commuting.

　イ　We can prevent the spread of infection.

　ウ　It is easier to balance work and family.

　エ　It enables us to be more creative.

Question (W) : No. 2　Which is true about the passaee?

　ア　Telecommuting is different from remote work in terms of the place of work.

　イ　All knowledgeable workers should work remotely.

　ウ　Remote work is being introduced in manufacturing industries.

　エ　Remote work requires a specific location or equipment.

以上で聞き取りテストを終わります。次の問題に進みなさい。

(☆☆☆◎◎◎)

【２】次の各文の(　　)に入る最も適切なものを次のア〜エの中からそれぞれ一つ選び，記号で答えよ。

1　I(　　) some of my old photos when I was clearing out my room.

　ア　brought about　　イ　came across　　ウ　caught up

エ turned on

2　A (　　) is a small, useful, and cleverly-designed machine or tool.

　　ア　broom　　イ　clipper　　ウ　gadget　　エ　threshold

3　If you would only just listen, you (　　) something.

　　ア　might learn　　イ　learn　　ウ　learned　　エ　are learning

4　CEFR is an international (　　) for describing language ability on a six-point scale, from A1 for beginners, up to C2 for those who have mastered a language.

　　ア　conference　　イ　recognition　　ウ　standard　　エ　treaty

5　The Ministry of Education, Culture, Sports, Science and Technology defined (　　) to be fostered in schools in the following three pillars: knowledge and skills, abilities to think, make judgement and express oneself and motivation to learn, and humanity, etc.

　　ア　communication　　イ　compensation　　ウ　competencies

　　エ　curriculum

(☆☆☆○○○○)

【3】英語の「聞くこと」の力を高めるために，どのような授業中の活動が考えられるか。その活動の手順と具体的な効果を明確にして，80語程度の英語で説明せよ。なお，使用した語数を記入すること。

(☆☆☆☆○○○○)

【4】次の英文を読んで，以下の問に答えよ。

　　Underachievement in groups of children in the UK is recognized in international studiest － and successive governments have sought to address the issues in a range of ways. Reading to dogs, so far, has not been among ①them, but it's time to look at the strategy more seriously. Many children naturally enjoy reading and need little encouragement, but if they are struggling, their confidence can quickly diminish － and with it their motivation. This sets in motion ②the destructive cycle whereby reading

53

ability fails to improve. So how can dogs help?

Reading to dogs is just that — encouraging children to read alongside a dog. The practice originated in the US in 1999 with the Reading Education Assistance Dogs scheme and initiatives of this type now extend to a number of countries. The presence of dogs has a calming effect on many people. Many primary schools are becoming increasingly pressurized environments and children generally do not respond well to such pressure. ⌈ あ ⌉ Reading can be a solitary activity, but can also be a pleasurable, shared social event. Children who are struggling to read benefit from the simple pleasure of reading to ③a loyal, loving listener.

Children who are struggling to read, for whatever reason, need to build confidence and rediscover a motivation for reading. A dog is a reassuring, uncritical audience who will not mind if mistakes are made. Children can read to the dog, uninterrupted; comments will not be made. For more experienced or capable readers, they can experiment with intonation and "voices", knowing that the dog will respond positively — and building fluency further develops comprehension in readers. ⌈ い ⌉ For children who are struggling, reconnecting with the pleasure of reading is very important. As Marylyn Jager-Adams, a literacy scholar, noted in a seminal review of beginner reading in the US: "If we want children to learn to read well, we must find a way to induce them to read lots." Reading to a dog can create a helpful balance, supporting literacy activities which may seem less appealing to a child. Children with dyslexia, for example, need focused support to develop their understanding of the alphabetic code (how speech sounds correspond to spelling choices). But this needs to be balanced with activities which support (A) reading and social enjoyment, or the child can become (B).

Breaking a negative cycle will inevitably lead to the creation of a virtuous circle — and sharing a good book with a dog enables children to apply their reading skills in a positive and enjoyable way. However, research evidence in

54

this area is rather limited, despite the growing popularity of the scheme.
う There clearly is more work to do, but interest in reading to dogs
appears to have grown through the evidence of case studies. The example,
often cited in the media, is that of Tony Nevett and his greyhound Danny.
Tony and Danny's involvement in a number of schools has been
transformative, not only in terms of reading but also in promoting general
well-being and positive behavior among children with a diverse range of
needs.

So, reading to dogs could offer ④many benefits. As with any approach or
intervention, it is not a panacea ― but set within a language-rich literacy
environment, there appears to be little to lose and much to gain.

問1　下線部①の説明として最も適切なものを次のア～エの中から一
つ選び，記号で答えよ。

ア　ways to understand feelings of animals

イ　ways to advance students' performance

ウ　ways to build good relationships with dogs

エ　ways to enhance students' reputations

問2　下線部②の内容を本文に即して50字程度の日本語で書け。

問3　下線部③について，次の問に対する答を本文に即して20字程度
の日本語で書け。

Why is a dog a loyal loving listener?

問4　本文中の(　A　)，(　B　)に入る語の組合せとして最も適切なも
のを次のア～エの中から一つ選び，記号で答えよ。

ア　A：dependent　　　B：motivated

イ　A：independent　　B：motivated

ウ　A：dependent　　　B：demotivated

エ　A：independent　　B：demotivated

問5　次の英文が入る最も適切な箇所を　あ　～　う　の中から一
つ選び，記号で答えよ。

A dog, however, creates an environment that immediately feels more relaxed and welcoming.

問6　下線部④について，本文の内容と一致しないものを次のア〜エの中から一つ選び，記号で答えよ。

　ア　affection for small loving animals

　イ　health and happiness in general

　ウ　confidence and motivation for reading

　エ　positive attitudes towards various things

問7　本文のタイトルとして最も適切なものを次のア〜エの中から一つ選び，記号で答えよ。

　ア　Reading to Dogs as a Perfect Learning Method

　イ　How Dogs Could Make Children Better Readers

　ウ　Advantages and Disadvantages of Reading to Dogs

　エ　The Latest Dog Training Method Originated in the US

問8　教師が子供たちに自信を付けさせるための取組として，どのようなことが考えられるか。具体的な取組とその理由を50語程度の英語で書け。ただし，本文と同じ取組は除く。なお，使用した語数を記入すること。

（☆☆☆☆◎◎◎）

【中学校】

【１】次の英文を読んで，以下の問に答えよ。

When you're in a medical emergency, you don't typically think of calling a statistician. However, the COVID-19 outbreak has shown just how necessary a clear understanding and appropriate use of data is to help prevent the spread of disease. One person understood ①this a long time ago. Were she alive today, Florence Nightingale would understand the importance of data in dealing with a public health emergency. Nightingale is renowned for her career in nursing, but less well known for her pioneering work in medical statistics. But it was actually her statistical skills that led to Nightingale saving many more lives.

Nightingale was one of the first female statisticians. She developed an early passion for statistics. As a child she collected shells and supplemented her collection with tables and lists. Nightingale was home-schooled by her father but insisted on learning maths from a mathematician before she trained as a nurse. Upon arriving at the British military hospital in Turkey in 1856, Nightingale was (A) at the hospital's conditions and the lack of clear hospital records. Even the number of deaths was not recorded accurately. She soon discovered three different death registers existed, each giving a completely different account of the deaths among the soldiers. Using her statistical skills, Nightingale set to work to introduce new guidelines on how to record sickness and mortality across military hospitals. This helped her better understand both the numbers and causes of deaths. Now, worldwide,

B

.

The ability to compare datasets from different places is critical to understanding outbreaks. One of the challenges in monitoring the COVID-19 pandemic has been the lack of standardised datasets experts can compare on the number of people infected. This is due to differences in testing rules in different countries. More than 150 years after Nightingale pointed out the need to standardise datasets before comparing them, we are certain she would have something to say about ②this. With her improved data, Nightingale put her statistical skills to use. She discovered deaths due to disease were more than seven times the number of deaths due to combat, because of unsanitary hospital conditions. However, knowing numbers alone have limited persuasive powers, Nightingale used her skills in statistical communication to convince the British parliament of the need to act. She avoided the dry tables used by most statisticians of the time, and instead created graphs to illustrate the impact of hospital and nursing practice reform on army mortality rates. Today, graphs remain one of the most effective ways to understand the effects of health care interventions, including those used to illustrate the effectiveness of physical distancing to curb COVED-19's spread.

Nightingale was engaged in improving public health in many countries, including Australia. She wrote papers on the (　C　) of pavilion-style hospital building designs, which were later incorporated into Australian hospitals. This style consists of small wings, or pavilions, leading off a central corridor — this is convenient for nursing staff and encourages good ventilation. In 1868, Lucy Osburn headed the first team of nurses sent to Australia to establish Nightingale-style nursing. Nightingale never visited Australia herself, but this did not stop her using her usual tactics of requesting data from her wide network of contacts and drawing conclusions from what she found. She was a prolific correspondent — we have more than 12,000 of her letters, and those are only the ones which haven't been burned, lost or otherwise destroyed.

In 1858, Nightingale's achievements in statistics were recognised by the Royal Statistical Society in the UK, when she became the first woman Fellow of the Society. After Nightingale's fellowship, it would be more than 100 years before a woman was elected President of the Royal Statistical Society. As in many STEM (Science, Technology, Engineering and Mathematics) disciplines, female statisticians are still fighting for equal recognition. To date, only two women have received the Statistical Society of Australia's highest honour, the Pitman Medal. But it's clear female statisticians are still making headway. In 2019, five major statistical associations had women presidents. Today, on her 200th birthday, ③Nightingale would have been proud.

問1　下線部①の内容を本文に即して40字程度の日本語で書け。

問2　本文中の(　A　), (　C　)に入る最も適切な語を次のア～ウの中からそれぞれ一つ選び，記号で答えよ。

　　A：　ア　horrified　　　イ　delighted　　　ウ　relieved
　　C：　ア　restrictions　　イ　disadvantages　ウ　benefits

問3　本文中の　　B　　に入る最も適切なものを次のア～ウの中から一つ選び，記号で答えよ。

ア　the Royal Red Cross praises those who have contributed to the world's health issues

イ　there are similar standards for recording diseases, such as the International Classification of Diseases

ウ　patients with serious illnesses are immediately sent to isolation facilities

問4　下線部②の内容を本文に即して70字程度の日本語で書け。

問5　本文の内容に合うように，次の英文の(　a　)～(　c　)に入る適切な英語1語をそれぞれ書け。

Nightingale realised that far more soldiers died of (　a　) than combat, and used (　b　) graphs to persuade the British parliament into reforming hospital and nursing operations to reduce (　c　).

問6　How did Nightingale help her team establish Nightingale-style nursing without visiting Australia? Answer in English.

問7　下線部③のように筆者が述べているのは，どのような経緯があるからか。本文を踏まえて75字程度の日本語で書け。

問8　本文のタイトルとして最も適切なものを次のア～ウの中から一つ選び，記号で答えよ。

ア　The Healing Power of Data: Florence Nightingale's True Legacy

イ　The Battle in the Military Hospitals: Florence Nightingale's Deep Grief

ウ　The Importance of STEM Education: Florence Nightingale's Prediction

(☆☆☆○○○○)

【高等学校】

【1】次の英文を読んで，以下の問に答えよ。

　The 23 October 2015 issue of the journal *Science* reported a feel-good story about how some children in India had received cataract surgery and were able to see. On the surface, nothing in this incident should surprise us. Ready access to cataract surgery is something we take for granted. But the story is not that simple.

The children had been born with cataracts. They had never been able to see. By the time their condition was diagnosed ― they came from impoverished and uneducated families in remote regions ― the regional physicians had told the parents that it was too late for a cure because ①the children were past a critical period for gaining vision. Nevertheless, a team of eye specialists arranged for the cataract surgery to be performed even on teenagers. Now, hundreds of formerly blind children are able to see.

The concept of a critical period for developing vision was based on cats and monkeys. The results showed that without visual signals during a critical period of development, vision is impaired for life. For humans, this critical window was thought to close tight by the time a child was eight years old. (For ethical reasons, no comparable studies were run on humans.) Hubel and Wiesel were awarded the Nobel Prize in 1981 for their work. And physicians around the world stopped performing cataract surgery on children older than eight. The data were clear. But they were wrong.

In this light, an apparent "feel-good" story becomes a "feel-bad" story about innumerable other children who were denied cataract surgery because they were too old.

②The theme of excessive faith in data was illustrated by another news item. A team of researchers set out to replicate 100 high-profile psychology experiments that had been performed in 2008. They reported their findings in *Science*. Only about a third of the original findings were replicated and even for these, the effect size was much smaller than the initial report.

Other fields have run into the same problem. A few years ago, *Nature* reported that most of the cancer studies selected for review could not be replicated. Many other teams of researchers have begun examining how to reduce the chances of unreliable data.

I think this is the wrong approach. It exemplifies the bedrock-bias: a desire for a firm piece of (③A) that can be used as a (③B) for deriving inferences.

Scientists appreciate ④the tradeoff between Type Ⅰ errors (detecting effects that aren't actually present ─ false positives) and Type Ⅱ errors (failing to detect an effect that is present ─ false negatives). When you put more energy into reducing Type Ⅰ errors, you run the risk of increasing Type Ⅱ errors.

The bedrock-bias encourages us to make extreme efforts to eliminate false positives, but that approach would slow progress. A better perspective is to give up the quest for certainty and accept the possibility that any datum may be wrong. After all, skepticism is a mainstay of the scientific enterprise.

I recall a conversation with a decision researcher who insisted that we cannot trust our intuitions; instead, we should trust the data. I agreed that we should never trust intuitions (we should listen to our intuitions but evaluate them), but I didn't agree that we should trust the data. There are too many examples where the data can (⑤) us.

What we need is the ability to (⑥A) their validity. We need to be able to form anticipations in the face of ambiguity and uncertainty. And to do that, we will need to (⑥B) the data.

I'm not arguing that it's OK to get the research wrong. My argument is that we shouldn't ignore ⑦the possibility that the data might be wrong. The team of Indian eye specialists responded to anecdotes about cases of recovered vision and explored the possible benefits of cataract surgery past the critical period.

The heuristics-and-biases community has done an impressive job of sensitizing us to the limits of our heuristics and intuitions. Perhaps we need a parallel effort to sensitize us to the limits of the data. A few cognitive scientists have performed experiments on the difficulty of working with ambiguous data, but I think we need more: a larger, coordinated research program.

Such an enterprise would have implications beyond the scientific community. In a world that is increasingly data-centered, there may be value in learning how to work with imperfect data.

問1　下線部①のように当時考えられていた理由を本文に即して日本語で書け。

問2　下線部②に関して，研究雑誌に掲載された内容を二つ，本文に即して日本語で簡潔に書け。

問3　本文中の(③A)，(③B)に入る最も適切な語を次のア～ウの中からそれぞれ一つ選び，記号で答えよ。

　　③A　ア　advice　　　　　イ　evidence　　　ウ　machinery
　　③B　ア　foundation　　　イ　fiction　　　　ウ　fertilizer

問4　下線部④の内容を本文に即して具体的に50字程度の日本語で書け。

問5　本文中の(⑤)に入る適切な英語1語を書け。

問6　本文中の(⑥A)，(⑥B)に入る最も適切なものを次のア～ウの中からそれぞれ一つ選び，記号で答えよ。

　　ア　free ourselves from the expectation that we can trust

　　イ　make a proper judgement based on our intuitions paying no attention to

　　ウ　draw on relevant data without committing ourselves to

問7　As for the underlined part ⑦, how can teachers reduce this possibility in schools? Answer in 10 to 15 words in English.

(☆☆☆☆☆◎◎◎◎)

解答・解説

【中高共通】

【1】Part 1　1　ア　　2　ウ　　3　エ　　4　エ　　5　イ

　　Part 2　1　ア　　2　エ　　3　ウ　　4　No. 1　ウ　　No. 2　ア

〈解説〉Part 1では対話に対する質問について，印刷されている選択肢の中から対話の答えとして適切なものを1つ選ぶ。Part 2ではモノローグに関する質問に対して，印刷されている選択肢の中から答えとして適切なものを1つ選ぶ。ともに放送は1度のみであるため，聞き逃さないこと。実際に放送される表現と選択肢の表現は異なるので，どのように言い換えられているか即時に判断できなければならない。

【2】1　イ　　2　ウ　　3　ア　　4　ウ　　5　ウ

〈解説〉1 「部屋の整理をしていたら昔の写真が出てきた」とする。come across A「Aに偶然遭遇する」が適切。bring about A「Aを引き起こす，Aをもたらす」，catch up A「(withを伴って)Aに追いつく，(onを伴って)Aの遅れを取り戻す」，turn on A「Aをつける，Aのスイッチを入れる」。　2 「ガジェットとは，小さくて便利で，巧妙に設計された機械や道具のことである」となる。broom「箒」，clipper「爪切り」，threshold「敷居，出発点」。3つ以上の語を並列させる場合には，A，B，and Cのようにカンマが2つ入ることが多い。cleverly-designedのように，複数の語から成る形容詞は前置修飾の際にハイフンが用いられる。3 「聞くだけで，何か学べるかもしれない」。if節の主節では助動詞を伴うため，might learnとするのが正解。　4 「CEFRとは，言語能力を初心者のA1から熟練者のC2までの6段階で表す国際基準である」となる。conference「会議」，recognition「承認」，treaty「条約」。CEFR(Common European Framework of Reference for Languages)はヨーロッパ言語共通参照枠と訳される。　5 「文部科学省は，学校で育成すべき資質・能力を『知識及び技能』，『思考力・判断力・表現力等』，

『学びに向かう力，人間性等』の3つの柱で定義した」。新学習指導要領の英訳版は，2021年11月末現在，小学校および中学校では「第1章総則」のみ，高等学校では教科・科目名一覧のみ公布されている。文部科学省のホームページから入手し，日本語の文言がどのように訳されているか確認されたい。

【3】It will be useful to introduce "dictation," one of the bottom-up activities, in my lesson. In the dictation activity, students will first listen to a new text. Then, they write down the whole or part of it. The most notable effect of this activity is that they will notice the changes of sounds, such as omission or assimilation when they listen to the next repeatedly to accomplish the task. This activity may be very effective in improving their listening skills. (80 words)

〈解説〉解答例で取り上げているディクテーション活動は，語彙や文法を解析してメッセージを理解するボトムアップ活動の一種である。まず音声を聴かせ，音声の全体もしくは一部を書き取らせる。書き言葉にする過程で1語ずつ聴き取るために，弱く読まれる語(例：be going toのto)にも注意を向けることとなり，omission(省略)やassimilation(同化)，linking(連結)など，音声変化のルールの学習に効果がある。

【4】問1　イ　　　問2　子供が読むことにつまずくと，自信ややる気を失くして，読む能力が向上せずに，再びつまずくという悪循環。(50字)
問3　犬は批判せず安心でき，邪魔もしないから。(20字)　　　問4　エ
問5　あ　　問6　ア　　問7　イ　　問8　Teachers can give specific roles to each student and praise their achievements when they accomplish their tasks. Students can feel that they are needed when they have some duties. Also, they can feel fulfilled and have confidence in themselves after their achievements. It is very important and effective for students. (50 words)

〈解説〉問1　直前の文章では，イギリスの子供たちの成績が低いこと，それに対して政府は様々な取組を模索してきたと述べられている。よ

って，代名詞themの指示対象は，イ「生徒のパフォーマンスを向上させる方法」が適切である。　問2　the destructive cycle「破壊的な循環」の内容は直前の文で表されているため，Many children naturally…の内容を日本語でまとめる。　問3「なぜ犬が忠実で愛らしい聴き手なのか？」に対する答えは，第3パラグラフ2文目参照。reassuring「安心させるような」，uncritical「無批判な」，not mind if mistakes are made「間違ったとしても気にしない」と具体的に述べられている。　問4　第3パラグラフでは(文字を覚え始める)小学生やディスレクシア(読み書き障害)の生徒に対して，犬への読み聞かせが効果的であることを述べている。その理由は，アルファベットの規則(音と綴りがどのように対応しているのか)に関する意図的な焦点が当てられた活動に偏重せず，バランスを取ることができるためである。犬に読み聞かせるのは教師から独立した読解活動であるので，Aはindependent(独立した)が適切。or(さもなくば)で対比されているBには否定的な語が入ると考えられるので，demotivated(やる気を失わせるような)が適切。　問5　挿入文の文意は「しかし，犬がいることでリラックスした心地よい雰囲気になる」。よって，学習環境について述べている第2パラグラフが適切である。挿入文にディスコースマーカーのhoweverが用いられていることからも，犬がいない状態での読解指導について扱っているかどうかの対比という視点で，空所の前後を読むとよい。　問6　アの「小さな愛らしい動物への愛情」は，犬への読み聞かせの利点として言及されていない。　イ「一般的な健康と幸せ」は，第4パラグラフのTonyとDannyの例で，promoting general well-being「一般的な健康を促進する」と述べられていることから適切である。ウの「読解への自信と動機付け」は第3パラグラフ，エの「様々なことへの肯定的な態度」は第4パラグラフでそれぞれ述べられている。　問7　本文は生徒が犬に対して読み聞かせをすることの利点を述べたものであることから，イ「犬が子どもの読解能力を向上させる方法」が適切。　ア　第5パラグラフでit is not a panacea「それ(犬への読み聞かせ)は万能薬ではない」と述べている。よって，Perfect Learning Methodとは言えない。　ウ　本

文中にdisadvantagesは述べられていない。　エ　第2パラグラフで，犬への読み聞かせは1999年にアメリカで生まれたとあるが，「最新の犬の訓練法」については述べられていない。　問8　モチベーションや自己効力感といった概念を正しく把握しておき，それらを肯定的な方向に高める具体的な内容を記述する。解答例では「生徒一人一人に具体的な役割を与え，課題を達成したときにはその成果を褒めること」を挙げている。

【中学校】

【１】問1　病気の拡大を防ぐには，データの明確な理解とその適切な使用がとても重要であること。(40字)　問2　A　ア　　C　ウ
問3　イ　　問4　各国の検査規制が異なるため，専門家が新型コロナウイルス感染症の拡大を監視するための，感染者数について比較できる標準化されたデータがないこと。(70字)　問5　a　disease(s)
b　new　c　mortality/deaths　　問6　She collected data from her wide network of contacts and shared her conclusions by exchanging letters.
問7　統計分野において，男性と対等に認められるために女性が努力してきており，最近では統計学会の会長に女性が選出されるなど，対等な評価を得つつあるという経緯。(75字)　　問8　ア
〈解説〉問1　直前の文のhow necessary以下を簡潔にまとめる。
問2　A　統計学はこれまでに手に入ったデータを利用して，これからの予測などを行う学問である。この統計学に興味のあったナイチンゲールが，トルコのイギリス軍病院の状況と明確な記録の欠如を知って，「愕然とした，ぞっとした」と考えられる。よってhorrifiedが適切。
C　ナイチンゲールがパビリオン形式の病棟について書いた論文によれば，看護スタッフにとって便利であり，風通しがいいというbenefits「利点」がある。　問3　第2パラグラフではナイチンゲールが統計学を用いて，病院での病気や死亡の記録方法を開発したことが述べられている。よって，「International Classification of Diseases(ICD：国際疾病分類)のように，病気の記録に関する同様な基準が用いられている」が

適切。　問4　150年前にナイチンゲールが指摘した点は「データセットを比較する前に標準化する必要性」である。下線部②のthisは、それよりも前の文の内容を受けているので、第3パラグラフの前半部分をまとめればよい。　問5　第3パラグラフの後半参照。空所補充後の文意は、「ナイチンゲールが病院でのデータを取ることによって気づいた点は、戦死者よりも病死者(a)の数が多いことである。ナイチンゲールは、死亡率(c)を減少させるため病院や看護業務を改善するよう、新しい(b)グラフを使って英国議会を説得した」となる。　問6　質問は「ナイチンゲールはオーストラリアを訪れることなく、どのようにしてチームにナイチンゲール式看護を確立させたのか？」。第4パラグラフの「幅広い人脈から資料を取り寄せる」、「文通をよくしていた」という記述をもとにまとめる。　問7　第5パラグラフでは女性の統計学者について述べられている。ナイチンゲール自身が統計学の学会にて女性初のフェローとなっており、現在まで女性の統計学者が前進していることを誇りに思うだろう、と書かれている。よって、第5パラグラフの後半部分をまとめればよい。　問8　本文はナイチンゲールが統計学に詳しかったことを述べているので、ア「データの持つ癒しの力：フローレンス・ナイチンゲールの真の遺産」が適切。イは「軍病院での戦い：フローレンス・ナイチンゲールの深い悲しみ」、ウは「STEM教育の重要性：フローレンス・ナイチンゲールの予言」。

【高等学校】

【1】問1　動物実験により、視覚発達の臨界期までに視覚刺激がなければ、視力が一生損なわれると判明し、人間の場合その臨界期が8歳までであると考えられていたから。　問2　・2008年に行われた注目度の高い心理実験のうち、3分の1しか再現性がなく、あったとしても当初想定された程の効果量はなかったということ。　・再検証のために選ばれたガン研究のほとんどに再現性がなかったこと。
問3　③A　イ　　③B　ア　　問4　実在しない効果を認識する誤りを減らせば、実在する効果を見過ごす可能性が高まり、逆もまた真であ

ること。(50字)　　問5　blind(deceive, mislead)　　問6　⑥A　ウ
⑥B　ア　　問7　・When teachers mark tests, it is better to check them
twice.(11 words)　　・They can collect various data without depending on a
single set of data. (13 words)

〈解説〉問1　第1パラグラフと第2パラグラフでは，critical period「臨界
期」を過ぎて白内障の手術を受けた子供の目が見えるようになったと
いう報告が研究雑誌*Science*に投稿されたことが述べられている。続く
第3パラグラフでは，この臨界期についてはネコやサルを使った研究
に基づいていることが述べられている。動物実験の結果，発達の臨界
期までに視覚刺激が得られないと視力が損なわれることが示され，人
間の場合には臨界期が8歳であると考えられた。これらの内容を日本
語で述べる。　　問2　*Science*と*Nature*のそれぞれに掲載された内容を
まとめる。前者は，100件の心理学実験結果のうち，再現(実験と同じ
結果を得ること)できたのは約3分の1であり，その効果量(ある現象に
対する効果の大きさを表す指標)は報告されていたものよりも小さかっ
た。後者はガン研究のほとんどが再現できなかったことを報告してい
る。それぞれを日本語でまとめる。　　問3　空所はbedrock-biasの説明
である。第6パラグラフまでは心理実験とガン研究の例を示し，いず
れも実験の再現性には疑問が残ることを述べている。このことから，
bedrock-biasでは推論を導き出すための「基礎」となる確たる「証拠」
を重視していると言える。　　問4　下線部直後にbetweenがあるため，
提示されている2種類のerror「(統計用語)過誤」について日本語でまと
め，それらがトレードオフの関係(どちらかが高くなれば，どちらかが
低くなる)にあることを述べる。　　問5　データを信じることについて
懐疑的な著者が述べている主張としては，データが自分たちのことを
欺いたり，惑わせたり，盲目にさせたりすることが挙げられる。
問6　直前のパラグラフではデータに対する批判的な視点が重要であ
ることを述べており，空所Aの直後には「データの妥当性」，空所Bの
直後には「データ」が続いている。それぞれの選択肢の意味は，ア
「〜を信頼できるという期待感から逃れる」，イ「〜を気にせず，直観

で適切な判断を下す」，ウ「～に関わることなく，関連するデータを利用する」。イは直前のパラグラフ1文目で直観による判断が否定されているため誤り。候補はアとウのいずれかである。Aは恣意的にデータを選択することなく関連するデータを収集すること，Bはデータそのものを信じることへの注意を述べていると考えられる。　問7　教師はどうすればデータが誤っている可能性を低下させられるか，学校での具体例を述べる英作文問題である。教育現場で得られるデータの例には，テストの結果や授業評価アンケートなどがある。解答例では，テストの採点の際にデータの信頼性を高めるために2回採点することや，1つのデータに依存するのではなく様々なデータを収集することが重要であることを挙げている。

2021年度　実施問題

【中高共通】

【１】聞き取りテスト

　　これから1〜7の対話と8〜10の英文を1回ずつ放送します。それぞれの英語の後に，その内容について質問を一つします。その質問に対する答として適切なものを次のア〜エの中からそれぞれ一つ選び，記号で答えよ。

1　W : Hey, Nick, what are you doing this Sunday?

　　M : I don't know. I'll probably stay home and read books to finish my homework. Why?

　　W : There's a soccer game at Kamoike Stadium. I have two tickets. Do you want to come with me?

　　M : Sure, why not?

　　Question (W) : What is the man going to do this Sunday?

　ア　　Stay home and just relax.

　イ　　Read books to finish his homework.

　ウ　　Buy two tickets for the soccer game.

　エ　　Watch soccer at Kamoike Stadium.

2　M : What are you having for dinner tonight?

　　W : I guess I'll get some food at a convenience store or order some food for delivery. I don't feel like cooking today.

　　M : Then, how about going together to the Italian restaurant that opened near my house. I heard that it's very good.

　　W : That sounds nice.

　　Question (M) : What is the man most likely to do after the conversation?

　ア　　Go to a convenience store.

イ　Order some food for delivery.

ウ　Make Italian food.

エ　Make a reservation at the restaurant.

3　W : Hi, this is room 417. I want to take a shower right now, but I can't get any hot water.

M : We apologize for the inconvenience. I'll send someone to your room to check it.

W : How long will it take? I'm in a hurry because I have an appointment with a client.

M : If you don't mind, we'd like to move you to another room. We'll help you carry your baggage to the room as soon as possible.

W : OK. Thank you.

Question (M) : What is the woman most likely to do after the conversation?

ア　Ask someone to fix the shower.

イ　Cancel the appointment with her client.

ウ　Move to another room.

エ　Call the front desk clerk.

4　W : I'd like to send this package to London. How long will it take?

M : Let's see. It'll take about 10 days.

W : 10 days? It's a birthday present for my cousin, and his birthday is this Saturday.

M : Well, if you send it by express mail, I'm sure your cousin will get his birthday gift by then.

Question (W) : What did the man suggest that the woman do?

ア　Send the package by express.

イ　Visit London to surprise her cousin.

ウ　Ask her cousin what he wants.

エ　Tell her cousin about the delayed arrival.

5　M : Hello. This is ABC Animal Hospital. What can I do for you?

W : Our cat has been refusing to eat food for three days. Will you have a look at her today?

M : Sorry, we have a full schedule today. How about at 9:00 a.m. tomorrow?

W : Sure. That's fine. Thank you very much.

Question (M) : Why did the woman call?

ア　To ask someone to look for her cat.

イ　To order extra cat food.

ウ　To make an appointment with a vet.

エ　To get information about cat diseases.

6　W: Have you seen my smartphone? I can't find it. I don't remember where and when I used it last.

M : Again? Shall I ring your smartphone?

W : Yes, please. But I keep my phone on vibrate mode, so we may not hear the sound.

M : Well, let's be quiet then. Oh, I think I hear something vibrating in your bag. You should decide which pocket to put it in.

Question (W) : What did the man tell the woman to do?

ア　To decide where her smartphone belongs.

イ　To take notes to remember what she did.

ウ　To set her smartphone to silent mode.

エ　To put her smartphone in her bag.

7　W : Excuse me. Can I borrow this book?

M : Yes, if you have a library card.

W : Oh, really? Can I apply for one?

M : Of course. You need to fill out this form and show us some identification, like a driver's license. Oops, I'm sorry. You can't take this book out, but you can read and photocopy it in the library.

Question (W) : Why couldn't the woman borrow the book?

ア　She didn't have a library card.

イ　She forgot her driver's license.

ウ　It was forbidden to remove the book.

エ　The book had already been borrowed.

8　Now more and more foreigners live and work in Japan. Additionally, the number of children whose parents don't understand Japanese is increasing. Because they don't speak Japanese at home, their chance to use it is limited and they can't use it properly or they have some trouble communicating with other people. It is necessary to improve their Japanese language level to increase their chances of employment in Japan in the future. In order to support them, we have language classes organized by volunteers. If you are interested in helping, please contact us.

Question (M) : What is the purpose of the speech?

ア　To collect good news about foreigners.

イ　To increase the number of the employment.

ウ　To look for language volunteers.

エ　To share ideas to improve English.

9　Landmines are bombs placed on or under the ground, which explode when people or vehicles move over them. Since it is difficult and dangerous to detect and eliminate them, a lot of landmines remain and many people are killed or injured every year. Nowadays, giant rats called "Hero Rats" are getting attention. They are trained for about 9 months to identify the smell of landmines. They are too light to explode landmines even if they walk over them. Their small size also means they can be transported easily.

Question (W) : Which is true about "Hero Rats"?

ア　They are trained for about nine years.

イ　They help us find and remove landmines.

ウ　They are heavy enough to explode landmines.

エ　They are easily affected by cold weather.

10 Ladies and gentlemen, thank you very much for taking this train tour today. Please enjoy the beautiful scenery including the ocean view from the windows. This train has a restaurant which provides a special lunch for you. This is the highlight of the tour. Our chef prepares the lunch using fresh local ingredients. You can use the bar at any time and order alcohol if you pay an extra charge. Because we collaborate with local businesses along the train line, you can buy local products as souvenirs. We hope you'll have a wonderful time. Thank you.

Question (M) : Which is true about the train tour?

ア　People can order drinks for free at the bar.

イ　People can enjoy a beautiful ocean view from the windows.

ウ　The train stops at every station for taking photos.

エ　People can start local businesses along the train line.

以上で聞き取りテストを終わります。次の問題に進みなさい。

(☆☆◎◎◎◎)

【２】次の各文の(　　)に入る適切な英語を下のア～エの中からそれぞれ一つ選び，記号で答えよ。

1　The room was so (　　) you could hear a pin drop.

　　ア　composed　　イ　sophisticated　　ウ　sound　　エ　still

2　In our daily lives, we meet lots of (　　) in English. Many of them are adjectives and one common way of making them is by adding a prefix, like *in-*, *un-* and *dis-*, such as *comfortable* and *uncomfortable.*

ア　acronyms　　イ　antonyms　　ウ　pseudonyms
エ　synonyms

3　He has a great sense of humor and he's extremely good at telling stories. I was completely (　　) by him.

ア　taken down　　イ　taken in　　ウ　taken off　　エ　taken over

4　It was surprising that he (　　) any of it even though he's a leading figure in that field.

ア　has been heard　　イ　has not heard　　ウ　had been heard
エ　had not heard

5　A key principle of Task-based Language Learning is that even though learners are primarily concerned with constructing and comprehending messages, they also need to attend to (　　) for learning to take place.

ア　content　　イ　form　　ウ　interlocutors　　エ　lessons

(☆☆☆○○○○)

【3】生徒の学習意欲が高まる要因の例として，「教師のやる気が感じられること」，「やりがいのある課題が与えられること」，「学習内容が興味深いこと」，「教室が笑いにあふれていること」がある。この中であなたが最も効果的だと思うものはどれか，理由や根拠を明確にして80語程度の英語で書け。なお，使用した語数を記入すること。

(☆☆☆○○○○)

【4】次の英文を読んで，後の問に答えよ。

Snow days are ①routine for many teachers; some school calendars are planned with the assumption students will miss classes because of bad weather. But ②school closures, especially lengthy ones, may cause some teachers to worry if lost time will keep them from completing the curriculum or put students at a disadvantage when writing standardized tests.

Many schools prepare by creating distance learning opportunities to ensure classes continue even when bad weather closes schools. In New Hampshire for example, (a state that is no stranger to stormy Nor'easters), several school districts have adopted ③Blizzard Bag days. Students work from home when schools are closed because of bad weather. They access lessons online; students who don't have Internet access are provided with paper materials. The days aren't wasted time. Schools need to submit a plan to the Department of Education requesting how many Blizzard Bag days they'd like (the maximum is five per school year), and provide details about how they plan to deliver lessons on those days. Department of Education guidelines say the schoolwork assigned "must be equivalent in effort and rigor to typical classroom work." At least 80 percent of students must participate for a day to be an approved school day.

Similar programs exist in regions not necessarily known for colder weather, like Kentucky. School districts across the state have introduced Non-Traditional Instruction (NTI) days for the past few years. They're similar to Blizzard Bags days. [A] More than 70 of the state's 173 districts participate in the program.

It's especially important in rural areas where cities may not have enough snow ploughs to remove snow from roads, said Carla Whitis, Assistant Superintendent at Graves County School District in southwestern Kentucky. Geographically, it's one of the state's largest school districts and many students live on rural roads that may be (B) for buses to travel on after storms. Graves County began offering NTI days during the 2015-2016 school year. Students complete review assignments during those days; no (C) material is introduced. The work is supposed to take about three hours for students to complete. Whitis said that's comparable to the amount of time students spend on schoolwork in the classroom. Students have up to three days to hand in the assignments after the NTI day. The district ranked as one of the top districts in the state at the end of 2015-2016 year, said Whitis, coming in at 28. "We don't think that it had a negative impact," she said. If students' scores had decreased after the year, the district would have "definitely" considered if NTI days had had a negative influence on the students, said Whitis. That's not to say there weren't some challenges. Some students couldn't access the assignments on certain devices. Others had limited access to devices because parents needed to use their computers to work from home, or there weren't enough devices for all the children in a household to access the material at the same time. ④These are lessons the district will keep in mind as it prepares for future NTI days, Whitis said.

問1　本文中での下線部①の意味に最も近いものを次のア～エの中から一つ選び，記号で答えよ。

　　ア　boring　　　イ　exceptional　　　ウ　important　　　エ　ordinary

問2　下線部②について，次の問に対する答えを本文に即して60字程度の日本語で書け。

　　What are likely to be concerns to some teachers?

問3　次の英文は下線部③の説明である。(1)～(3)に入る与えられた文字で始まる適切な英語1語をそれぞれ書け。

　　They are (1)(o　　　) school days, when students take lessons via the Internet at their homes while students with no Internet access (2)(w　　　) with paper materials, up to five days depending on the (3)(p　　　) rate.

問4　本文中の　　A　　には，次のア～ウの文を並べ替えてできる一つのまとまった文章が入る。正しい順に並べ替えよ。

　　ア　On the NTI day, students get lessons through the school websites or use paper materials if they don't have access to the Internet.

　　イ　Teachers contact the students during the day to offer assistance, if needed.

　　ウ　When the forecast predicts bad weather, districts decide if the next day will be an NTI day.

問5　本文中の(B)，(C)に入る最も適切な語を次のア～ウの中からそれぞれ一つ選び，記号で答えよ。

　　B：　ア　narrow　　　イ　possible　　　ウ　unsafe

　　C：　ア　difficult　　　イ　new　　　ウ　recycled

問6　下線部④の内容を本文に即して95字程度の日本語で書け。

問7　次は本文を読んだALTと教師の対話である。空所に入るものと
　　して最も適切なものを下のア～エの中から一つ選び，記号で答えよ。

　　　　ALT : This article is interesting.

　　Teacher : Really? What is it about?

　　　　ALT : This article illustrates (　　　) for students in the United States.

　　ア　wind and snow damages to education

　　イ　distance learning opportunities

　　ウ　the drawbacks of online education

　　エ　future prospects of rural education

問8　日本の英語教育において，オンラインでの学びを積極的に活用
　　することに関して，あなたが考える良い点を50語程度の英語で書け。
　　なお，使用した語数を記入すること。

(☆☆☆☆○○○)

【中学校】

【１】次の英文を読んで，後の問に答えよ。

　　Are quiet people more outgoing online? Do we test out a more extroverted personality on social media? For several years now, psychologists have been trying to figure out whether people act the same way online as they do in real life. In one study, scientists analysed the Facebook profiles and pages of a group of university students. They found that the extroverts had more wall posts, photos and friends; they sought out social interactions and engaged more with the crowd. The introverts, on the other hand, were more often watchers. In other words, ⎣　①　⎦.

　　Many introverts I spoke to told me that they didn't post often, but that they often checked in and chatted with friends online. Virtual networks were a way of maintaining or even strengthening their real relationships. In 2012, a group of scientists from the University of California, Irvine, discovered ②similar trends when they studied how teens use online communication. The scientists questioned 126 secondary school students about how they engaged with one another through social media, and they found that for most kids, their online and offline friends were one and the same.

Noah is perhaps an (A): he has made new friends online with people all over the world—without ever meeting them face-to-face. 'I made some weird and surprising connections with people online on MMORPGs [massively multi-player online role-playing games] like EverQuest, or World of Warcraft, where you're playing with thousands of people at once, and everyone has an avatar. I was always inspired by the story, or the creative elements of the game, so we would bond over that.' For Noah, these friendships were often less stressful than his friendships with classmates, with whom he felt pressure to be fun and cool on the spot. あ

③Befriending people online has its ups and downs. Studies show that these virtual friendships can be positive and empowering, but they can also be a barrier to finding friends in real life. One fourteen-year-old boy we met was part of a virtual team in a combat game online; his team was made up of boys from across the country. Although he referred to these boys as some of his (B) friends, they never shared their stories or real-world experiences, and he had no plans to meet any of them in person. In some cases he didn't even know their real names.

④Always keep in mind that most people present an airbrushed version of their lives online. Think about what gets posted to Instagram: photos of vacations, or of delicious meals, or of moments at parties when we're mid-laughter and flanked by friends. What about those less glamorous moments eating cereal in pyjamas on a Sunday morning? Or more vulnerable moments when we're feeling lonely or nervous? If you only get to know people through their social media presence, you might not see that they feel just as fragile as you do—including the extroverted ones! い

Child psychologist Aimee Yermish counsels her patients to examine their relationships thoughtfully. If a friendship consists mostly of gaming or of an online connection, then it has limitations. That's because the term *friend* only *partly* represented online. A true, mature bond includes a personal and social connection, of the kind you develop sitting across from someone, chatting over a snack. Yermish tells her patients to approach their digital friendships the same way they approach friendships offline: look for people who might become true friends over time. It's helpful to think of digital communities, from Facebook to online gaming, not as complete worlds in and of themselves. ⎿　う　⎤

Since the Internet is open to everyone, there are a lot of creeps and criminals out there, and bullies too. Be careful about what you say online and don't be quick to trust a stranger. And remember that there's always a chance that a photo or video you post will be shared without your (　C　). Make sure that you aren't texting or Snapchatting a photo that you wouldn't want a stranger to see. No matter how loud and proud your online persona is, please make sure you're also staying safe!

問1　本文中の　①　に入る文として最も適切なものを次のア〜エの中から一つ選び，記号で答えよ。

ア　introverts had difficulty acting the same way online as they do in real life

イ　introverts tended to behave more active online than extroverts

ウ　introverts and extroverts usually behaved like themselves online

エ　introverts and extroverts tried to get close to their ideal images online

問2　下線部②の内容を本文に即して35字程度の日本語で書け。

問3　本文中の(　A　)〜(　C　)に入る最も適切な語を次のア〜カの中からそれぞれ一つ選び，記号で答えよ。

ア　applicant　　イ　best　　ウ　consent　　エ　encouragement

オ　exception　　カ　temporary

問4　次の英文が入る最も適切な箇所を　あ　〜　う　の中から

80

一つ選び，記号で答えよ。

Think of them as a way to forge stronger connections in the real world.

問5　下線部③とはどういうことか，研究結果をもとに本文に即して50字程度の日本語で書け。

問6　次の英文が下線部④における筆者の意図を表すものとなるように，（　a　）～（　c　）に入る最も適切な語を下のア～オの中からそれぞれ一つ選び，記号で答えよ。

> You have to remember that people hide their (　a　) lives and try to show off their fulfilling days through social media so as to make their lives seem more (　b　). However, there is a possibility that we can't understand their real (　c　), because we see the only positive aspects of their lives.

ア　attractive　　イ　destructive　　ウ　meals　　エ　personalities
オ　true

問7　次の問に対する答えを本文に即して60字程度の日本語で書け。

Why does Aimee Yermish think digital friendships have limitations?

問8　本文のタイトルとして最も適切なものを次のア～エの中から一つ選び，記号で答えよ。
ア　Glamorous Moments　　イ　Online Crime
ウ　The Digital Crisis　　エ　Wi-Fi Friendships

(☆☆☆◎◎◎)

【高等学校】

【1】次の英文を読んで，後の問に答えよ。

Sleep *before* learning refreshes our ability to initially make new memories. It does so each and every night. While we are awake, the brain is constantly acquiring and absorbing novel information. Passing memory opportunities are captured by specific parts of the brain. For ①fact-based information learning such as memorizing someone's name, a new phone number, or where you parked your car, a region of the brain called the hippocampus helps apprehend these passing experiences and binds their details together. A long, finger-shaped structure tucked deep on either side of your brain, the hippocampus offers a short-term reservoir, or temporary information store, for accumulating new memories. Unfortunately, ②the hippocampus has a limited storage capacity. Exceed its capacity and you run the risk of not being able to add more information or, equally bad, overwriting one memory with another.

How, then, does the brain deal with this memory capacity challenge? Some years ago, my research team wondered if sleep helped solve this storage problem. We examined whether sleep shifted recently acquired memories to a more permanent, long-term storage location in the brain, thereby freeing up our short-term memory stores so that we awake with a refreshed ability for new learning.

We began testing ③this theory using daytime naps. We recruited a group of healthy young adults and randomly divided them into a nap group and a non-nap group. At noon, all the participants underwent a rigorous session of learning (one hundred face-name pairs) intended to ④tax the hippocampus, their short-term memory storage site. As expected, both groups performed at comparable levels. Soon after, the nap group took a ninety-minute siesta in the sleep laboratory with electrodes placed on their heads to measure sleep. The no-nap group stayed awake in the laboratory and performed menial activities. Later that day, at six p.m., all participants performed another round of intensive learning where they tried to cram yet another set of new facts into their short-term storage reservoirs (another one hundred face-name pairs). Our question was simple: Does the learning capacity of the human brain decline with continued time awake across the day and, if so, can sleep reverse ⑤this saturation effect and thus restore learning ability?

Those who were awake throughout the day became progressively (A) learning, even though their ability to concentrate remained stable. In contrast, those who napped did markedly (B), and actually improved in their

82

capacity to memorize facts. The difference between the two groups at six p.m. was not small: a 20 percent learning advantage for those who slept.

Having observed that sleep restores the brain's capacity for learning, making room for new memories, we went in search of exactly what it was about sleep that transacted the restoration benefit. Analyzing the electrical brainwaves of those in the nap group brought our answer. The memory refreshment was related to NREM (non-rapid eye movement) sleep, and specifically the short, powerful bursts of electrical activity called sleep spindles. The more sleep spindles an individual obtained during the nap, the greater the restoration of their learning when they woke up. Importantly, sleep spindles did not predict someone's innate learning aptitude. Instead, it was specifically the *change* in learning from before relative to after sleep that spindles predicted.

Perhaps more remarkable, as we analyzed sleep-spindle bursts of activity, we observed a strikingly reliable loop of electrical current pulsing throughout the brain that repeated every 100 to 200 milliseconds. The pulses kept weaving a path back and forth between the hippocampus, with its short-term, limited storage space, and the far larger, long-term storage site of the cortex. In that moment, we had just become privy to an electrical transaction occurring in the quiet secrecy of sleep: one that was shifting fact-based memories from the temporary storage depot (the hippocampus) to a long-term secure vault (the cortex). In doing so, sleep had delightfully cleared out the hippocampus, replenishing this short-term information repository with plentiful free space. Participants awoke with a refreshed capacity to absorb new information within the hippocampus, having relocated yesterday's imprinted experiences to a more permanent safe hold. The learning of new facts could begin again, anew, the following day.

We and other research groups have since repeated this study across a full night of sleep and replicated the same finding: the more sleep spindles an individual has at night, ___C___ when the next morning comes.

問1　下線部①の具体例をすべて本文に即して日本語で書け。

問2　下線部②がもたらす問題について，本文に即して65字程度の日本語で書け。

問3　下線部③の内容を本文に即して80字程度の日本語で書け。

問4　本文中での下線部④の意味に最も近いものを次のア～エの中から一つ選び，記号で答えよ。

　　ア　overburden　　イ　overcome　　ウ　overestimate
　　エ　overpay

問5　下線部⑤の内容を本文に即して40字程度の日本語で書け。

問6　本文中の（　A　），（　B　）に入る語の組み合わせとして最も適切なものを次のア～エの中から一つ選び，記号で答えよ。

　　ア　A : less interested in　　　B : faster
　　イ　A : worse at　　　　　　　B : better
　　ウ　A : better at　　　　　　　B : worse
　　エ　A : more interested in　　　B : slower

問7　次の問に対する答えを本文に即して日本語で書け。

　　What was it that sleep spindles predicted in the study?

問8　本文中の　　C　　に入る英語7語を本文中から抜き出して書け。

問9　本文のタイトルとして最も適切なものを次のア～エの中から一つ選び，記号で答えよ。

　　ア　The moderate time when the hippocampus activates learning
　　イ　The relationship between sleep and the cortex
　　ウ　The role intensive learning plays in making new memories
　　エ　The significance of NREM sleep before learning

（☆☆☆○○○○）

84

解答・解説

【中高共通】

【1】1　エ　　2　エ　　3　ウ　　4　ア　　5　ウ　　6　ア　　7　ウ
　　8　ウ　　9　イ　　10　イ

〈解説〉1〜7は，男女間で2，3回やり取りされる日常会話を聞いて質問に
　答えるもの。質問は「男性は日曜日に何をする予定か」，「この会話の
　後，女性は何をするだろうか」などから成る。8〜10は，90語前後の
　英文から成るスピーチやアナウンスを聞いて質問に答えるもの。「ス
　ピーチの目的は何か」や「内容について正しいものを選択せよ」など
　の質問から成る。特に難しい内容ではないが，放送文は1度のみなの
　で聞き逃さないこと。

【2】1　エ　　2　イ　　3　イ　　4　エ　　5　イ

〈解説〉1　「部屋はとても静かで，ピンが落ちても聞こえるほどだった」。
　still「〈人・物が〉じっと動かない，静かな」。hear a pin drop「シーン
　としている，(ピンが落ちる音が聞こえるくらい)静まり返っている」。
　2　comfortableとuncomfortableの例を挙げ，反意語の作り方を説明して
　いる。antonym「反意語」。なお，acronymは「頭字語」，pseudonymは
　「仮名，ペンネーム」，synonymは「同義語」である。　3　「彼はすばら
　しいユーモア感覚を持っていて，作り話をするのが極めて得意だ。私
　は完璧に彼に騙された」。take in「(うそを)真に受ける，信じ込む」。
　4　「彼はこの分野で主要な人物であるにもかかわらず，それについて
　聞いていなかったことは驚きだった」。hear of 〜「〜について聞く」。
　主節の動詞が過去形なので，過去完了が適切。　5　Task-based
　Learningを説明している。学習者は「形式」にも注意を払う必要があ
　る。interlocutorは「対話者」。

85

【３】Teachers' eagerness to teach is the most important factor for motivating students. Motivated teachers prepare lessons and offer clear objectives for learning. In addition, since they will give a lot of options in their lessons, students can choose what they'd like to do. Thus, students will work more enthusiastically. So, the possibilities to achieve goals will be greater, and their motivation will increase, too. In other words, teachers' eagerness to teach is very influential for students' motivation. (77 words)

〈解説〉「やりがいのある課題が与えられること」,「学習内容が興味深いこと」などに関しては, 課題を解決していく活動などを通して得られる「楽しい」,「使えた」,「役に立つ」という経験を積み重ねることで学習意欲の高まりが期待できること,「教室が笑いにあふれていること」に関しては, 間違っていたり不完全であったりしても, 安心して発言や発表ができる環境を作り上げることで, 自分の考えを伝えたいという内的動機付けにつなげていくことなどに触れて書くことができる。

【４】問1　エ　　　問2　授業時間が失われたことが履修課程の修了を妨げたり, 生徒を共通(標準, 統一)テストで不利な状況に置いたりするのではないかという懸念。(65字)　　　問3　(1) official　　(2) work (3) participation　　問4　ウ→ア→イ　　問5　B　ウ　　C　イ問6　生徒が課題を入手する機器を持っていなかったり, 親が在宅勤務でコンピュータを使うため生徒の機器の使用が制限されたり, 家に全員の子どもたちが同時に使える十分な数の機器がなかったりしたこと。(92字)　　問7　イ　　　問8　English classes using an online environment will allow Japanese students to practice speaking English with foreign students in real time so they are more motivated to learn English, and such cross-cultural communication will also help both Japanese and foreign students understand each other's cultures, which results in young students respecting foreign cultures. (52 words)

〈解説〉問1　routine「ありふれた, いつもの」。　　問2　学校閉鎖をする

ことによる教師たちの懸念は何かを答える。下線部②の文中の，worry if lost time …の内容を日本語でまとめる。　問3　ブリザードバッグデイズの説明は，第2段落に書かれている。「それらは公の授業日である。その日には，生徒は家庭でインターネットを通じて授業を受ける。一方インターネットにアクセスできない生徒は紙素材を使って勉強する。参加率に応じて5日までとなる」。　問4　空所には，ブリザードバッグデイズに似通ったNTIの説明が入る。ウ「予報が悪天候の時，次の日をNTIの日にするかを地域が判断する」→ア「NTIの日に，生徒は学校のウェブサイトを通して授業を受けるか，インターネットにアクセスできないならば，紙素材を使う」→イ「必要があれば補助するために，教師はその日に生徒にコンタクトをとる」。　問5　空所Bは，NTIなどを必要としている地域について述べており，「多くの生徒は，嵐の後バスが通るには危険な田舎道に依存して生活している」となる。空所CはNTIの教材について述べており，「生徒はその期間中，復習課題を仕上げる。新しい教材は取り入れられない」となる。　問6　下線部「これらは」は，NTIが現在抱える課題を指す。2文前のSome students …以降の内容を日本語でまとめる。　問7　本文の内容を端的に表している語句を選ぶ。「この記事は，合衆国の生徒たちのための遠隔地の学習機会について説明している」。　問8　オンラインでの学びの利点はさまざまあるが，一般的な内容ではなく英語教育について言及すること。解答例では「海外の学生とリアルタイムにやり取りすることで，学習意欲が増すことや異文化理解に役立つ」ことを挙げている。

【中学校】

【1】問1　ウ　　問2　仮想ネットワークは，実際の人間関係を維持したり，強めたりさえすること。(35字)　　問3　A　オ　　B　イ　C　ウ　　問4　う　　問5　インターネット上の友情は健全で活力を与えうるし，実際の生活で友達を見つける障壁にもなりうること。(48字)　　問6　a　オ　　b　ア　　c　エ　　問7　真の深い絆は個人的，

社会的なつながりを含むものであり，オンライン上での友達という言葉は一部の意味しか表さないから。(57字)　　問8　エ

〈解説〉問1　第1段落参照。フェイスブックのプロフィールや学生グループのサイトの分析により，外交的な人は社会的交流を求め人と関わろうとするのに対し，内向的な人はウオッチャーであることが多いことがわかったとある。したがって，ウ「内向的な人と外交的な人は，たいていオンラインでも自分らしく振舞っていた」が適切。　問2　下線部②の「同様の傾向」とは，1文前のVirtual networks …以下の文の内容を指す。　問3　A　第3段落4文目参照。ノアにとって，オンラインの友達関係は，同級生の友達関係に比べストレスがない。一方第2段落では，たいていの子どもにとってオンラインの友達とオフラインの友達は同じだとある。よって，「ノアはおそらく例外である」となる。　B　第4段落ではオンラインの友達について肯定的な点と否定的な点の両方が述べられている。ある少年の例を取り上げて，「(筆者が会った14歳の)少年は，(ネット上のチームに属する)少年たちを親友と呼んでいる」。　C　第7段落はネット犯罪やいじめなどの危険性について述べている。よって，「掲載した写真やビデオが同意なしに共有される可能性が常にあることを覚えておくべきだ」となる。

問4　挿入文は「それら(デジタルコミュニティ)を，現実世界の中でより強い関係を築く方法だと考えなさい」。think of A as Bで「AをBとみなす，考える」に着目する。第6段落最終文では，この挿入文と同じ言い回しを使って「フェイスブックからオンラインゲームまで，デジタルコミュニティをそれ自体で完璧な世界だと考えない方が有益だ」と述べている。よって「う」に挿入するのが適切。　問5　下線部③の文意は「オンラインで友達になることは，良いことも悪いこともある」。この直後の文が，下線部③の研究結果を示しているので，50字程度に日本語でまとめる。　問6　下線部④の文意は「たいていの人はオンラインで自分の生活を修正バージョンで提示していることを常に心にとめておきなさい」。よって，a「人々はありのままの生活を隠している」，b「自分の生活がもっと魅力的に見えるように」，c「私た

ちは本当の人柄を理解できない可能性がある」とすればよい。

問7　質問は「エイミー・イェルミッシュはデジタルの友人関係になぜ限界があると考えているか」。第6段落3文目参照。That's because … の文が答えに当たる。　問8　第2段落ではonline friends，第6段落ではdigital friendshipなど，表現を変えながらも，face-to-faceではない友人(関係)について述べている。

【高等学校】

【1】問1　人の名前や新しい電話番号，またはどこに車を駐車したかを暗記すること。　問2　短期記憶を司る脳の部位は，その容量を超えると，それ以上の情報を追加できない，又は，ある情報の上に別の情報を上書きする恐れがあるという問題。(69字)　問3　睡眠が最近獲得した記憶を長期記憶の貯蔵場所へ移動させ，それにより新しい学習のために能力が回復された状態で目覚めるように短期記憶の貯蔵場所を空にするという理論。(79字)　問4　ア　問5　日中起き続けている時間が長くなると，人間の脳の学習容量は減少するということ。(38字)　問6　イ　問7　寝る前から寝た後にかけての学習における変化。　問8　the greater the restoration of their learning　問9　エ

〈解説〉問1　下線部①の直後の，such as ～以下に具体例が挙げられている。　問2　下線部②の文意は「海馬は限られた記憶容量しかない」。直後の文に，容量を超えるとどうなるかが書かれているので，日本語でまとめる。　問3　筆者たちが検証した理論は，直前の第2段落3文目に説明されている。　問4　tax「～に負担をかける，～を酷使する」。overburden「過度の負担をかける」。　問5　下線部⑤this saturation effectは，直前の内容を指す。下線部⑤を含む文意は「人間の脳の学習容量は昼間長時間起き続けていると低下するのか。もしそうなら，睡眠はこの飽和効果を覆し記憶能力を回復させるのか」。　問6　第4段落には，昼間の睡眠が学習に与える影響を調べた結果が書かれている。昼間起きていた人は次第に学習成績が，A「悪化して」いった。対照的に，昼寝をした人は著しく，B「よく」なった。　問7　英文の意味

は「この研究で，睡眠紡錘波は何を予測していたか」。第5段落の最終文に答えが述べられている。　問8　最後の段落では，夜の睡眠の実験でも昼寝と同様の結果になったとある。「個人が夜に睡眠紡錘波を多く現せば現すほど」に続く空所なので，第5段落4文目後半のthe greater the restoration of their learningを入れるのが適切。　問9　本文では，学習には睡眠が重要であることを述べている。

2020年度　実施問題

【中高共通】

【1】聞き取りテスト

　　これから1〜10の英文を1回ずつ放送します。それぞれの英語のあとに，その内容について質問を一つします。その質問に対する答として適切なものをア〜エの中からそれぞれ一つ選び，記号で答えよ。

1　W : I have a terrible backache.

　　M : Umm, the X-ray doesn't show your backbone is broken.

　　W : But I can't keep standing while doing housework

　　M : Okay, if the painkiller doesn't work, come again and stay in the hospital.

　　Question(W) : What is the woman likely to do after the conversation?

　　ア　Stay in the hospital.

　　イ　Take the medicine

　　ウ　Keep standing.

　　エ　Do housework.

2　M : How much does it cost to send this package to Canada?

　　W : If you sand it by ship, the postage is seven forty. It costs ten dollars more by air.

　　M : I want to send it by air. Can I use a credit card?

　　W : Sorry. There is something wrong with the machine now.

　　Question(M) : How, and how much does the man have to pay?

　　ア　$7.40 with a card.

　　イ　$7.40 in cash.

　　ウ　$17.40 with a card.

　　エ　$17.40 in cash.

3　W : Hi, Dave. We are going for a drive and going to a hot spring during *Platinum Week.*

　　M : Really?　I don't believe it's worth going all that way to a crowded place. I'll stay at home and watch movies.

　　W : Emma and Justin want to go to the sand-steamed hot spring in Ibusuki.

　　M : What?　Why didn't you say she was going, too?　Do you have enough room for me in the car?

Question (W): What does Dave want to do during *Platinum Week?*

ア　Join his friends for a drive.

イ　Watch movies at home.

ウ　Go to the movies with his friends.

エ　Help Justin with his work.

4　M : What's the matter with you?

　　W : My computer has shut down suddenly. It may be too old. I'm wondering about buying a new one.

　　M : How about having the buttery checked?　sn't it time to replace it?

　　W : Yeah, 1 will. Oh, look at the outlet. It's unplugged.

Question (M): What was the problem?

ア　The computer needed repairing.

イ　The computer broke down.

ウ　The woman forgot to plug in the computer.

エ　The woman didn't know how to use the computer.

5　M : Here are this month's newly released books.

　　W : Umm... mystery, romance and science fiction...

　　M : This mystery novel is my recommendation. It will be made into a movie next year.

W : Well, I usually don't read these kinds of novels, but I will borrow it.

Question(M): Which statement is true?

ア　The woman is recommended a love story.

イ　The woman often borrows mystery novels.

ウ　The woman will read the recommended novel.

エ　The woman isn't interested in new books.

6　W : You've lost weight, haven't you?　Do you still walk every day?

M : No, I go to the gym several times a week.

W : You seem to enjoy exercising at the gym.

M : Yeah, training and chatting with my friends is fun for me.

Question(W): Which statement is true?

ア　He feels his current routine is good for him.

イ　He wants to continue his walking habit.

ウ　He doesn't like to chat with his friends.

エ　He thinks training at the gym is too hard.

7　W : I don't know how to apply for the exam on the Internet.

M : That's easy. All you need is a digital picture.

W : Can I use a picture saved on my smartphone?

M : Of course. And don't forget to print out the application form just in case.

Question(W): What does the man advise the woman to do?

ア　Print her picture.

イ　Surf the Internet.

ウ　Print the application form.

エ　Apply for the exam on paper.

8　Recently, there have been more and more exchange students and foreign workers in Japan. Some universities have dormitories where exchange students can live with their families. On the other hand, the preparation to receive the foreign workers' families is not good enough. It is urgent that we resolve the issue because we will need their labor for a long period of time.

Question (M): What is the title of the passage?

　ア　The increasing number of exchange students.

　イ　A decline in Japanese tourism.

　ウ　A rejection of students from overseas.

　エ　The current situation of foreign workers in Japan.

9　This is a story about an old Californian couple who became millionaires. The old man used to be a professor at a university and he had a lot of books. One day, his grandson visited their house to look for some books in order to do his history homework. When he opened one of the books, he found a lottery ticket between the pages. The old couple had forgotten about it. The grandson checked and found it was a winner!

Question (W): What made the old couple millionaires?

　ア　A lottery ticket found by their grandson.

　イ　A discovery in a university library.

　ウ　An achievement by the professor.

　エ　A book on California rolls.

10　Ladies and gentlemen, thank you very much for coming today. The concert was going to start at 7:00, but we really must apologize to you for the 30-minute delay. You can enjoy free drinks in front of the entrance while waiting. A shuttle bus to Kagoshima Station can be taken after the concert. It costs 2 hundred yen. Please wait until the concert starts.

Question (M): Which is true about the announcement?

　ア　The audience can take the shuttle bus without paying a fare.

　イ　The concert will start as scheduled.

　　ウ　Free drinks are available.

　　エ　The audience can receive a refund for their tickets

以上で英語の聞き取りテストを終わります。次の問題に進みなさい。

(☆☆☆○○○○○)

【2】次の各文の(　　)に入る適切な英語をア～エの中からそれぞれ一つ選び，記号で答えよ。

1　When teachers design a lesson plan, they should (　A　) a course of study, which is (　B　) great importance for them.

　　ア　A : fall short of　　　　　B : on

　　イ　A : take into account　　B : of

　　ウ　A : catch hold of　　　　B : on

　　エ　A : come up to　　　　　B : of

2　*Scanning* is a reading technique where the reader (　　　) rather than trying to absorb all the information.

　　ア　looks for specific information

　　イ　grasps all the information

　　ウ　summarizes the entire passage

　　エ　reads the passage intensively

3　"*The Old Man and the Sea*" was written by the author of "(　　　)".

　　ア　*Of Mice and Men*

　　イ　*For Whom the Bell Tolls*

　　ウ　*The Great Gatsby*

　　エ　*The Grapes of Wrath*

4　The JTE suggested to the ALT that they (　　　) the next lesson plan.

　　ア　discuss about

　　イ　discussed about

　　ウ　discuss

　　エ　discussed

95

5　Yuri has (　　) her to study in Canada for a year.
　ア　persuaded her father to let
　イ　persuaded her father of allowing
　ウ　talked to her father into letting
　エ　talked her father into allowing

(☆☆☆◎◎◎◎)

【3】英語には「聞くこと」,「話すこと」,「読むこと」及び「書くこと」の4技能がある。英語の授業において，それらの技能を統合的に活用させる指導例と，その指導から期待される効果を80語程度の英語で書け。なお，使用した語数を記入すること。

(☆☆☆☆◎◎◎◎)

【4】次の英文を読んで，後の問に答えよ。

There is now an active field of research into how the Internet is changing what we learn and remember. Start with the "Google Effect." In a 2011 experiment helmed by Daniel Wegner of Harvard, volunteers were presented with a list of forty trivia facts—short, pithy statements such as "An ostrich's eye is bigger than its brain." Each person was instructed to type all forty statements on a computer. Half the volunteers were told to remember the facts. The other half weren't. Also, half were informed that their work would be stored on the computer. The other half were told that it would be erased immediately after ①the task's completion.

The volunteers were later given a quiz on the facts they'd typed. Those instructed to remember the information scored no better than those who hadn't been told to do so. But those who believed that their work would be (　A　) scored much better compared to those who believed it would be (　B　). This was true, whether they were trying to remember the facts or not.

Proust was not the first to propose that memory is a great mystery. We remember the madeleine dipped in tea and forget many experiences and facts of greater consequence. The (C) mind exercises little choice in remembering and forgetting. Nobody decides to forget a client's name or to remember forever the lyrics of a detested pop tune. It just happens.

The Harvard experiment's results are consistent with a pragmatic system of memory. It is impossible to remember everything. The brain must constantly be doing triage on memories, without conscious intervention. And apparently it recognizes that there is less need to stock our minds with information that can be readily retrieved. (It may be a very long time before you need to know how big an ostrich's eyeball is.) So ②facts are more often forgotten when people believe the facts will be archived. This phenomenon has earned a name —the Google Effect—describing the automatic forgetting of information that can be found online.

If you take the Google Effect to the point of absurdity, selfies would cause ③amnesia. But a 2013 study conducted by Linda Henkel of Fairfield University pointed in that direction. Henkel noticed that visitors to art museums are obsessed with taking cellphone shots of artwork and often are less interested in looking at the art itself. So she performed ④an experiment at Fairfield University's Bellarmine Museum of Art. Undergraduates took a docent tour in which they were directed to view specific artworks. Some were instructed to photograph the art, and others were simply told to take note of it. The next day, both groups were quizzed on their knowledge of the artwork. The visitors who snapped pictures were less able to identify the works and to recall visual details.

Our unconscious curators of memory must be aware of how quickly and easily any needed fact can be called up. This implies that our broadband networks have created a new regime of learning and memory, one in which facts are less likely to be retained and are more quickly forgotten. In a few years, we'll probably all be wearing devices that shoot a 24-7 video stream of our lives. Will social media make amnesiacs of us all?

問1　下線部①のtaskの内容を30字以内の日本語で書け。

問2　本文中の(A)，(B)に入る語の組合せとして最も適切なものを次のア～エの中から一つ選び，記号で答えよ。

ア　A : stored　　　B : saved

イ　A : stored　　　B : erased

ウ　A : erased　　　B : deleted

エ　A : erased　　　B : saved

問3　本文中の(C)に入る1語を本文中から抜き出して書け。

問4　次の英文が下線部②の説明となるように，(1)，(2)に与えられた文字で始まる適切な1語を書け。

　　You are less likely to (1)(r　　　　) facts, given that you assume they will be (2)(r　　　) on the Web.

問5　下線部③の定義として最も適切なものをア～エの中から一つ選び，記号で答えよ。

ア　a type of mental illness that causes long periods of unhappiness

イ　an abnormal growth of the tissue in the brain

ウ　loss of the ability to remember

エ　a sudden change in the blood supply

問6　下線部④の結果を80字程度の日本語で書け。

問7　The Google Effectの例を示すものとして最も適切なものをア～エの中から一つ選び，記号で答えよ。

ア　You find it easy to memorize the information on the Internet.

イ　When you become friends with someone new online, you can easily memorize his or her name.

ウ　If you upload a file to the cloud, you sometimes have a hard time browsing it.

エ　You repeatedly look up the same recipe for the same dish on the Web.

問8　「知りたいことはすべてインターネットで検索すればよい」という意見に対するあなたの考えを60語程度の英語で書け。なお，使用した語数を記入すること。

(☆☆☆☆○○○○)

【中学校】

【1】 次の英文を読んで，後の問に答えよ。

When I was ten years old, I came home from school one day to find my father awake, which was (A) enough. He was a driver for a car service at night in the city. He often came home as my sister Sabrina and I were getting up for school, and slept until it was time to work again that evening. But that day he was up.

I was so excited by my father being home that I (B) to notice his packed bag in the hall. But I wouldn't have thought much about it. "Where are you going?" asked Sabrina, who had noticed. "My mother is sick," he replied, "I am going home to visit her." "Will she be okay?" I asked. ①I had never met my grandmother. She was too weak to travel, and my mother said we didn't have enough money to afford the tickets to Ethiopia. "She will be fine," my father said. "When are you coming back?" Sabrina asked. "Soon, Sabrina." "How soon?" she asked. "Soon," he repeated, "Is there anything you want me to bring back?" "Will you bring us one of these white dresses?" I asked. I'd seen them in the pictures of my cousins. They were beautiful with delicate embroidery. He smiled, "I promise." He looked at Sabrina. "Do you want me to bring you one?" "No, thank you," she said.

He stood to leave. He had tears in his eyes as he held me close and sang to me. "Tschay Hailu," the lullaby he used to sing to me every night. *Eshrurururu, eshrurururu, ye binyea enate tolo.* "Sing with me, dear," he said, and I did. When the song, was over, he pushed me away to arm's length, tears streaming down his face. "Promise me you will never stop singing." I said what I always said—that I promised. He wiped his face, picked up his suitcase and left.

②My grandmother died five weeks later. I cried, not because I was sad but because my father would be staying for the funeral and to settle her affairs. And the weeks (C) him had already been enough. With him absent, my family was like a three-legged chair.

"How much longer?" I asked over the phone line when he'd been gone for two months. "Not much longer," he said. "And you won't forget the white dress?" "I won't forget," he replied. I hung up the phone. Sabrina was standing there. "He's not coming back," she said. "Yes, he is!" I screamed at her. "You're just jealous because he loves me more. Because I can sing. He's coming back!"

A few months after that, I received a package in the mail. Inside was a white dress. It was beautiful and fit me perfectly. There was a note from my father. *I promised*, it said. And that was when I knew ⬚ D ⬚. I threw the dress into the trash. Then I went to my room and began to cry.

"What's gotten into you?" Mom asked when she found me there that night. It was still several weeks before she would sit me and Sabrina down and solemnly announce ③what we already knew: that she and our father were getting divorced; that he was staying in Ethiopia for foreseeable future. I just kept crying into my pillow. "I don't know what's with her," I heard my mother tell Sabrina. "Or how to snap her out of it."

I was still crying when I heard the door creak open. It was Sabrina. Silently, she climbed into the bed, and then my sister, who did not like to be hugged or kissed or even touched, wrapped her body around mine. "Don't worry. I'll take care of you now," she murmured. Then she began to sing to me. *Eshrurururu, eshrurururu, ye binyea enate tolo.* I had never heard my sister sing. I didn't know she could sing. And yet she sang the lullaby in a clear, pure voice. She sang it as if she too had been born singing. "Sing with me," she said. I did. We lay together, singing, harmonizing without even trying. Our voices blended perfectly, easily. We sang and I stopped crying. ④I believed that as long as we sang together, I would be okay.

問1　本文中の（　A　）～（　C　）に入る適切な語を次のア～カの中から それぞれ一つ選び，記号で答えよ。

ア　failed　　イ　common　　ウ　with　　エ　without
オ　came　　カ　unusual

問2　下線部①の理由を50字程度の日本語で書け。

問3　下線部②を知って筆者はどうしたか。その理由を含めて50字以内の日本語で書け。

問4　本文中の　　D　　に入る最も適切な英語を次のア～エの中から一つ選び，記号で答えよ。

　ア　my father was right

　イ　my mother was right

　ウ　Sabrina was right

　エ　I was right

問5　下線部③の具体的内容を50字程度の日本語で書け。

問6　次の英文が下線部④における筆者の心情を表すものとなるように，（　a　）～（　c　）に入る最も適切な語をア～オの中からそれぞれ一つ選び，記号で答えよ。

　　At first, I had thought it impossible to overcome my （　a　） over my father's absence. However, when I heard Sabrina sing and we sang the lullaby together, I felt the same kind of （　b　） as I did when I was with my father. Sabrina filled the hole my father's silence had left. Now I can be （　c　） if we sing together.

　ア　sorrow　　イ　positive　　ウ　surprise　　エ　pessimistic

　オ　relief

問7　あなたがこれまで誰かからもらったものの中で心に残っているものを1つ挙げ，その理由を60語程度の英語で書け。なお，使用した語数を記入すること。

（☆☆☆☆○○○○）

【高等学校】

【1】次の英文を読んで，後の問に答えよ。

　Communication exercises and assignments have traditionally put introverts at a disadvantage by design. The regular contributor to discussions in history, the first student to explain or write out the solution in math, and the student who offers to explain their experiment to the rest of the class in science will always be showered with positive reinforcement and generally rewarded with high praises. But what about the students who know the answer but prefer one-on-one conversations? Or the ones who are comfortable speaking to the class but prefer time to process their thoughts before answering a question? Or the ones that do their best critical thinking when it's not spontaneous? Presentations in geography, class discussions in careers, and pick-up games in gym are not just the wrong format for introverts to display their skills, they can be (　A　) to their education. As curricula move away from an emphasis on content to skills, the time is right to use that move as an opportunity to better serve introverts in school.

　　Communication tasks and assignments are hardest on introverts. Historically, participation marks hurt introverts, but now, with subjects like English shifting from language into a communication strand, that can make up to one-quarter of a student's in-class mark; 　B　 . To better serve introverts and provide them with the best opportunities to demonstrate their skills, we need to carefully plan communication tasks so that they don't unintentionally put introverts at a disadvantage. A communication exercise that allows introverts to flourish is ①circle discussion. For example, in an English class, instead of asking a question about a short story and having students raise their hands to respond or calling on them at random, a teacher could organize the class in a circle, propose a question and work around the circle one student at a time. This is a great set-up for introverts because they know exactly when their turn will be, allowing them time to process and consider how they want to respond. Everyone has a voice and everyone makes an equal contribution. Having the teacher sit with students where everyone participates in a predictable order eliminates the feeling of being put on-the-spot that inhibits introverts from demonstrating all their skills.

　　Anotherr assignment that better serves introverts is a podcast. I've used a podcast as the culminating assignment for my Grade 11 English class recently and found it great as ②a platform for introverted students to excel. While recording one's thoughts may be daunting, the forum of a podcast has many benefits for introverts. First, it allows for a student to work from notes or a script. As an aside, this proved to be an unexpectedly beautiful writing task as many students revised their scripts to perfection and that provided me with a mechanism to suggest that all writing requires such revision. Writing the notes or scripts allows the processing time that introverts prefer. As well, a podcast can be recorded multiple times before the final product is shared. This removes the-on-the-spot feel of traditional presentations that often cloud an introvert's true ability. By encouraging critical thinking and requiring a revision process that benefits all students, podcasts provide the opportunity for introspective thinking that traditional presentations do not.

As a whole, society is doing a better job of recognizing that introverts have been set up for second place by a world that rewards charming, outgoing people. For example, my wife is a lawyer and she recently told me ③how many private sector businesses are changing their interview process in an effort to better reach introverts. Introverts may actually be the best candidates for jobs long-term, but the traditional process unintentionally favours extroverts and allows them to appear to be the beat candidates. To account for this bias, before the interview, many companies now provide their questions in advance allowing time for processing their thoughts to evaluate the candidate's problem-solving ability.

As education strives more than ever to provide opportunities for all students to achieve success, the time is right to reconsider how introverts can best display their communication skills. The use of circle discussion and podcasts are just two examples. Teachers can create platforms for introverts to excel, at communication tasks with some innovative lesson planning.

問1　次の英文はintrovertsの特徴について書かれたものである。本文の
　　　内容に合うように(　a　)〜(　c　)に適切な1語をそれぞれ本文中か

ら抜き出して書け。

　　Introverts prefer one-on-one conversations and are better at　（　a　）thinking. They need time to （　b　） what they think, and they cannot demonstrate their ability well in a （　c　） way.

問2　本文中の（　A　）に入る適切な語を次のア～エの中から一つ選び，記号で答えよ。

　　ア　active　　　イ　counteractive　　　ウ　productive

　　エ　counterproductive

問3　本文中の　　B　　に入る英語を次のア～エの中から一つ選び，記号で答えよ。

　　ア　language learning skills are more taken into consideration

　　イ　communication assignments count more than ever before

　　ウ　students' communicative competence is not evaluated

　　エ　English teachers hardly emphasize communication skills

問4　下線部①の活動の利点を65字程度の日本語でまとめよ。

問5　下線部②が本文で意味するものを次のア～エの中から一つ選び，記号で答えよ。

　　ア　a raised flat area beside the track at a station

　　イ　a tool for teachers to convey their feelings at classrooms

　　ウ　a type of computing system or a software

　　エ　an opportunity for somebody to express their opinions

問6　下線部③の具体例を本文から探し，80字程度の日本語で書け。

問7　本文の内容を踏まえたとき，あなたはどのような英語の授業を心がけるか。60語程度の英語で書け。なお使用した語数を記入すること。

（☆☆☆○○○○）

解答・解説

【中高共通】

【1】1 イ　2 エ　3 ア　4 ウ　5 ウ　6 ア　7 ウ
　　8 エ　9 ア　10 ウ

〈解説〉短い英文とその内容についての質問を聞き，問題用紙に印刷され
　た選択肢から適切な答えを選ぶ4択問題である。問題は男女の会話7問
　と50〜80語程度のモノローグ3問からなる。それぞれ放送は1度だけな
　ので，集中して聞く必要がある。放送前に，問題用紙の選択肢に目を
　通し，問われそうな情報を予測しておくとよい。リスニング問題開始
　1分前には予告アナウンスが，設問ごとには約8秒の間隔があるため，
　その時間を有効に活用したい。　　1 男性(医者)が「痛み止めが効かな
　かったら入院してください」と話していることから，女性(患者)は痛
　み止めを飲んで様子を見ると考えられる。したがってイ「薬を飲む」
　が適切。アの「入院する」は，痛み止めが効かない場合の話なので誤
　り。ウ「立ち続ける」，エ「家事をする」は，女性の腰痛のため不可
　能なので，ともに誤り。　　2 男性(客)は航空便で荷物を送ることを希
　望し，その料金は船便($7.40)より$10高いので$17.40となる。また，男
　性はクレジットカード払いを希望したが，女性(店員)がカード読み取
　り機が故障していると答えたため，現金払いにしたと考えられる。
　3 男性(Dave)は最初自宅で映画を観ると話していたが，女性がEmma
　と一緒に車で温泉に行くと聞き，自分も女性の車に乗れるかを確認し
　た。したがって，ア「友人と一緒にドライブに行く」が適切。イ「自
　宅で映画を観る」は上記の説明から誤り。ウ「友人と映画を観に行く」
　は，行先が違うため誤り。エ「Justinの仕事を手伝う」は会話の中で言
　及されていないため誤り。　　4 電源につながるコードがコンセント
　から抜けていたため，ウ「コンピュータをコンセントにつなぎ忘れた」。
　この理由から，ア「コンピュータは修理が必要だった」，イ「コンピ
　ュータが壊れた」は誤り。エ「コンピュータの使い方がわからなかっ

た」は会話の中で言及されていないため誤り。　5　男性がミステリー小説を薦めたのに対し，女性はミステリー小説を普段はあまり読まないものの，男性が薦めた小説を借りると言っているため，ウ「薦められた小説を読む」が適切。ア「恋愛小説を薦められた」は本のジャンルが異なり，イ「よくミステリー小説を借りる」は女性の発言と一致しないため誤り。エ「新しい本に興味がない」は会話の中で言及されていないため誤り。　6　男性は週に数回ジムに通っており，女性からジム通いを楽しんでいると言われるとそれを肯定しているため，ア「現在の習慣を自分にとって良いものだと感じている」となる。イ「散歩の習慣を続けたいと思っている」は，女性から毎日散歩しているかと聞かれたときに男性が否定しているため誤り。ウ「友人とおしゃべりするのが嫌い」，エ「ジムでのトレーニングはつらいと考えている」は，男性がどちらも楽しいと感じているため誤り。　7　男性は女性に「念のため忘れずに申請書を印刷してください」と言っているので，ウ「申請書を印刷する」が適切。ア「彼女の写真を印刷する」，イ「ネットサーフィンをする」，エ「紙面で試験の申請をする」は会話の中で言及されていないため誤り。　8　英文では，海外からの留学生については家族と同居できる寮が提供されているが，労働者の家族については受け入れ態勢が不十分で早急な対応が必要とされている。英文で特に問題視されているのは労働者の家族の受け入れについてなので，エ「日本における外国人労働者の現状」が適切。ア「留学生の増加」は言及されているが，上記の理由からタイトルとしては誤り。イ「日本観光の衰退」，ウ「海外からの学生の拒否」は英文で言及されていないため誤り。　9　老夫婦は宝くじを買ったことを忘れていたが，老夫婦の家を訪れた孫が本に挟まっていたのを見つけ，それが当選していたことがわかった。したがって，ア「孫が見つけた宝くじ」が適切。イ「大学図書館での発見」，ウ「教授の業績」，エ「カリフォルニアロールの本」は誤り。　10　入り口前で無料のドリンクを飲めるため，ウ「無料ドリンクが入手可能」。ア「コンサートへの来場者は無料でシャトルバスに乗れる」は，200円かかるため誤り。

イ「コンサートが予定通り始まる」は，30分遅れで始まるため誤り。エ「コンサートへの来場者はチケットの払い戻しができる」は英文で言及されていないため誤り。

【2】1 イ　2 ア　3 イ　4 ウ　5 エ

〈解説〉1　空欄Aには "take into account" を入れ，「学習指導要領を考慮に入れる」とするのが適切。また，空欄Bには "of" を入れて「of 抽象名詞」"of(great)importance" とすると，形容詞 "important" と同じ意味になる。"fall short of" は「～に及ばない」，"catch hold of" は「～をつかむ」，"come up to" は「～に達する」の意味なので，文脈に合わず誤り。2　スキャニングの意味は，ア「特定の情報を探す」。なお，文章全体にざっと目を通して概要を理解する読み方をスキミングという。
3　「老人と海」と「誰がために鐘は鳴る」はいずれもヘミングウェイの小説である。ア「ハツカネズミと人間」，エ「怒りの葡萄」はスタインベックの小説，ウ「グレート・ギャツビー」はフィッツジェラルドの小説であるため誤り。　4　discussは他動詞で直後に目的語をとるため，前置詞aboutを伴っているアとイは誤り。また，空欄は提案の動詞suggestのthat節の中にあるため，"(should)動詞の原形" が入る。したがって，過去形のエは誤り。　5　空欄にはエを入れ，「ユリは父親を説得して1年間のカナダ留学を許可させた」とする。選択肢の最後はletかallowが入るが，適切な用法は "let＋目的語＋do" と "allow＋目的語＋to do" なのでアとウは誤り。また，「を説得して～させる」を表すフレーズは "persuade＋人＋to do" や "talk＋人＋into ～ing" であるため，イとウは誤り。

【3】At first students should listen to the entire text, and then read it. By doing so, they can grasp the outline of the text before reading it intensively and connect the sounds and letters. After reading the text, they can summarize or write their own opinions about it, and discuss their ideas with their classmates. They can improve their four skills through these activities, learn how to interact well with others, and broaden their ways of thinking. (77 words)

〈解説〉実際の場面では，「聞くこと」，「話すこと」，「読むこと」，「書くこと」を組み合わせてコミュニケーションをとることが多く，授業でもこれら4技能を統合的に活用させることが重要である。その際，一度に全ての技能を詰め込むより，一つひとつの活動で焦点を当てる技能を明確にし，それらをどのようにつなげていくのかを考える必要がある。公式解答のように，インプットからアウトプットへとスムーズに進められる指導例を考えられるとよい。

【4】問1　四十個の雑学的知識の文章をコンピュータに入力すること。(27字)　問2　エ　問3　conscious　問4　(1) remember
(2) recorded　問5　ウ　問6　芸術作品を鑑賞する際に，作品の写真を撮るよう指示された集団の方が，ただ注意して鑑賞するように指示された集団よりも，作品を識別できず，見た目の詳細を思い出せなかった。(82字)　問7　エ　問8　Easy access to all the information you want to find via the Internet has advantages and disadvantages. One of the good points is that the Internet provides you with information you need anytime as long as you have Internet access. However, information on the Web is not always reliable, it being sometimes difficult to know who wrote what you are reading. (61 words)

〈解説〉問1　taskは「課題」などの意味であるが，ここではHarvard大学の実験参加者に課された課題を指す。また，下線部①では "the task" と定冠詞theがあることから，このtaskは書き手と読み手が特定できるものであり，英文の中で既に言及されている。以上のことを考慮に入れると，第1パラグラフ3，4文目から，「四十個の雑学的知識の文章をコンピュータに入力すること」がtaskの内容だと考えられる。　問2　第1パラグラフ7，8文目から，Harvard大学の実験参加者はコンピュータに入力した雑学的知識が保存されると言われたグループと，すぐに削除されると言われたグループに分けられた。そして，空欄A，Bでは後

で実施された雑学的知識に関するクイズの成績をグループ間で比較している。第4パラグラフ1文目には「Harvard大学の実験結果は記憶の仕組みと一貫している」とあり，同パラグラフ4文目を見ると「(容易に検索できない情報に比べ)容易に検索可能な情報は記憶しておく必要性が低い」とある。したがって，Harvard大学の実験ではコンピュータに情報が保存されると言われたグループの方が削除されると言われたグループより，クイズの成績が低かったと考えられる。　問3　空欄Cを含む第3パラグラフを見ると，記憶と忘却は人間が自分でコントロールできるものではないことが記述されている。したがって，空欄には本文中の語conscious「意識的な」を入れるのが適切。　問4　下線部②の意味は「人々が保存されると思っているとき，事実はより頻繁に忘却される」。(1)は直前に"less likely to"とあるので，下線部②のforgetと反対の内容となる単語を考える。(2)は「保存(保管)する」を「記録する」と言い換える。　問5　下線部③の前文で，Google Effectとは「ウェブで入手できる情報は自動的に忘れてしまう現象である」と説明している。したがって，amnesiaの定義として適切なのは，ウ「記憶能力の喪失」。ア「長期間の憂鬱な精神状態を引き起こす精神病」，イ「脳組織の異常な成長」，エ「血液供給の急激な変化」は誤り。

問6　下線部④an experimentの説明は第5パラグラフ5〜8文目に記述されており，その内容を指定字数内でまとめる。　問7　本文はGoogle Effectについて書かれたもので，Harvard大学やHenkelの実験をあげながら説明を行い，第6パラグラフがまとめとなっている。第6パラグラフ1，2文目から，Google Effectとはインターネット上に保持されている情報がすぐに，かつ容易に人間の記憶から忘却される無意識的な現象だといえる。したがって，エ「付け合わせ料理の同じレシピを何度もウェブ上で調べる」が適切。アは，インターネット上の情報を容易に記憶できるとあるため誤り。イ「インターネット上で友人になると，その人の名前を簡単に覚えることができる」，ウ「ファイルをクラウドにアップロードすると，閲覧が難しいことがある」は本文で言及されていない内容なので誤り。　問8　自分の考えを書けばよいので，

提示された意見に賛成／反対する立場から書く他に，解答例のように「長所短所の両方があるため注意した上でインターネット検索を利用する」という意見を書くのも1つの方法である。ただし，どの立場から意見を書く場合でも，自分の意見に合致した説得力のある理由や具体例を添えることが求められる。

【中学校】

【1】問1　A　カ　　B　ア　　C　エ　　問2　祖母は旅行をするには体が弱く，私の家族はエチオピアへの航空券を買う経済的余裕がなかったから。(46字)　　問3　父親が祖母の葬式と，遺品整理のためにエチオピアに滞在することになったから泣いた。(40字)　　問4　ウ　問5　母親と父親が離婚することになることと，父親はしばらくの間エチオピアから帰って来ないということ。(47字)　　問6　a　ア　b　オ　c　イ　　問7　I will never forget the watch my father gave me when I entered high school. I was really happy about it because it was the first watch of my own, and it was very cute. The watch meant a lot to me: I felt like I was becoming more and more independent every time I wore it. I'm going to treasure it forever. (63 words)

〈解説〉問1　A　空欄Aの前の関係代名詞whichは，「ある日筆者が学校から帰宅すると父親が起きていた」という節の内容を指す。第1パラグラフ2，3文目から，筆者の父親は夜間に運転手として働いており，筆者とSabrinaが起床して学校に登校するころに帰宅し，夜まで寝ているとある。したがって，筆者が学校から帰宅するころに起きているのはunusual「珍しい」と考えられる。　B　空欄Bはthat節中の主語の直後で動詞が入る。"fail to do"は「～できない」の意味で，筆者は父親の荷物でいっぱいのバッグに気づかなかった。一方，第2パラグラフ3文目からSabrinaはそれに気づき，多くの荷物を持ってどこに行くのかを父親に尋ねている。　C　第4パラグラフ1，2文目から，父親が家を出て5週間後にエチオピアの祖母が亡くなり，葬式や事後処理でさらに長期間父親がエチオピアに滞在することになったため筆者は泣いた。

したがって，エのwithoutをCに入れると，第4パラグラフ3文目の意味
は「彼(父親)がいない期間は既に十分だった」となる。　問2　下線部
①の理由は直後の第2パラグラフ7文目に記述されており，その内容を
字数内でまとめればよい。　問3　下線部②を知った筆者の行動とそ
の理由は，直後の第4パラグラフ2文目に記述されている。

問4　第2パラグラフの9文目以降における父親と娘たち(筆者と
Sabrina)とのやり取りの中で，父親は筆者に白いドレスを届けると約
束したが，Sabrinaにいつ帰ってくるのかを聞かれると，具体的な日程
を約束しなかった。Sabrinaはこの時点で父親が長期間帰ってこない可
能性が高いことを悟っていたと考えられる。その後，第5パラグラフ
で筆者は父親と電話で話をしたが，父親が帰らないと言うSabrinaと口
論になる。第6パラグラフでは，白いドレスが父親から筆者に届いた
が，筆者は “*I promised*” と書かれた紙を見て，家に戻る日程は約束さ
れておらず，父親が当分の間は戻ってこないことを悟る。したがって，
空欄Dにはウ「Sabrinaが正しかった」が入る。　問5　下線部⑤の詳し
い内容は直後のコロンの後に書かれているので，that she and〜の文と，
that he was〜の文の内容をまとめる。　問6　第6パラグラフで筆者は
父親がしばらくの間エチオピアから戻らないことを悟り，部屋で泣き
出してしまう。第8パラグラフでSabrinaが筆者を慰め，筆者は父親と
歌っていた子守唄をSabrinaと歌い，泣き止むに至った。以上のことか
ら，空欄aにはsorrow「悲しみ」，空欄bにはrelief「安心」，空欄cには
positive「前向きな」を入れる。ウ「驚き」，エ「悲観的な」は文脈に
合わないため誤り。　問7　誰からもらったものか，もらったものが
何か，なぜ心に残っているのかを，最低限解答に入れなければならな
い。その際，それをもらった際の具体的なシチュエーションや，具体
的なエピソードを入れると，よりわかりやすくなる。

【高等学校】

【1】問1　a　critical　　b　process　　c　spontaneous　　問2　エ
　　問3　イ　　問4　生徒が自分の発言の順番がわかり，どのように答え

るか考えをまとめる時間を持つことができる。また全員が等しく発言できるため公平である。(65字)　　問5　エ　　問6　内向的な者に不利にならないように，面接の前に，多くの会社が質問を渡し，就職志願者が予め考えをまとめる時間を与えている。それにより志願者の問題解決能力を測っている。(81字)　　問7　To encourage introverts in large classes, I organize students into pairs or small groups. I also make time for them to process their ideas before the activities. I would like to have students perform in pairs, then in small groups, and finally perform in front of the whole class. This will help every student have confidence and improve their performances. (60 words)

〈解説〉問1　第1パラグラフでは2文目で外向的な生徒(extroverts)の具体例があげられており，逆接の接続詞butをはさんで6～9文目には内向的な生徒(introverts)の具体例があげられている。その内容からintrovertsは「一対一の会話を好む，解答前に考えをまとめる時間を望む，求められたときに最もよい批判的な思考を行う」などの特徴があることがわかる。したがって空欄aには「批判的な」，空欄bには「過程」，空欄cには「自発的な」を入れるのが適切。　　問2　空欄Aを含む文の前半では，いくつかの指導形態を例示し，それらが「内向的な生徒たちが能力を示すには不適切であるだけでなく，(　　　)である」と述べている。よって，続く後半ではさらにネガティブな内容が書かれていると考えられる。したがって，空欄Aにはエ counterproductive「逆効果の」が入る。ア active「能動的な」，イ counteractive「反作用の」，ウ productive「生産的な」は文脈に合わず誤り。　　問3　第2パラグラフ2文目の空欄B前の部分には，「英語などが言語を教える科目からコミュニケーションを教える科目に変わってきており，それが生徒の授業内評価の1/4を占めるほどになってきた」と述べられている。したがって，その内容に合致するのはイ「コミュニケーションの課題が以前より重要になっている」。他の選択肢は，言語の教育からコミュニケーションの教育に代わってきているという内容に合わないため誤り。

問4　circle discussionの利点は，第2パラグラフ12文目の "This (circle

discussion) is a great set-up for introverts because…" に続く部分から14文目に記述されている。この内容を65字程度にまとめる。

問5　platformには「意見発表の機会」の意味があるため，エ「誰かが意見を表現する機会」が適切。第3パラグラフ2文目では，筆者は英語の課題にポッドキャストを利用しており，内向的な生徒たちがすぐれたパフォーマンスを示すよい機会と考えている。　問6　下線部③の文意は「いかに多くの民間企業でその就職面接のプロセスが変わってきているか」。この具体例が第4パラグラフ3，4文目に記述されている。

問7　「本文の内容を踏まえたとき」と指定されていることに注意。本文ではcircle discussionやポッドキャストの事例があげられているが，内向的な生徒たちに配慮した英語の授業を考える必要がある。その際，問1の解説で述べたようなintrovertsの性質を考慮し，字数以内にまとめる。

2019年度　実施問題

【中高共通】

【1】聞き取りテスト

　これから1〜10の英語を1回同ずつ放送します。それぞれの英語のあとに，その内容について質問を一つします。その質問に対する答として適切なものをア〜エの中から一つずつ選び，その記号で答えよ。

1　M：I'm terribly busy these days. Risa, you also work really hard. So, I think we need some fresh air. Why don't we plan a trip this weekend?

　　W：I'd like to, Ben, but I have something to finish by Saturday. So, I can't take a trip.

　　M：O.K, but we need a break. How about going to a movie and shopping on Sunday?

　　W：That sounds good.

　　Question(M)：What does the man suggest to the woman that they do on Sunday?

　　ア　Work harder than before.

　　イ　Take a ride in an airplane together.

　　ウ　Try to cancel watching a movie.

　　エ　Have time to relax together.

2　W：What's happening? We're not moving. This road isn't usually like this at night on weekends.

　　M：Yeah, this road is busy only early in the morning. Come to think of it, I wonder if an accident happened near here.

　　W：Maybe you're right. Oh, look at the sign. It says road repairs have started today.

M : Oh, that explains it.

Question (W): Why is there so much traffic now?

ア　There is a terrible car accident.

イ　It is rush hour right now.

ウ　The road is being fixed.

エ　It is a night on the weekend.

3　W : Welcome to Kagoshima Book Store. Can I help you? We have an abundant line up of new books.

M : I'm not looking for books. I saw you were hiring, but are you still accepting applications for the part-time job?

W : Oh yes, of course. I will talk to our manager, so please fill out this form and wait a moment.

M : Sure.

Question (W): What is the man's purpose for visiting this bookstore?

ア　To look for some new books at the store.

イ　To get a job at the book store.

ウ　To ask the manager for a wage increase.

エ　To wait for one of his friends at the store.

4　W : I'm full. That was so delicious, Tom.

M : I'm happy to hear that. You didn't expect I could cook, did you?

W : Actually, I didn't, so I was very surprised. How come you are so good at cooking?

M : My mother taught me the ABCs of cooking when I was a kid. Since then, I have been into it. Actually, I'm thinking of going to France to brush up my skills. I want to be a three-star chef someday.

W : I'm sure you will be.

Question (M): What did the man's mother do for him when he was young?

ア　She taught him how to cook.

イ　She taught him how to speak French.

ウ　She taught him how to date girls.

エ　She taught him how to write letters.

5　W : Excuse me, but could you tell me the way to the Satsuma Building?

　　M : Satsuma Building? It's very far from here.

　　W: Really? I want to go to my friend's office. It's in the Satsuma Building. He told me its address, and I wrote it down. I entered the address and I followed my smartphone's GPS navigation.

　　M : Do you have a memo of the address?

　　W : Yes. Here you are.

　　M : Thank you. Can I take a look at your smartphone? Let me see... Oh, you put in the wrong address. You should check the address carefully and type it again.

　　Question (W): Why did the woman get lost?

　　ア　Her friend told her the wrong address.

　　イ　She didn't type the address correctly.

　　ウ　She lost the paper she wrote the address on.

　　エ　Her GPS navigation system wasn't working properly.

6　M : Hello, Aozora Police Station. How can I help you?

　　W: My bicycle was stolen! I'm standing in front of Aozora Mall, where I left it before I went shopping.

　　M : OK, Please calm down. All the bicycles are supposed to be registered when they are bought. So your bicycle must have a number. Could you tell it to me?

　　W : Oh, I don't remember it, but I have the registration documents at my house. So, I will call you later.

　　Question (M): What is the woman going to do next?

　　ア　Return to her house.

イ Look for the bicycle.

ウ Complain to the police.

エ Buy a new bicycle.

7 M : What a hot day! How about going for a swim?

W : Oh, I'm sorry, Ken, but I must go to the library to borrow some books for my homework.

M : Oh, Cindy, it's Sunday today. The library is closed. Why don't we go there tomorrow? I have some books to return.

W : Oh, I see. Since the library is closed, I'll go with you.

Question (M): What is the woman most likely to do on Monday?

ア Go swimming.

イ Go shopping with Ken.

ウ Go to the library.

エ Return some books to Ken.

8 Hello, everyone. Today I would like to talk about smartphones. Many parents usually think smartphones are not good for children even if parents allow their children to have them. However, whether smartphones become good or bad depends on how they are used. Not only children, but parents should use them in an appropriate manner. Each family should talk about the use of smartphones and make some rules. For example, children have to put them on the table in the living room and they cannot use them after 9:00 pm. Also a filtering system can prevent children from using harmful websites. Before letting your children have smartphones, why don't you make some rules?

Question (W): Which is the best title for this passage?

ア The Good and Bad Points of Smartphones.

イ The Correct Way to Talk with Children.

ウ The Influence of Smartphones on Children.

117

エ　The Smart Rules of Smartphones.

9　When I was young, classes were mostly taught in a lecture format, but I heard that the average learning retention rate is only 5 percent in that way. By reading, the rate is 10 percent, by demonstration, it is 30 percent, and by discussion, it is 50 percent. By practicing, it is 75 percent, and the highest is teaching others. That percentage is 90 percent. When we teach something to others, we may find we don't know as much as we thought and we can recognize what we have learned. Teaching is a good method of learning.

Question (W): What is the man talking about?

ア　About how to teach something effectively.

イ　About how to learn something effectively.

ウ　About how to read the text carefully.

エ　About when to start learning foreign languages.

10　Attention, please. For passengers waiting for Satsuma Airlines Flight 333 to London, the flight is overbooked, so we're looking for passengers who are willing to give up their seats in exchange for a travel voucher. For those passengers who agree to our proposal, we ask that you report to the passenger-service desk in terminal 2. We are sorry for the inconvenience, but we would appreciate your cooperation.

Question (M): Who can get a travel voucher?

ア　Passengers who will not accept the suggestion from the Airlines.

イ　Passengers who are eager to take Flight 333 to London.

ウ　Passengers who will voluntarily not take Flight 333 to London.

エ　Passengers who are not going to the passenger-service desk.

以上で英語の聞き取りテストを終わります。次の問題に進みなさい。

(☆☆○○○○)

【2】次の(　　)に入る適切な語をア～エの中から一つずつ選び，記号で
答えよ。

1　For this concert, tickets will be allotted in (　　) of application.

　　ア　turn　　イ　degree　　ウ　order　　エ　series

2　Emi is sick in bed. If she had not walked home in the rain yesterday, she
　　(　　) camping with her friends now.

　　ア　can go　　イ　could go　　ウ　can have gone

　　エ　I could have gone

3　James doesn't like the rude way (　　) Nancy spoke to his sister.

　　ア　in which　　イ　which　　ウ　in that　　エ　where

4　(　　) learning focuses on the use of authentic language through
　　meaningful activities such as visiting the doctor or a telephone call. This
　　method encourages meaningful communication and is student-centered.

　　ア　Content-based　　イ　Task-based　　ウ　Meaning-based

　　エ　Form-based

5　Debates are a great way for students to get involved in class. Students
　　have to find (　　) topics, prepare for the debate with their team, and think
　　on their feet as they practice public speaking.

　　ア　arrogant　　イ　introverted　　ウ　controversial

　　エ　conventional

(☆☆◎◎◎◎)

【3】次の英語のことわざを参考にして，授業を通して，英語教師は生徒
にどのように関わっていけばよいか。自分の考えを80語程度の英語で
書け。なお，使用した語数を記入すること。

"You can lead a horse to water, but you cannot make it drink."

(☆☆☆☆◎◎◎)

【4】次の英文を読んで，後の問に答えよ。

　　Ellie Colegate, 15, spent five years studying French at school in Kent, but opted not to continue beyond Year 9. "Learning a new language was never something my teachers made appealing or entertaining. My French teacher just made us copy and complete exercises from books. And during lessons, she spent little time speaking the language herself and would only ever get a handful of the best students to speak in class." ①The British approach to language education has failed to engage her.

At the same time, the industry around Teaching English as a Foreign Language (TEFL) is exploding with activity and seeing increasing success across the globe. TEFL teachers teach English abroad to people whose first language is not English. There are TEFL courses offered by a number of accredited course providers across the globe.

How is it that the TEFL industry is booming while the British language learning system is in a state of crisis?

Benny Lewis, a travel blogger who teaches English, believes the TEFL approach is successful because it emphasizes alternative elements of language learning. "TEFL teachers are forced to step outside of a failed academic system that never helped them speak a language at school, and ②they do things completely differently." he explains.

The secret to TEFL methodology is simple: teachers create natural situations for students to interact in. Every student speaks throughout the lesson, and physical movement is exploited to avoid boredom and fatigue. Traditional grammar tables and confusing linguistic terminology are often abandoned, but that doesn't mean it gets ignored. "Grammar is explained by use of examples in such a way that it doesn't feel like grammar," says Lewis. "It can and likely must be taught, but in a (　A　) context."

Speaking becomes easier if the physical setup of a classroom allows direct communication between teacher and student, and interaction between students. TEFL teachers aim for a (　B　) atmosphere by organizing desks in a horseshoe shape or "cafe-style", rather than arranging a classroom in (　C　) rows.

However this is dependent on delivery by a native speaker. "It's easier and less exposing for non-native speakers teaching a language to hide behind a text book or grammar book than it is to engage in activities a TEFL teacher would engage in," says Johnny Harben, who has taught English as a foreign language in the UK. "Unless somebody is absolutely fluent, there's always the temptation to speak in a common language with students," Harben adds. ③"The TEFL methodologies are absolutely for the native English speaker."

The key component of TEFL's triumph seems to be in ④the immersion concept. Carol Syder, director at The English Experience School of English, agrees that immersion with a native speaker is an integral part of the process. "We only employ English mother tongue speakers at both our school and on the camps we run abroad every year. Why? Because this is the best way to ensure that the students gain confidence and it gives them the best opportunity to improve their language skills in a short period of time."

Hannah Garrard taught in South Korea for two years. She believes communication and temperament are pivotal. "Trying to communicate can be an embarrassing experience for both student and teacher [in TEFL], so you really have to bring your personality to each lesson," she says. "I got to know my students and established what they wanted from their learning. I asked what they wanted to know about in terms of subject, and built the technical language skills from there."

Immersion and communication are the buzzwords and concepts that could drive British language education forward. "Immersion pushes students to ⑤find lateral solutions to problems," Garrard says. "They have to think 'how am I going to make myself understood?', so communication and problem-solving are taken - quite naturally - to the next level."

問1　下線部①の具体的理由を60字程度の日本語で書け。

問2　後の英文が下線部②の説明となるように，(a)，(b)に与えられた文字で始まる適切な英語1語をそれぞれ書け。

　　For the purpose of developing students' (a)(s　　) skills, TEFL teachers give English classes using (b)(p　　　) approaches which are different from traditional ones.

問3　本文中の(　A　)に入る最も適切な語を次のア～ウの中から一つ選び，記号で答えよ。

ア　critical　　イ　grammatical　　ウ　communicative

問4　本文中の(　B　)，(　C　)に入る語の組み合わせとして最も適切なものを次のア～エの中から一つ選び，記号で答えよ。

ア　B：monotonous　　　C：democratic

イ　B：democratic　　　C：monotonous

ウ　B：riotous　　　　C：multiple

エ　B：multiple　　　　C：riotous

問5　下線部③のように述べた具体的理由を65字程度の日本語で書け。

問6　次の英文が下線部④の説明となるように，(a)，(b)に適切な英語1語をそれぞれ書け。

　　This concept states that students are able to improve their language skills in a short time,　by putting them in an (a)(　　　) situation where they (b)(　　　) to use only that language.

問7　下線部⑤の意味に最も近いものを次のア～ウの中から一つ選び，記号で答えよ。

ア　think from many different points of view

イ　stick to traditional ideas to solve problems

ウ　give students the single right answer naturally

問8　次の質問に対するあなたの考えを60語程度の英語で書け。なお，使用した語数を記入すること。

　　What do you think about bringing your personality to each lesson?

(☆☆☆◎◎◎)

【中学校】

【1】次の英文を読んで，後の問に答えよ。

　　This is the blog written by Tom. He feels nervous about his schoolmates,

Luke Williams and Ryan Colby. Luke is a new student from a big city. Ryan hates Tom, and he is always teasing Tom about ①his problem.

22/09/2015   22：21

...I'm afraid of the letter 'W'. It is difficult for me to say the sound, and I often repeat it. So what?

22/03/2016   21:30

Today was a good day. I had a talk with Dad. He told me there's a new drug for my problem. But guess what? I like the way I talk. ②So does Dad. He told me it's made me a better person because I think carefully before I speak. We decided I don't need drugs.

07/04/2016   7:51

What a day! It started badly. The phone rang while I was having breakfast. I was so excited but (A) − an important day for me!!! So I answered it without thinking. Bad idea! It was Luke Williams. I thought, 'How has he got my number?'

When I saw him yesterday, he probably only wanted to ask me what I was doing in the science fair, but I couldn't speak. He always makes me so nervous, so I just walked away. He probably thought I was a stupid person. So I thought, 'Why is he calling me now?'He said, 'Hello ... hello? Is this Tom?'

Did I tell you 'H'is a problem for me too? So, trying to say 'hello'was my second bad idea. Then I heard someone laughing. It sounded like Ryan. I put the phone down. OK, so they were calling to laugh at me. Anyway, I've got to go. The science fair is waiting for me!

07/04/2016   22:51

Today was a really big day for me. The last time I spoke in class was three years ago, and it was such an embarrassing and (B) moment that I would never forget it. I tried to say a 'W'and made that strange sound. Everyone laughed and I haven't spoken in class since then. After that I've had special support from my teacher, and he lets me use my laptop in class all the time. I got an app that turns text into speech. It's really cool!

And guess what? [a] When I listen to music with my headphones, I've found I can speak without having my problem!!

I arrived at school early this morning to practice with my group. Luke Williams was waiting by the entrance. He was smiling. Ryan was there too. He said, 'Hey, Tom, guess what?'[b] I tried to say, 'What?'and got stuck on the 'W'and Ryan and his friends started laughing. I turned and ran.

I wasn't going to do the science fair after that, but I got a text from Dad saying good luck. [c] I thought "OK, I'm not going to let people like Ryan make me feel bad any more."

Unfortunately, I was so nervous that I chose the wrong music on my MP3 player. So instead of Mozart I was listening to dance music. The problem is that when I listen to dance music with my headphones. I can't stop myself talking in the same rhythm as the music. So ③it just sounds like I'm rapping!

Most people in school have never heard me speak. They were really surprised when I started doing a rap about bacteria that eat plastic. I could see they were laughing at me, but when I finished, they all stood up and cheered.

After we finished, everyone wanted to be my friend. I didn't see Ryan or Luke right after the science fair.

Luke came to my house this afternoon. I couldn't believe it! ④I was wrong. He wasn't laughing at me this morning. He was calling to say 'good luck in the science fair'. And that wasn't Ryan laughing on the phone, it was Luke's dog barking! We thought that was really (C)! Dad invited him to stay for dinner. Then when I said goodbye to him at the door he turned around and said, 'Guess what?'And I said, '(D)?'

問1　下線部①の具体的な内容を50字程度の日本語で書け。

問2　下線部②の具体的な内容を25字程度の日本語で書け。

問3　本文中の(　A　)～(　C　)に入る最も適切な語をア～カの中から一つずつ選び，記号で答えよ。

　　ア　courageous　　イ　cowardly　　ウ　terrible　　エ　funny

　　オ　suspicious　　カ　worried

問4　次の英文が入る最も適切な箇所を[　a　]～[　c　]の中から一つ選び，記号で答えよ。

　　　I have another great thing to tell you!

問5　下線部③の状況を具体的に60字程度の日本語で書け。

問6　次の英文が下線部④を説明する内容となるように，(　ア　)～(　ウ　)に適切な英語1語をそれぞれ書け。

　　　When I got a phone call from Luke this morning, I thought he and Ryan called to make (　ア　) of me. In fact, however, Luke wanted to (　イ　) me about the science fair on the phone. Besides, I (　ウ　) Luke's dog barking for Ryan's laughter.

問7　本文中の(　D　)に入る英語1語を本文中から抜き出して書け。

問8　あなたが苦手としていたことを克服した経験とその経験から学んだことを60語程度の英語で書け。なお，使用した語数を記入すること。

(☆☆☆◎◎◎)

【高等学校】

【1】次の英文を読んで，後の問に答えよ。

　　Of all the people I have ever interviewed, Mathilda Spak has to be one of the most extraordinary. At close to 100, Mathilda is out there volunteering every day from morning till night. This strong lady has more energy than people half her age even though she has severe arthritis and suffers from black-outs. Yet Mathilda completely relishes life. She told me, ①"I'm having a ball！"

　　"I made a promise to my mother that I would work on myasthenia gravis － the fatal debilitating illness which causes abnormal weakness of certain muscles that she died from — till I found out what caused it and how to cure it. I have been asking questions ever since. Twenty-five years ago, I started a research project and we are getting closer to finding out the causes. We have been able to cut the death rate from 85% to 5%. However, that's not enough!"

②"I fundraise for the City of Hope so as to put my promise to my mother into action. Each year we have a Grand Prix fundraiser for 20 different charitable organizations. Hundreds apply to be included but the rule is that each organization can only take part in it every three years. A few years ago, I made a deal with them to keep myasthenia gravis on their schedule every year. How did I convince them? I told them that I am in my nineties and I can't afford to wait around three years between cycles."

"I also work at the Children's Hospital in Long Beach, California. When babies who have been abused are brought to the clinic, their sailed clothes are thrown out and they end up being released wrapped in a shabby towel. Can you imagine? When I saw that, ③I lost my temper. I told the people at the hospital. These children need decent clothes! So they put me in charge. I convinced a yarn company to contribute balls of yarn. Now I have members of different churches knitting beautiful blankets and sweaters for the babies. I also accept contributions of new clothing. Now every single baby goes home properly clothed, with a pretty new blanket."

"There are 6 days a week, and I try to fit it all in. What I can't do at the office I take home on Sundays. You have to stay busy, otherwise you get bored and you start to feel sorry for yourself. I also serve as a guide for the Long Beach Symphony, helping out when the children visit from schools."

"I got started on this path because my mother taught me from the time I was a child that you must always give back to the community in service. We had a little store in a poor neighborhood and my mother was always helping people. I learned it from her."

"My advice to this generation is — give of yourself. There's no one who cannot give something. You can take care of a child, volunteer, or help your neighbor. No excuses. My mother taught me you never say *can't*, and that's how I live. I have to walk with a cane. Big deal. ④<u>So I buy myself fancy canes.</u>"

"Only by giving do you get back. My mother also taught me to only use the dollar for what good you can do with it, and to never turn away a hungry person."

"I get people to do all kinds of things. I go to the nursing home and have the older women knit for the babies. If someone says they can't help out, I ask for one Wednesday. But people started saying, '[A] or you'll be doing one Wednesday for the rest of your life!' I have one man who has been doing one Wednesday for 40 years."

More than ever, the world needs all of us to care about each other and demonstrate our care through our actions. How can you use your life to make the world a better place? Small deed or large, what most matters is opening your heart and making a (B) in any way you can.

問1　下線部①とほぼ同じ意味の英文を次のア〜エから一つ選び，記号で答えよ。
ア　I'm really tired of working!
イ　I'm fed up with my life!
ウ　I'm addicted to kicking a ball!
エ　I'm really enjoying myself!

問2　次の英文が下線部②の内容を表すように，(a), (b)に与えられた文字で始まる適切な英語1語をそれぞれ書け。

I had a deal with companies which (a)(d　　) much money for studying of certain diseases. I told them to (b)(l　　) my disease every year because I was so old.

問3　Mathildaが下線部③のようになった理由を本文中から探し，65字程度の日本語で書け。

127

問4　下線部④にはMathildaの物事に対するどのような姿勢が表れているか，本文に即して40字程度の日本語で書け。

問5　文字の[　A　]に入る最も適切なものを次のア～エから選び，記号で答えよ。

ア　Get her to help you for one Wednesday

イ　Don't let her ask you for one Wednesday

ウ　Tell her to do volunteer on Wednesday

エ　Don't ask her to work on Wednesday

問6　本文中の(　B　)に入る適切な英語1語を書け。

問7　あなたは教師として生徒にボランティア活動を通してどのようなことを学んで欲しいか，本文の内容を踏まえて，50語程度の英語で書け。なお，使用した語数を記入すること。

(☆☆☆◎◎◎)

解答・解説

【中高共通】

【1】1　エ　　2　ウ　　3　イ　　4　ア　　5　イ　　6　ア　　7　ウ
　　8　エ　　9　イ　　10　ウ

〈解説〉音声は1回しか流れないが，設問の選択肢は問題用紙に印刷されているので，事前に目を通し，問われる内容を予想しておくこと。設問1～7は短い会話，設問8～10は説明文である。いずれも平易な英語なので，落ち着いて臨めば正答できる問題である。リスニングが苦手な人は各種検定試験等のリスニング対策教材を使って，短い会話文や説明文を聞いて練習しておくとよいだろう。　1　男性の2回目の発言の「日曜日に映画と買い物に行きませんか？」に対して女性が「いいですね」と答えている。　2　女性の2回目の発言で「道路補修工事が

今日始まった」と言っている。　3　男性の1回目の発言で「まだアル
バイトの応募は受け付けていますか」と店員に尋ねている。　4　男
性の2回目の発言で「私の母は，私が子どもの時，料理のいろはを教
えてくれた」と言っている。the ABC(s) ofは「〜の初歩，入門」の意
味。　5　男性の3回目の発言で「住所が間違っていますよ」と言って
いる。　6　女性が2回目の発言で「登録書が家にある」と言っている。
7　質問文は「女性は月曜日に何をしますか」。男性は2回目の発言で
「今日は日曜で図書館は休館だから，明日一緒に行こう。返す本があ
るから」と誘っている。　8　第5文目以降で子どもたちのスマートフ
ォンの使用ルールについて書かれていることがわかる。　9　第2文目
に授業内での活動別に生徒たちが学んだことの記憶率が示されてい
る。ここから，男性はどのように授業を行えば生徒たちの定着率が上
がるかを説明しようとしていることがわかる。　10　空港でアナウン
スが流れている場面である。2文目に「席を譲っていいただける方」
とある。

【2】1　ウ　　2　イ　　3　ア　　4　イ　　5　ウ
〈解説〉1　in order of「〜の順番」という意味。　2　If節は仮定法過去完
了の形だが，帰結節は文末にnowがあるので仮定法過去の形にする。
3　空欄の後ろをNancy spoke to his sister in the rude wayと考えれば，前
置詞＋関係代名詞だとわかる。　4　目標とする言語が実際使われる
場面を想定した様々な活動を通じて，学習者間のインタラクションや
コミュニケーションを重視する指導法のことを，タスクベースの言語
指導法という。　5　debateではどのような話題を扱うのかを考えてみ
るとよい。controversialは「議論の余地のある，論争を呼ぶ」という意
味。

【3】Teachers should not force students to study, but they should provide an
inclusive environment for students to learn. If students enjoy learning English
and are willing to use it as a communication tool, they can definitely learn

English by themselves. With this perspective, teachers should organize their lessons well so that students can feel that learning is fun and finally become autonomous learners. Teachers are able to help students become responsible for their own learning in school and in life. (80 words)

〈解説〉ことわざの意味は，「馬を水際まで連れて行っても，無理に水を飲ませることはできない」。つまり「周囲で何を言おうとも，肝心なのは本人の気持ち」という意味。解答例では，教師は生徒たちに強制的に勉強させるのではなく，楽しみながら学習し，コミュニケーションツールとして使わせ，ひいてはそれが自律学習者育成につながると述べられている。指導要領におけるコミュニケーション重視の傾向や昨今の「自律学習促進」の流れを踏まえ，様々な場面を想定して自分の意見を整理しておくことが大切である。語数制限に慣れるために，それらを短文にまとめる練習も併せて行おう。

【4】問1　教師の外国語使用はほとんどなく，教科書の演習中心のおもしろくない授業が進み，生徒たちもその言語を話せるようにはならないから。(62字)　　問2　(a) speaking　　(b) practical　　問3　ウ　問4　イ　　問5　教える言語を母語としない教師は文法中心の授業をする方が負担が少なく，その言語が流暢でない限り学生と共通の言語で話す誘惑があるから。(65字)　　問6　(a) intensive　　(b) have　問7　ア　　問8　Since language teachers teach the core details of communication, they should bring their personality to each lesson. This is because it is an important part of communication in everyday situations. If students come to communicate in the way their teacher does and then tell him/her what they really want to learn about, it is easier for the teacher to understand the students' needs. (63 words)

　(出典：The Guardian 2013 *What We Can Learn from Teaching English Abroad*　一部改作)

〈解説〉問1　第1段落第3文と第4文より，Ellieのフランス語教師が教科書の問題をさせるだけで，その教師自身も授業でフランス語をほとんど

話さず，何人かの優秀な生徒を指名し発表させていることがわかる。これを字数制限に従ってまとめる。　問2　直前の文より，do things completely differentlyが表す内容は，スピーキングの技術向上に役立たない既存の教育システムからの脱却である。practicalは「実用的な」の意味。　問3　第5段落第1文より，外国語として英語を教える教授法の秘訣は，生徒たちがその言語を使う自然な状況を作り出すことである。文法指導も同じで，同段落第4文より，文法が文法だと感じないような方法で具体例を挙げながら教えられるべき，すなわち実際のコミュニケーションを想定して指導されるべきだと述べている。

問4　第6段落第1文より，生徒と教師，生徒と生徒の間でコミュニケーションが取れる環境を作れば，スピーキングスキルを向上させやすいと述べられている。monotonousは「単調な」という意味。

問5　第7段落第2文，第3文で述べられている内容を字数制限に従ってまとめる。temptationは「誘惑」という意味。　問6　the immersion conceptの内容は第8段落第3文以降に述べられている。つまり，校内やキャンパス内で，対象とする外国語のみを使用することにすることで，短期間でスキルアップを目指すという考え方である。intensiveは「短期集中的な」という意味。　問7　lateralは「横の，側面の」という意味。lateral solutionとは「多角的観点から物事を見ることによる解決法」を表している。　問8　解答例では教師は自分の人格を授業に持ち込むべきだとして，その理由は生徒たちが教員と同じような方法で意思を伝えようとすれば，お互い理解しやすいからと述べている。

【中学校】

【1】問1　Wの発音が難しく，しばしば繰り返してしまうことがあり，Hも上手く発音ができないということ。(45字)　問2　自分の話し方を父親も気に入っているということ。(23字)　問3　A　カ　B　ウ　C　エ　問4　a　問5　ヘッドフォンで，ダンス音楽を聴いているときの話し方が，その音楽と同じリズムになってしまい，ラップのように聞こえる状況。(59字)　問6　ア　fun

イ　encourage　　ウ　took [mistook]　　問7　What　　問8　When I was a junior high school student, I was poor at English. My test scores were always bad, but I liked to listen to English songs and watch movies in English. I enjoyed English through these things and my English was gradually improving. Through my experience, I learned that it was very important to enjoy something to improve my skills. (61 words)

　　　（出典：Brendan Dunne *Guess What?*　一部改作）

〈解説〉問1　22:21のブログの内容と7:51のブログの第3段落第1文，第2文にTomが抱える問題が述べられている。　問2　So does Dadは「私の父もそうです」という意味で，直前のI like the way I talkを受けている。　問3　Aの直後のimportant dayとは，7:51のブログの第2段落第1文目より，an important dayとはサイエンスフェアで発表する日のことだとわかる。筆者はワクワクしていたものの，「不安」でもあったので，カが適切である。Bは，空欄の直前にembarrassing「ばつの悪い，気まずい」とあるので，選択肢の中でこれと意味の近い単語としてはterribleが適切。Cは，22:51のブログの第8段落第5文，第6文より，Lukeが今朝電話してきたのはTomをからかうためでなく，発表を控えているTomを励ますためであり，電話から聞こえたRyanの笑い声は実はLukeの犬の鳴き声だったとわかるので，エが正解となる。
問4　another great thingが指す内容が後に続くと考えると，空欄直後に続く説明として適切なのはaである。　問5　itが指す内容が直前の一文である。これを字数制限に従ってまとめる。　問6　ア　7:51の第2段落，第3段落より，最初TomはLukeから電話をもらった時，からかわれていると感じたことがわかるので，funを入れる。make fun of 〜は「〜をからかう，ばかにする」という意味。　イ　22:51のブログの最終段落第5文より，LukeはTomに電話してサイエンスフェアで頑張るよう励ますつもりだったことがわかる。　ウ　22:51のブログの最終段落第6文より，TomがLukeの犬の鳴き声をRyanの笑い声と勘違いしたのである。mistake A for Bは「AをBと間違える」という意味。
問7　第3段落22:51のブログの第3段落第5文，第6文を参考に答える。

問8　問われていることは2点で，苦手なことを克服した経験とそこから学んだこと。この順番で書くとまとめやすい。解答例では，英語が苦手だったが，英語の音楽を聞いたり，英語の映画を見たりするのは好きだったので，好きな音楽や映画を通じて英語の点数が上がったと述べている。さらにこの経験から，何か自分のスキルを向上させる楽しいことをするのが大切だと言っている。

【高等学校】

【1】問1　エ　　問2　(a) donated　　(b) list　　問3　虐待されている赤ん坊が病院に連れてこられたとき，汚れた洋服は捨てられ，最後は薄汚れたタオルにくるまれて病院を出されるのを見たから。(65字)
問4　杖で歩くことは大変なことだが，できないと言わずに特別な杖で前向きに歩こうという姿勢。(42字)　　　問5　イ　　　問6　difference
問7　Students have to contribute to the society they belong to after they graduate from school. Through volunteer activities, I want my students to notice the problems in our society, and then find out their own solutions. Those experiences would lead them to realize there is something they can do for their society. (52 words)

　　　(出典：Naomi Drew　*LEARNING PEACE*　一部改作)

〈解説〉問1　第1段落第3文，第4文より，Mathildaは病気を患っていたが，人生を楽しんでいたことがわかる。relishは「楽しむ」という意味。have a ballで「大いに楽しむ」。　　問2　fundraiseは「資金を集める」という意味。第3段落第2文より，資金集めのパーティーを慈善団体のために行っていたことがわかるので，aにはdonatedが入る。bについて，my promiseが表す内容は，第2段落第1文より，Mathildaが，亡き母の死因であった重症筋無力症の原因を突き止めることだとわかる。さらに，第1段落第3文より，Mathildaが母と似た病気にかかっていると推測できる。したがって，特定の病気の原因追究のためにお金を寄付してくれる企業に対し，自分の病気を毎年「(対象の病気として)リストするよう」依頼したと考えられる。put ～ into actionは「～を実行に移す」

という意味。　問3　第4段落第2文に理由が書かれている。soiledは「汚れた」，shabbyは「使い古した，薄汚れた」，lose one's temperは「かんしゃくを起こす」という意味。　問4　第7段落第5文に母から教わったことが書かれており，これがMathildaの姿勢に影響を与えたと考えられる。　問5　直前の文のask for one Wednesday は，「相手が持つ時間の1日をください」という意味である。つまり，Mathildaが誰かに何かをするよう依頼し，それが断わられた場合，彼女はその人の持つ1日を自分が依頼したことに当てて欲しいと言うのである。one Wednesdayはone day of their timeという意味である。これを受けて逆接を表すbutに続くように空所に入るものを考える。　問6　この話のまとめの部分に当たるのが第10段落で，文全体をよく読んで，空所に入る語を考える。make a differenceは「違いをもたらす」という意味。問7　解答例では，ボランティア活動をすることで社会の問題が見えてきて自分なりの解決法を探る姿勢が養えることが示されている。

2018年度　実施問題

【中高共通】

【1】聞き取りテスト

　　これから1〜10の英語を1回ずつ放送します。それぞれの英語のあとに，その内容について質問を一つします。その質問に対する答として最も適切なものを次のア〜エの中から一つずつ選び，記号で答えなさい。

1　M : Chester Police Station.

　　W : Hello. I'm calling because I think my mountain bike was stolen.

　　M : OK. When did you see it last?

　　W : I parked it in front of my house last night, but when I woke up, it was gone.

　　Question(M) : Why is the woman calling the police?

　　ア　She heard a loud noise.

　　イ　She lost her wallet last night.

　　ウ　She saw a strange car outside.

　　エ　She found her bike gone.

2　W : Excuse me. I'm looking for *Dark Nights*, the new novel by Lucy Williams. Do you have it?

　　M : Yes, we do. It just came in yesterday.

　　W : Where can I find it?

　　M : It's in the new-release section over there.

　　Question(W) : Where does this conversation probably take place?

　　ア　In a bank.　　　　　　　イ　In a bookstore.

　　ウ　In a computer shop.　　エ　In a grocery store.

3 W : How was your weekend, Mark?

M : It was OK. I went to the art museum.

W : I didn't know you liked art.

M : Actually, I don't. My grandmother wanted to go, so I took her there.

Question (W) : Why did Mark go to the art museum on the weekend?

ア　He wanted to see the paintings.

イ　He went there to see his grandmother.

ウ　His grandmother wanted to go.

エ　His paintings were there.

4 M : Hi, I'd like five ten-cent stamps and two one-dollar stamps, please.

W : Sorry? Could you please repeat that?

M : Five ten-cent stamps and two one-dollar stamps.

W : All right.

Question (M) : How much will the man pay for the stamps?

ア　$2.50　　イ　$2.15　　ウ　$3.50　　エ　$3.15

5 W : Can you help me with my homework, Glen?

M : Sure, Cathy. As long as it doesn't have anything to do with math.

W : Actually, I was hoping you could help me with biology.

M : I'm not that good at it, but I'll try.

Question (W) : What will Glen try to do?

ア　Help Cathy finish her math homework.

イ　Help Cathy choose which classes to take.

ウ　Help Cathy find her biology textbook.

エ　Help Cathy do her biology assignment.

6 M : What are you going to study in college, Sarah?

W : I've always wanted to study art, but my parents think I should major in something like economics or marketing.

M : Why is that?

W : Well, they think that if I study a subject related to business, it'll be easier for me to find a job. But I'm going to stick to my original plan.

Question (M) : What does Sarah want to study at college?

ア　Business.　　イ　Art.　　ウ　Economics.　　エ　Marketing.

7　W : Excuse me. Could you tell me how to get to the Royal Hotel?

M : It's quite far from here. It would be better to take a taxi.

W : I don't mind walking. I'm not in a hurry.

M : OK. Go all the way down this street until you get to the station. Then turn left. It's on the next block.

W : Thank you very much.

Question (M) : What will the woman probably do next?

ア　Take a taxi to the station.　　イ　Walk to the hotel.

ウ　Go home by bus.　　エ　Get a train to the hotel.

8　Meg works for an American company that makes furniture, and she regularly travels all around the United States to sell the company's products. Next mouth, she will go on her first overseas business trip. Meg's company wants to start selling furniture to companies in Thailand, so she will go there to talk to some possible customers.

Question (W) : What will Meg do next month?

ア　Travel to Thailand on business.

イ　Design new furniture in Thailand.

ウ　Write a report about the United States.

エ　Attend a job interview in the United States.

9　OK, the supermarket will open in an hour, so let's get ready for the first customers. There is a special offer on vegetable soup, so make sure there are enough packs on the shelves. Also, we should announce that we've changed where some of the items are. In particular, remind customers that bread is now in Aisle 5.

Question (M) : What is one thing employees should tell customers today?

ア　They are sold out of soup.

イ　Bread is on sale at half price.

ウ　Some items have been moved.

エ　The opening times will change.

10　Computers, smart phones, and video games are very valuable. They've become more and more important to our daily lives. As our world depends more on these technologies, we need to take care when using them. They're just tools. Nobody can say whether they're good or bad in themselves. We should learn to make good use of these tecbnologies. That is, the success of these technologies depends on our wisdom.

Question (W) : What is the main idea of this passage?

ア　How to use new technologies wisely.

イ　New technologies in the future.

ウ　Health hazards of new technologies.

エ　The importance of new technologies.

以上で英語の聞き取りテストを終わります。次の問題に進みなさい。

(☆☆☆◎◎◎)

【2】次の各文の(　　)に入る最も適切な語(句)を下のア～エの中から一つずつ選び，記号で答えよ。

1　George was an (　　) student who was able to master advanced English from a very young age.

ア　exceptional　　イ　aesthetic　　ウ　uptight　　エ　applicable

2　Thomas made an (　　) speech that impressed most people in the hall, but the content dissatisfied some.

ア infectious　　イ eloquent　　ウ incurable　　エ available

3　Joe (　　) his lack of an extensive background knowledge in English by studying hard every night to master the subject.

ア　goes through with　　イ　looks down on　　ウ　makes up for

エ　comes down with

4　Employers should try to create an environment (　　) all the employees can work comfortably.

ア　which　　イ　where　　ウ　when　　エ　that

5　(　　) competence is the ability of speakers to compensate for breakdowns in communication or to improve the effectiveness of communication.

ア　Strategic　　イ　Discourse　　ウ　Sociolinguistic

エ　Grammatical

(☆☆☆☆○○○○)

【3】ディスカッションやプレゼンテーションなど英語による言語活動を生徒にさせる際，あなたはどのようなことに気を付けて指導するか，理由を含めて80語程度の英語で書け。なお，使用した語数を記入すること。

(☆☆☆☆○○○○)

【4】次の英文を読んで，後の問に答えよ。

Stanford psychologist Carol Dweck, along with other education researchers interested in ①growth mindset, have done, numerous studies showing that when students believe their intelligence can grow and change with effort, they perform better on academic tests. These findings have sparked interest and debate about how to encourage a growth mindset in students both at home and at school.

Now, a national study of tenth-graders in Chile found student mindsets are correlated with achievement on language and math tests. Furthermore, students from low-income families were less likely to hold a growth mindset than their more ②affluent peers. However, if a low-income student did have a growth mindset, it worked as a buffer against the negative effects of poverty on achievement.

"This is not a sample; this is everyone in school," said Susana Claro, a doctoral candidate at Stanford's Graduate School of Education and lead author of the article "Growth Mindset Tempers the Effects of Poverty on Academic Achievement," published in the Proceedings of the National Academy of Sciences. Claro, along with Stanford scholars David Paunesku and Carol Dweck, wanted to know if growth mindset would correlate with academic performance on a large-scale (168,000 students). They found that ③it did at almost every school in Chile, a correlation stronger than they expected to find.

When students in Chile take national exams measuring language and math, they are also obligated to fill out ④a lengthy survey from the Ministry of Education on a range of subjects, from bullying to healthy eating, sports and how well they got along with their teachers. The survey questions change every year, and in 2012 Claro convinced the ministry to include two questions on growth mindset. Teachers and parents are also surveyed, which is why Claro and her colleagues have such detailed income information for each student.

"This is the first time that we can see the landscape of growth mindset in a complete population," Claro said. "We'd always used samples before." She and her colleagues wanted to know if a study this large would reveal the same correlations seen in representative samples in the U.S. or whether the large sample size would be "too noisy." To Claro's surprise, the findings were very clear.

"This is the first time that we measured that there is a growth mindset gap across socioeconomic groups," she said. Researchers are convinced that growth mindsets are (A), not (B) created, so these findings suggest that something in the environment of children from poor families is fostering a fixed mindset.

"Children are capturing messages that are in their environment," Claro said. Whether those messages are coming from parents, teachers, the general environment or all of the above is unknown, but Claro said pinpointing where the messages are coming from and trying to change them could be an important strategy for improving academic achievement. The easiest place to start is (C).

"We don't really know if changing students' mindsets is possible on a larger scale, and we aren't sure how to work with teachers," Claro said. She acknowledged that even when teachers are well-intentioned, they might be sending messages to students that don't promote a growth mindset. "However, good teachers ⑤do this naturally," she said. "They send growth mindset messages, and we are learning from them and trying to disaggregate what they do."

Claro acknowledged that whether students achieve academically or not is a result of a complicated mix of factors that include poverty, trauma and motivation, among other factors. She believes that these growth mindset findings indicate that, at the very least, focusing on building growth mindsets in students should be part of the conversation.

問1　下線部①とはどのような考えか。本文に即して30字程度の日本
　　語で書け。

問2　下線部②の意味に最も近い語を次のア～ウの中から一つ選び，
　　記号で答えよ。

　　ア　healthy　　イ　worthy　　ウ　wealthy

問3　下線部③の具体的内容を20字程度の日本語で書け。

問4　次の英文が下線部④について説明したものになるように，（　　）
　　に与えられた文字で始まる適切な英語1語を書け。

　　　The contents of the survey range from bullying to healthy eating, sports
　　and students' (r　　) with their teachers.

問5　本文中の（　A　），（　B　）に入る語の組み合わせとして最も適切

なものを次のア～エの中から一つ選び，記号で答えよ。

ア　A : naturally　　　　B : artificially

イ　A : artificially　　　　B : naturally

ウ　A : socially　　　　　B : biologically

エ　A : biologically　　　　B : socially

問6　本文中の（　C　）に入る最も適切な語を次のア～ウの中から一つ選び，記号で答えよ。

ア　home　　イ　school　　ウ　community

問7　下線部⑤の具体的内容を30字程度の日本語で書け。

問8　生徒の "growth mindset" を形成するために，あなたは生徒とどのように接するか。そして，その結果どのようなことが期待されると思うか。50語程度の英語で書け。なお，使用した語数を記入すること。

(☆☆☆☆◎◎◎)

【中学校】

【1】次の英文を読んで，後の問に答えよ。

My life was dramatically transformed because ①a simple three-word phrase was delivered at the right time in just the right way. When I was three years old, my parents discovered I was totally deaf, a situation which forced them to make crucial decisions about my education.

After consulting with numerous specialists and doctors, they made a decision that would forever alter my future. Instead of sending me to a private school for the deaf, they decided to "mainstream" me. All of my peers and teachers would have normal hearing.

From the time I started going there in 3rd grade, I was the only deaf child at Blue Creek Elementary School in the small, quiet town of Latham, New York. From almost the first day there, the other kids ②taunted me and called me names mainly because of my hearing aid and the way I talked.

I remember thinking, "What have I done wrong?"

My hearing aid was a rectangular box that was harnessed to my shoulders and hung from my neck like an albatross. It created a big lump on my chest with wires running from the box to my ears.

I experienced ③great anxiety throughout elementary school because, in addition to the problems of "fitting in" with the other students, I also struggled mightily with most of my schoolwork. I seemed to spend every spare moment doing homework just so I could keep up. The teachers didn't know what to do with me.

Because of my hearing disability, I was constantly asking everyone, "What did he/she say?" I worried that everyone would soon grow tired of repeating everything back to me. Since fitting in was so important to me, every time people around me laughed or smiled, I did the same even though I usually had no idea what was going on.

When the kids made fun of me, I internalized all of it. I was sure that I was a bad person; I felt I deserved their sneers. On the surface, I was gregarious, outgoing and happy-go-lucky, but in reality, my self-esteem was quite (A). I saw myself as an ugly buck-toothed kid wearing a weird-looking box around his neck who wasn't smart enough to keep up with the rest of the kids.

Mrs. Jordan, my 5th grade teacher, changed all of that with a simple three-word phrase. A large woman with salt and pepper hair, and twinkling brown eyes, Mrs, Jordan had a voice that boomeranged off the walls of her tiny classroom.

One morning, she asked the class a question. I read her lips from my front-row seat and immediately raised my hand. I couldn't believe it—for once I knew the answer. However, when she called on me, I was (B). Here was an opportunity to impress this powerful teacher and show her I was worthy of her love, maybe even impress my classmates a little. I didn't want to blow ④it.

Despite my fears, I felt uncharacteristically confident because—for once—I was sure I had the right answer. I took a deep breath and nervously answered Mrs. Jordan's question.

I will never forget what happened next.

Her response was (　C　). It startled all of us.

Mrs. Jordan enthusiastically slammed her right foot on the floor and whirled her right finger in a full circle until it pointed directly at me. With sparkling eyes and a wide smile she cried, "That's right Stephen!"

For the first time in my young life, I was an instant star.

My heart burst with pride as an ear-to-ear grin filled my face. I sat a little taller in my chair and puffed out my chest. My confidence soared like never before. I decided right then and there that I would make a place for myself in this world. A simple three-word phrase delivered with incredible enthusiasm had totally transformed my young life.

From that day forward, my grades and speech improved dramatically. My popularity among my peers increased and my outlook on life did a complete turnaround.

And ⑤it all started with Mrs, Jordan.

問1　下線部①を表す英語3語を本文中から抜き出して書け。

問2　下線部②の意味に最も近い語を次のア～ウの中から一つ選び，記号で答えよ。

　　ア　teased　　イ　displeased　　ウ　relieved

問3　下線部③の具体的内容を40字以内の日本語で書け。

問4　本文中の(　A　)～(　C　)に入る最も適切な語を次のア～カの中から一つずつ選び，記号で答えよ。

　　ア　mild　　イ　low　　ウ　explosive　　エ　disobedient
　　オ　afraid　　カ　cooperative

問5　下線部④が指す内容を60字程度の日本語で書け。

問6　次の英文が下線部⑤の内容とほぼ同じになるように，(　a　)～(　c　)に適切な英語1語をそれぞれ書け。

　　　I did (　a　) at school than before. I became (　b　) among my

classmates and my attitude toward life (　c　).

問7　英語の学習に自信を持てない生徒に対して，あなたはどのよう
　　な学習指導の工夫をするか。50語程度の英語で書け。なお，使用し
　　た語数を記入すること。

(☆☆☆◎◎◎)

【高等学校】

【 1 】次の英文を読んで，後の問に答えよ。

About 6 months ago, I joined a gym. Every morning, there was one personal trainer there who worked out at the same time that my little group did our workout. He did his "routine" with such a quiet determination that he made it all look very easy; although I knew all too well how hard he was working. When I was tempted to whine and quit, I watched him push himself to his own limits, and I found myself (　A　) to work as hard and without complaining.

A couple of weeks ago, I was watching him do chin-ups. He made them look effortless. I broke away from my group and asked him if I could try a chin-up. I had never tried before, but he just made it look so easy. | B | encouraged me to step up to the bar. I pulled myself up without thinking...once...then twice. That was all I had in me; I had no strength left. I told him that was all I had, so he stepped up behind me and pushed me up for a third and fourth "pull." It felt so good. I felt strong, and I smiled from ear to ear.

The next day when I was done with my workout, I asked him to spot me again. Again, I did two, and so it continued for the rest of the week. I thought it was pathetic that I could only do two, but when I came to the gym at the end of the week, he was standing there just shaking his head. When I asked him what was up, he said he was impressed with my chin-ups. He told me that when they are training firefighters, the men are required to do 5 chin-ups, and women are required to do 1 or 2. He explained that most people can't do them

145

at all and that he was impressed that I could. He further told me that if I practiced every day, I would be doing 5 or 6 in no time. At this point, I should probably add that I am 50 years old and female.

The moral of this story is because I didn't know any better, because he told me I could, I saw no reason to doubt. I just jumped in and gave it a try — and I did it! I didn't see it as a great accomplishment because I didn't realize that it was difficult, and it was my goal to get stronger. No one told me I couldn't do it, in fact, I was encouraged to try. Had he told me initially how difficult it was, I more than likely would not have tried at all, or I might have tried, but given it only half the effort because failure would have been the expectation. I applaud him for letting me believe that it was not only a possibility, but that success was a realistic expectation.

How many times have we decided not to try at all because we were told that we couldn't? How many times have we told our children, our friends and our co-workers that they couldn't do something, that their ideas were impossible or beyond reach? How many times have we told ourselves that we would fail before we even started?

I started to ponder examples that I had witnessed and this came to mind: I recalled a conversation a friend of mine had with his daughter just prior to her heading off to university. He spoke to her (with good intentions) of how hard she would have to work in order to succeed, University wasn't like high school — this was the real world and now she would have to grow up. This child quit after two years. Another friend spoke to her daughter of the adventure she was embarking on and how proud she was. I remember how we laughed because the mother already had her outfit picked out for convocation day! This child just graduated with her degree in physiology. Looking back, neither daughter was more intelligent than the other. Was it the silent expectations or lack thereof that predicted the outcome?

I have a new approach now. I have experienced first hand how good it feels to rush in so innocently. To believe that we CAN do it and go on to accomplish exactly what we set out to do because no one told us we couldn't. I've learned how important it is to support others and ourselves in our endeavors and to let them know that we believe they can do it rather than telling them we think that they can't.

I personally want to be like my trainer; standing there behind the people that I love, encouraging them, believing in them and being ready to catch them when they get tired.

What a powerful lesson this has been for me! I'll be doing "5" in no time at all because I was told I (C).

問1　本文中の(A)に入る適切な語を次のア～エから一つ選び，記号で答えよ。

　ア　motivating　　イ　motivated　　ウ　depressing

　エ　depressed

問2　本文中の　　B　　に入る最も適切なものを次のア～エから一つ選び，記号で答えよ。

　ア　He explained its difficulty and

　イ　He warned me of the danger but

　ウ　He told me it would be reckless but

　エ　He eagerly stepped aside and

問3　次の英文が第3段落の内容を著すように，(a), (b)に与えられた文字で始まる適切な英語1語をそれぞれ書け。

　　The writer thought it was (a)(e　　) that she could do only two chin-ups, but the trainer thought her performance was very (b)(i　　).

問4　筆者がtrainerを賞賛している理由を本文中から探し，50字程度の日本語で書け。

問5　下線部のように筆者が考えるに至った出来事を，本文に即して65字程度の日本語で書け。

問6　本文中の(C)に入る適切な英語1語を書け。

問7　生徒が英語圏の国に留学したいと相談してきたら，あなたは教師としてどのような言葉を掛けるか。本文の内容を踏まえて，50語

程度の英語で書け。なお，使用した語数を記入すること。

(☆☆☆☆◎◎◎◎)

解答・解説

【中高共通】

【1】1　エ　2　イ　3　ウ　4　ア　5　エ　6　イ　7　イ
　　8　ア　9　ウ　10　ア

〈解説〉音声は1回しか流れないが，設問の選択肢は問題用紙に印刷され
ているので，あらかじめ目を通しておくことができる。英文は1〜7が
短い会話，8〜10が説明文である。いずれも日常会話レベルの英語な
ので，落ち着いて臨めば正答できる問題である。リスニングが苦手な
人はリスニング教材や，テレビ・ラジオなどの英会話講座で耳慣らし
をしておくとよいだろう。　1　Wの2回目の発言で「起きたら，(マウ
ンテンバイクが)なくなっていた」と言っている。　2　Wは「Lucy
Williamsの新しい小説を探しています。どこにありますか」と尋ねて
いる。　3　Mは2回目の発言で「祖母が美術館に行きたがったので，
連れて行った」と言っている。　4　Mは「10セント切手5枚と1ドル切
手を2枚ください」と言っているので，合計2ドル50セントとなる。
5　Wは1回目の発言で「宿題を手伝ってほしい」，2回目の発言で「生
物学」だと言っている。　6　Wは1回目の発言で「アートを勉強した
いと思っていた」，2回目の発言で「自分の最初の計画どおりにする」
と言っている。　7　Wは2回目の発言で「歩くのは構いません。急い
でいませんから」と言っている。　8　第3文の「Megの会社はタイの
企業に家具の販売を始めたがっている」から，ア「タイへ出張する」
が適切である。　9　第3文のthat以下で「商品の売り場を変えた」と
言っている。　10　第4文「所詮(テクノロジーは)道具である」，第6文
「テクノロジーの成功は我々の知恵にかかっている」から，テクノロ

148

ジーの使い方に関する内容だとわかる。

【2】1 ア　2 イ　3 ウ　4 イ　5 ア

〈解説〉1　who以下の意味を考えればよい。exceptional「例外的な」。

2　eloquent speech「雄弁な演説」の意味。　3　by以下は「その課目を毎晩一生懸命勉強することで」の意味。make up for「補償する，つぐなう」。　4　関係代名詞と間違えないように。後半の部分をall the employees can work comfortably in the environmentと考えれば，in以下が副詞句となるので関係詞副詞が正しいとわかる。　5　the ability以下の意味を考えればよい。competence「(言語)能力」。

【3】At first, I should set clear goals so that the students can understand what to do during activities. I also need to give them opportunities to recall what they have learned and how to express their opinions in English. That will help them tell the other students clearly what they want to say. During activities, I should have them cooperate with each other. After activities, I should have time for them to evaluate themselves, which will improve their performance. (79 words)

〈解説〉解答例では，まず活動時間内の目標を明確にすることを述べている。そして，振り返りの時間を設けて，ペアワークなどを行わせ，最後に活動の評価を行うことを述べている。学習指導要領におけるコミュニケーション重視の傾向を踏まえ，様々な場面を想定して自分の意見を整理しておくことが大切である。字数制限に慣れるために，それらを短文にまとめる練習も併せて行おう。なお，公式に示されている採点基準は①内容の適切さ，②論の展開の適切さ，③語彙・文法の適切さ，④分量，である。

【4】問1　知性は努力次第で，伸ばすことや変えることができるという考え。(30字)　問2　ウ　問3　成長思考が学業成績と関係していたということ。(22字)　問4　relationship(s)　問5　ウ　問6　イ

問7　成長思考を促すようなメッセージを生徒に送っているということ。(30字)　　問8　I would praise students as often as possible for their good work or behavior because they seek approval from their teachers. Once they feel that their desire for recognition is fulfilled, they will be motivated to learn and try to better themselves, which I believe will help students improve their performance. (51 words)

〈解説〉問1　第1段落第1文のwhen以下で「生徒が，知性は努力によって伸ばしたり変えたりすることができると信じるとき，彼らの学業成績はよくなる」と述べている。　　問2　下線部②の前のthan以下は，第2段落第2文のstudents from low-income families「収入の低い家庭の生徒」との比較であるので，wealthy「裕福な」が正しい。　　問3　下線部③は，直前の文である第3段落第2文のgrowthからperformanceまでを受けている。この部分を20字程度で訳す。　　問4　第4段落第1文のhow well they以下は「教師といかにうまくやっていくか」なので，relationship(s)「関係」が適切。　　問5　第6段落第1文のweからgroupsまでの「社会経済上のグループ間で成長思考に差がある」に注目する。つまり成長思考は社会的につくられるということである。　　問6　第7段落第2文に述べられている条件を満たすのは，選択肢の中ではイ「学校」である。　　問7　解答例の他には，「成長思考をしない生徒に対して，指導助言を行うこと」(24字)でもよい。　　問8　解答例では，生徒をほめることで「自己有用感」をもたせ，能力を出させることを記述しているが，第9段落第2文のfocusing以下のような観点(＝「生徒との会話により，生徒の成長思考の積み上げに焦点をあてる」)から記述することも可能である。

【中学校】

【1】問1　That's right Stephen(!)　　問2　ア　　問3　他の生徒達にうまく溶け込めるかという不安と，学業についていけるかという不安。(38字)　　問4　A　イ　　B　オ　　C　ウ　　問5　影響力のある先生に好印象を与え，私が愛されるに値する生徒だと示すと共に，同級生に

も少しは良い印象を与えることができる機会。(61字)

問6　a　better　　b　popular　　c　changed(improved)　　問7　I think such students should have many chances for success in their English study, so I will give them many opportunities to express themselves in easy English. Also, I will provide them with assignments which are easy enough for them to do. By doing so, they will feel confident. (49 words)

〈解説〉問1　第15段落の最後の部分にあるMrs. Jordanの言葉が解答である。　問2　tauntは「あざける，馬鹿にする」の意味なので，ア「からかう，いじめる」が適切。　問3　第6段落第1文のbecause以下が答えである。2か所のwith以下に注意すること。他の生徒たちに溶け込めるかどうかと学業についていけるかの2点について不安だったのである。　問4　Aは第8段落第4文に自分の外見が変だったと述べているので，自己評価が低かったとわかる。Bは，第9段落第2文の「Mrs. Jordanの声は教室中に響き渡るような大声」と，第11段落の冒頭のDespite my fears「私の不安にかかわらず」から，オの「心配した」が適切である。Cは，第13段落第2文と第14文の最初からfloorまでに，筆者が正解を答えたときMrs. Jordanが熱烈にほめてくれたことが述べられている。　問5　第10段落第5文が答えである。ここには3つの内容が含まれていることを訳出する。　問6　下線部⑤が指しているのは第18段落第1文と第2文の内容である。これらを問題文のように言い換えればよい。do a complete turnaroundは「豹変する」の意味。

問7　解答例では，成功体験を数多く与えて自信を持たせることを述べている。英語は4つの能力の技術教科なので，個々の生徒の能力を見極めて，例えばリーディングが得意な生徒には範読させるなどして，成功体験をさせることも大切である。

【高等学校】

【1】問1　イ　　問2　エ　　問3　(a) embarrassing　　(b) impressive　問4　懸垂ができるという可能性を示しただけでなく，その成功は現実的に見込みがあると筆者に信じ込ませたから。(50字)　　問5　大学

生活に対して何も先入観を持たずに入学した知人の娘は無事卒業した
が，大学は厳しい場所だと思いこんでいた別の娘は中退したこと。(63
字)　　問6　can (could)　　問7　You have been studying English very
hard, so you can do well abroad. You would learn a lot of things there, and it
would be a good opportunity to broaden your views. I'm sure you will enjoy
studying, living, and meeting people there. I believe you will be successful!
(49 words)

〈解説〉問1　第1段落第4文のI watchedからown limitsに注目。ジムのトレ
　　ーナーが限界までがんばるのを見て奮起したのである。　問2　空欄
　　直後のencouraged以下で，トレーナーはバーのところへ来るように言
　　っているので，ア，イ及びウは不適切である。　　問3　第3段落第3文
　　のIからdo twoまでと，同第4文のhe saidから最後までを問題文のように
　　言い換えればよい。patheticは「痛ましい，憐れな」。　　問4　第4段落
　　第5文に，筆者がトレーナーを賞賛する理由が述べられている。
　　realistic expectations「現実的な予測」。　　問5　下線部はit is〜that…の強
　　調構文であることに注意。第6段落第1文のI recalled以下から同第8文の
　　最後までに，能力が同じ女子に対して，一方には否定的なことを言っ
　　て，他方には肯定的なことを言った結果について述べている。これら
　　の内容をまとめればよい。　　問6　第7段落第3文に「誰もできないと
　　言わないのだから，できると信じていればできる」とある。
問7　解答例では，留学に積極的な姿勢を示している。いわゆる
positiveな姿勢と言葉が生徒を後押しすることを記述すればよい。

2017年度　実施問題

【中高共通】

【1】聞き取りテスト

　これから1〜10の英語を1回ずつ放送します。それぞれの英語のあとに，その内容について質問を一つします。その質問に対する答として最も適切なものをア〜エの中から一つずつ選び，記号で答えよ。

1　M : Hi, Tracy. Do you want to go to a barbecue party tonight?

　　W : Sounds good, but I think it will rain this evening.

　　M : Don't worry. We have a large tent.

　　W : Oh, that's good. I'll bring some vegetables and soft drinks.

　　Question (M): What are they going to do?

　　ア　Cancel the party.　　イ　Go to see a movie.

　　ウ　Buy a large tent.　　エ　Have a barbecue party.

2　W : Excuse me. I'm looking for a book by a female writer, but I forgot her name. It was published recently.

　　M : OK. Do you remember the title of the book?

　　W : No. I remember the book jacket is blue and gold. It's a mystery novel.

　　M : Hmm... it must be "Coral Reef" by Jenny Thomas. It's very popular right now.

　　Question (W): What is the woman asking for?

　　ア　A concert ticket.　　イ　A classical music CD.

　　ウ　A mystery novel.　　エ　A jacket.

3　M : How was your hike?

　　W : Terrible, Dad. It rained really hard and I got completely wet. I should

2017年度　実施問題

have brought a rain coat.

M : Oh, dear. I'm sorry to hear that. Why don't you take a hot shower. Mom is cooking beef stew in the kitchen.

W : That sounds great!

Question (M): What will the girl do first?

　ア　Take a shower.　　　　イ　Go swimming in the river.

　ウ　Go to the mountain.　　エ　Go to see a doctor.

4　W : Kagoshima Department Store.

M : Hello. Yesterday I bought an umbrella at your shop, but it doesn't open. Can I get my money back?

W : Yes, sir. Do you still have the receipt?

M : Yes. I'll come by your shop tomorrow evening.

Question (W): What does the man want to do?

　ア　Buy a new umbrella.

　イ　Throw the umbrella away.

　ウ　Exchange the umbrella for a bag.

　エ　Get a refund.

5　W : Hello. I booked a bus tour to Canada, but I broke my leg. So I can't go on the canoe trip.

M : Oh, I see. Would you like to cancel your tour or just change the plans?

W : I'd like to change them. What do you recommend?

M : A visit to the Niagara Falls is available. We can provide a wheelchair for you.

W : Thank you.

Question (M): What does the woman want to do?

　ア　Change her plans.　　　イ　Go canoeing.

　ウ　Book a tour to Australia.　エ　Cancel her trip to Canada.

6　W : Hello. I'd like to apply for the annual membership.

　　M : Thank you. We'll need an ID with a photograph, and your phone number and e-mail address.

　　W : OK. Here's my driver's license. How much is it?

　　M : It's 50 dollars.

　　W : Oh, I don't have enough money with me now. I'll come back later.

　　Question(M): Why couldn't she apply for the membership?

　　ア　She does not have any ID with her.

　　イ　She does not have enough money.

　　ウ　She left her driver's license at home.

　　エ　She forgot her e-mail address.

7　M : Hi, mom. I'll be back to New York earlier than I expected.

　　W : Oh, will you?　　When are you leaving Boston?

　　M : Tomorrow morning. Can you pick me up at Central Station tomorrow evening?

　　W : Well, I was going to have dinner with Amy, but I'll ask her if we can meet another day.

　　Question(M): What does the man want his mother to do?

　　ア　Go shopping with him.

　　イ　Ask Amy to cook dinner.

　　ウ　Pick him up at the station.

　　エ　Come to Boston to see him off.

8　M : Hello. This is Adam Kane in room 611. Something is wrong with the shower.　There is no hot water.

　　W : I'm really sorry about that Mr. Kane. If you wouldn't mind, we could move you to a different room. 1028 is open and it has a panoramic view of the city.

　　M : That sounds great. I'll move.

W : Thank you, sir. Our staff is coming to pickup your luggage in a few
　　minutes. Please wait there.

Question (M): What is Mr. Kane likely to do next?

　ア　Fix the shower.　　　　　イ　Carry his luggage.

　ウ　Move to another room.　　エ　Call the front desk.

9　Welcome to the Northfield Junior High School Charity Event. We have
　many performances tonight --- First-year students will sing, second-year
　students will dance, and third-year students will perform the play 'Snow
　Beauty.' Teachers will also join these performances. Before the
　performances, we are planning to have a concert by the school's brass
　band. After the concert, we will raise money to help the victims of
　refugees. We are most grateful for your kindness.

Question (M): What is the main purpose of this event?

　ア　To select the best performance.

　イ　To welcome new students.

　ウ　To invite elderly people.

　エ　To collect donations.

10　Thank you for riding with us. This is Southern Express No. 5 bound for
　Hakata. We're sorry to announce that we have a half-an-hour delay due to
　the heavy rain. We will arrive at Hakata Station at 8:15. We apologize for
　the inconvenience and thank you for your patience.

Question (W): What time does this train usually arrive at Hakata Station?

　ア　7:15.　　イ　7:45.　　ウ　8:20.　　エ　8:45.

以上で英語の聞き取りテストを終わります。次の問題に進みなさい。

【２】次の各文の(　　)に入る最も適切な語句をア〜エの中から一つずつ
　　選び、記号で答えよ。

1　I recently started jogging for 30 minutes every morning, so my friend tried to (　　) in for the Kagoshima Marathon.

ア　advise to me to go　　　イ　talk me into going
ウ　tell me to going　　　エ　propose me into go

2　It was hard to follow the diet plan (　　), but I stuck to it and eventually lost 20 pounds.

ア　at first sight　　イ　at first hand　　ウ　for the first time
エ　at first

3　In Japan during and after the Second World War, food was (　　), and many people were very hungry.

ア　scarce　　イ　little　　ウ　much　　エ　abundant

4　(　　) competence is knowing how to use and respond to language appropriately according to the setting, the topic, and relationships among the people communicating.

ア　Strategic　　イ　Linguistic　　ウ　Sociolinguistic
エ　Discourse

5　*A Midsummer Night's Dream* is a comedy written by (　　), and it portrays the events surrounding the marriage of Theseus, the Duke of Athens, to Hippolyta.

ア　Jonathan Swift　　　イ　Charles Dickens
ウ　William Shakespeare　　エ　Daniel Defoe

(☆☆☆◎◎◎◎)

【3】次の言葉はニューヨーク市立大学大学院センター教授のキャシー・デビッドソンの言葉である。この内容を踏まえて，教師は生徒にどのような力を育成する必要があると考えるか，80語程度の英語で書け。なお，使用した語数を記入すること。

　「2011年度にアメリカの小学校に入学した子どもたちの65％は，大学卒業時に今は存在していない職業に就くだろう。」

(☆☆☆☆◎◎◎◎)

157

【４】 次の英文を読んで，後の問に答えよ。

According to an Internet security developer's report, nearly 62% of children worldwide have had a negative experience online — nearly four in ten involving serious situations, i. e. cyberbullying or receiving inappropriate photos from strangers. A whopping 74% of kids active on social networks say they've found themselves in unpleasant situations alone, while additional surveys reveal that nearly eight in ten have witnessed acts of meanness or cruelty on social networking services. That's a serious problem when over three out of every four middle and high-school kids own a cell phone, yet a quarter of adolescents say parents know nothing about what they're doing on the Internet. Even more so when you consider that 20% of kids won't tell parents about negative online experiences for fear of getting into trouble, and nearly a fifth fear adults' overreacting as well.

Welcome to the digital age — an era increasingly defined by a growing gulf between those who grew up with technology and those to whom modern-day advancements such as apps, cloud computing and smartphones remain ①esoteric. And, for that matter, one where experienced role models able to provide positive, real-world solutions for addressing new and emerging problems are increasingly hard to find. For previous generations, parents and teachers could serve as a vital source of wisdom and learning for all things family- or life-related, but like many of today's educators and experts, they too are facing the stark reality of having never been confronted by life in a world of 24/7 online streaming downloads, instant mobile video sharing, and innocent mistakes that live on in infamy forever via the Internet.

Even technology experts presently struggle to decide how to define online rules and etiquette given the speed at which advancements now arrive and online trends shift. ②That's problematic for parents and instructors. As ever, the answer lies with education. However, growing worry surrounds the widening chasm that is appearing between the reality of connected life and the lack of online awareness being provided by our school system.

Based on recent surveys, parents and teachers largely agree that the Internet and technology should be better integrated into modern schools, college curriculums and university classrooms. According to non-profit and Homeland Security collaborator the National Cyber Security Alliance, however, schools are (　A　) to teach online safety, security and digital citizenship. Case in point: Over 80% of school administrators say they do an adequate job of preparing students to meet the challenges a digital world presents. However, when surveyed, a frightening 36% of teachers claim they've received zero hours of training in the previous year.

A moving target, keeping kids safe naturally requires ongoing effort and discussion from all sides — kids, parents, teachers and law enforcement officials alike — all of whom must actively work to provide families with support, and share learning and best practices. But make no mistake: We need basic training and ongoing education in digital citizenship and online safety in schools now — not in the near or distant future.

Some computer security software companies offer software solutions that block or filter questionable content. Others offer apps and Web browsers that provide clean content for children's usage. But as we know, ③truly determined kids can circumvent all, and as companies themselves will tell you, software is no substitute for parenting. Only by proactively teaching positive computing and digital lifestyle habits can such problems truly be addressed.

Discussion can, and must, occur surrounding digital citizenship and online safety starting at the earliest years, and continue into later phases of adolescent and even professional life. Moreover, we need to recognize the pressing importance of keeping these conversations going at homes, schools and boardrooms the globe over. Standardized educational solutions and training programs that teach high-tech safety rules and responsible online usage could provide the solution. Whether such programs come from the state, private or non-profit sector though, it is vital that we better equip kids and adults alike to meet the challenges of the modern world.

問1　次の英文が第1段落の内容と一致するように，(a)には数字を，(b)には与えられた文字で始まる英語1語を書け。

Problems involving children using social networks are serious because (a)(　　)% of children think their parents have no idea what their children are doing online, and because a fifth of children (b)(h　　) their unpleasant or frightening experiences from their parents.

問2　下線部①の意味に最も近い語をア～ウの中から一つ選び，記号で答えよ。

ア　dangerous　　イ　familiar　　ウ　puzzling

問3　下線部②について，親や教師にとってどのようなことが問題であるか，50字以内の日本語で書け。

問4　本文中の(　A　)に入る最も適切な語をア～ウの中から一つ選び，記号で答えよ。

ア　well-organized　　イ　ill-prepared　　ウ　fast-growing

問5　下線部③について，次の問に英語で答えよ。

How can we stop such kids from getting around computer security software?

問6　digital citizenship の定義として最も適切なものをア～エの中から一つ選び，記号で答えよ。

ア　the responsibility to act appropriately and safely with regard to technology use

イ　a software that companies provide to prevent children from negative experiences online

ウ　the legal right to belong to a particular country and keep children safe online

エ　the state of being a citizen and accepting the responsibilities of it

問7　インターネット上のコミュニケーションのあり方について，あなたはどのようなことを生徒に指導するか，50語程度の英語で書け。

なお，使用した語数を記入すること。

(☆☆☆☆○○○○)

【中学校】

【1】次のある教師のエッセイを読んで，後の問に答えよ。

It was two days before the first day of school. There was a thick excitement in the air about a new school year, new expectations, and new experiences. Kelsey and Alana showed up at my classroom door. We exchanged pleasantries about our summers and what we were looking forward to the next school year. As the girls prepared to leave, Alana looked me in the eyes and said, "I hope that I have you next year, because I can tell that you are a good teacher."

This was our first meeting, and we had talked for less than two minutes. Yet, in that short time the girls had decided that I was a good teacher. It made me wonder, "①What does it really mean to be a good teacher?　What do good teachers do that makes them stand out from the rest?　How do good teachers stay inspired to be successful year after year?"

This year marks my twelfth year teaching middle school math, and every year I ask myself these questions. Ever since I was a kid I knew I wanted to be a teacher — to empower others through education and to work with a diverse population of students. ②This can be challenging, as many students struggle to develop a sense of what they want to do, or even can do, in life, due to their background.

I once overheard one of my students, Stella, tell a friend how much she hated school. I asked her what she wanted to be when she grew up. She proceeded to tell me about the fact that people in her neighborhood don't really have good jobs, how her parents could not afford college, and how she still had not decided what she wanted to be when she grew up. Stella was hopeless, and she had decided that her current condition had determined her destiny. I told her that doing well in school was not about being smart but working hard. I encouraged her to think about what she wanted to do in the future. Since then, she has developed a more optimistic mindset toward school and has become more engaged in the classroom.

③Good teachers believe in every child, every day, no matter their race, religion, socio-economic status, or current living conditions. We believe that all children can and will learn. Our faith in our students' abilities is the foundation for so many inspiring, life-changing student-teacher relationships, the kind that continue beyond the classroom and through a lifetime.

A few months ago I received an email from a former student. He was a few days away from college graduation, and he was reflecting on his experiences in middle and high school. He thought about our class and how he learned to (A) challenges. From that experience, he gained the confidence to take honors level math classes, which helped lead to a full-paid college scholarship and the opportunity to (B) his dream of becoming an emergency - room physician. In that moment, with tears streaming down my face, I was reminded of the difference that teachers can make in the life of a child.

Good teachers motivate kids to be better than their best selves. We push them out of their ④comfort zones. Good teachers stay inspired — sometimes by learning from other teachers — even in a career that is so physically and mentally demanding. We find our persistence because we know that we are making a difference, changing lives, and, in part, changing the world.

問1　筆者はなぜ下線部①のような疑問をもったのか，本文に即して35字程度の日本語で書け。

問2　下線部②の理由を本文に即して35字程度の日本語で書け。

問3　Stellaは筆者の励ましでどのように変容したか，本文に即して35字程度の日本語で書け。

問4　次の英文が下線部③の意味になるように( )に与えられた文字で始まる英語1語を書け。

Good teachers have faith in their students regardless of their (b   ).

問5　本文中の（　A　），（　B　）に入る最も適切な語をア〜オの中から一つずつ選び，記号で答えよ。

ア　create　イ　explain　ウ　face　エ　pursue　オ　refuse

問6　下線部④を最もよく表すものを次のア〜エの中から一つ選び，記号で答えよ。

ア　places in which you don't feel any stress

イ　situations where you get a sense of dissatisfaction

ウ　favorable relationships you make with teachers

エ　things that you can get by trying hard

問7　次の質問に対するあなたの考えを60語程度の英語で書け。なお，使用した語数を記入すること。

How do good teachers stay inspired to be successful?

（☆☆☆◎◎◎）

【高等学校】

【1】次の英文を読んで，後の問に答えよ。

　Dr. Karyn Gordon is an expert on youth, a family consultant, an author and much more. In her upcoming speaking tour, she will present to eight schools in the Toronto District School Board on the topic of 10 Practical Strategies to Develop Empathy and Gratitude in Children. "There are ①three parts to empathy: the head, the heart, and the hand," Gordon says. The head is the intellectual part of understanding what empathy is and what it does, the heart feels what others are feeling, and the hand actually takes action after feeling empathy for someone.

　Gordon's first tip is called ②Fill Their Emotional Bucket. "When children get the sense that their parent, teacher, or coach has more empathy for them, that's the best form of teaching," Gordon says. When a child is upset, angry or frustrated, try to understand why they feel the way they do, instead of being angry, upset or defensive. If a child feels understood by the adults around them, they feel more loved and more secure, and ultimately, they learn to share their feelings in a calm manner.

Gordon's second tip is called Seek to Understand. Empathy is about trying to see something from another person's (　A　) and trying to feel what they feel. "When I'm coaching, I will try to jump in and see things from their (　A　)," Gordon says. "Can you help me understand how you see this?' It's a very comprehensive line. I love that line. That line has been extremely helpful."

Gordon's third tip, Ask Don't Tell, is very important to keep in mind when trying to understand a child's feelings. Gordon stresses that we never know for sure what the other person feels. "It's really important that we ask how they feel and don't tell them how they feel," she says. "It's really irritating for children when they're told how they feel." Avoiding statements like 'I know how you feel' and replacing them with '￼ B ￼' can make a world of difference.

③<u>A good exercise in understanding empathy</u> is Gordon's fourth tip, Switch Roles. "It's a great teaching method," Gordon says. Teachers divide their class into two groups and create a conflicting situation that must be resolved. Each group plays a different role, and after 10 or 15 minutes of discussion, the groups must switch roles and put themselves in the opposite group's shoes.

Gordon's fifth tip is about gratitude, Make 'Thank You' Part of Your Culture. Every country has a culture and every classroom has a culture, a common attitude, and an understood way of doing things. Gordon points out that it's very important to recognize and help foster a positive culture in the classroom. "Gratitude is very connected to empathy," says Gordon. "Really make sure your classroom is a thank-you classroom." From a simple thank you for holding the door, to a bigger thank you for sharing a secret, those two small words create a culture of gratitude in a classroom. Gordon says that when she teaches this model to educators, many of them feel that they don't need to do this, but it's a very easy way to create a positive culture of gratitude and empathy within the classroom.

Ultimately, creating empathy comes down to ④leading children by example. "We have to model what we want them to do," Gordon says. The schools selected for Dr. Karyn Gordon's upcoming speaking tour are being asked to fundraise in order to teach the students about the head, heart, and hand aspects of empathy, even before her arrival. The money will be donated to World Vision, and they will use the money to build a school in Haiti. "A lot of people have the head and the heart part, but they don't know what to actually do," says Gordon. "What I'm hoping is that they will be moved to actually take action and advance the project."

問1　下線部①はそれぞれどのような働きをするのか，40字程度の日本語で書け。

問2　下線部②の説明になるように，(a)〜(c)に与えられた文字で始まる英語1語をそれぞれ書け。

　　　When we adults say or do something that shows we (a)(c　　) about children, their emotional bucket will become full of (b)(p　　) feelings, and in the end, they will understand each other instead of losing their (c)(t　　).

問3　本文中の(A)に共通して入る最も適切な語をア〜エの中から一つ選び，記号で答えよ。

　　　ア　aptitude　　イ　indulgence　　ウ　maturity　　エ　perspective

問4　本文中の　B　に入る最も適切な1文をア〜エの中から一つ選び,記号で答えよ,

　　　ア　I actually don't understand how you feel in the least.
　　　イ　I don't think you should tell me your feelings.
　　　ウ　I imagine that you feel this way, am I right?
　　　エ　I know what's on your mind, should I tell you?

問5　下線部③の具体的な方法を70字以内の日本語で書け。

問6　下線部④の具体的な例を本文中から探し，20字以内の日本語で書け。

問7　本文の内容を踏まえて,あなたが学級経営をするときに大切にし
　　ていきたいことは何か，60語程度の英語で書け。なお，使用した語
　　数を記入すること。

(☆☆☆◎◎◎◎)

解答・解説

【中高共通】

【１】1　エ　　2　ウ　　3　ア　　4　エ　　5　ア　　6　イ　　7　ウ
　　8　ウ　　9　エ　　10　イ

〈解説〉1　今夜予定のバーベキュー・パーティーの相談である。Wによ
ると雨模様らしいが，Mは大きなテントがあるから大丈夫と言ってい
る。　　2　本屋の中での対話である。客(W)は著者の名前を忘れたが本
の体裁は覚えていて，ミステリー小説だと言っている。　　3　子(W)が
ハイキングに出かけたがびしょ濡れで帰宅した。父親(M)は「熱めの
シャワーを浴びたらどうだ」と言っている。Why don't you ～?という
表現に注意。「ぜひ～しなさい」の意味である。　　4　デパートの店員
(W)と客(M)の電話での会話である。客が返金を希望すると，店員はレ
シートを持っているかと聞いている。refundは「返金」の意味である。
5　骨折したツアー予定の客(W)と旅行代理店員(M)の電話での会話で
ある。客はツアーのキャンセルではなく，オプションの変更を希望し
ている。店員は車椅子の準備も可能だと言っている。I'd like to change
themの部分を聞き逃さないこと。　　6　年間メンバーの登録に来た客
(W)と店員(M)の会話である。客は費用の50ドルの持ち合せがないので
後で来ると言っている。apply for「申し込む」。　　7　子(M)と母親(W)
の電話での会話である。子は明日の晩に駅に迎えに来てくれと頼んで
いる。pick upは「(人を)車に乗せる」の意味。　　8　ホテルの客(M)が
部屋のシャワーについて苦情を言うと，担当者(W)は眺めのよい別の

部屋を提供すると言っている。客は了解して現在の部屋で待機する場面である。　9　中学校でのチャリティーイベントの場面である。学年ごとに教員も参加する出し物があり，ブラスバンドの演奏も予定されている。演奏の後で難民救済のための募金をすると述べている。raise money「金を集める」。　10　博多行きのサザンエクスプレス5号の車内放送である。大雨のために30分遅れていて，博多には8時15分に到着すると言っている。

【2】1　イ　　2　エ　　3　ア　　4　ウ　　5　ウ
〈解説〉1　正答のイは「(人に)話して～させる」の意味である。英文の意味は「私の友人は話をして私を鹿児島マラソンに参加させようとした」となる。アのadviseはadvise＋目的語＋to doの形をとる。ウのtellとエのproposeはtell / propose＋目的語＋to＋(代)名詞の形をとる。
2　アは「一見して」，イは「直接に」，ウは「初めて」，エは「最初は」の意味である。英文前半の意味は「最初はそのダイエット計画は難しかった」となる。　3　アは「欠乏して」という意味で，food以下の意味は「食料が欠乏して多くの人が非常に空腹だった」となる。イ「ほんの少し」，ウ「多量」，エ「豊富な」。　4　according to以下がヒントである。「コミュニケーションする人々の間での環境や話題や関係に従って」とあるので，ウ「社会言語学的な」が適切である。
5　『真夏の夜の夢』の著者はウのウィリアム・シェイクスピア。

【3】Japanese students are often quite indecisive and tend to accept whatever teachers say. Learning, however, is not memorizing but thinking for ourselves.

Change in modern society is incredibly rapid, and remarkable progress in scientific technology has recently enabled us to do what was thought to be impossible only ten years ago. Therefore, teachers need to build up the basis for learning throughout students' lives and to foster students' positive attitudes toward new things so that they can address various problems themselves.

(81 words)

〈解説〉解答例は，生徒が自ら積極的に学習する態度の育成という観点から記述されている。公式の採点基準では，内容・論の展開の適切さ，語彙，文法の適切さ，分量をみるので，これらが適切であればよい。以下に，柔軟な思考力の育成という観点から記述した別解を示すので，参考にしてほしい。This is very surprising information for us. The year will come only after 12 years. The entirely new occupations require children for completely new ways of thinking needed for their working. Now is the time teachers should enhance children to have ability for flexible thinking and how to act in their society. For the purpose of such flexible thinking, teachers' most important mission is to set various curricula which enables students to have zest for living.　(76 words)

【4】問1　(a)　25　　(b)　hide　　問2　ウ　　問3　専門家でも苦労している刻々と変化するインターネット使用上のルールとエチケットを定義すること。(46字)　　問4　イ　　問5　We can stop them from doing so by proactively teaching positive computing and digital lifestyle habits.　　問6　ア　　問7　I will tell my students to behave appropriately when they use the Internet. They should communicate with others online in the same way as they do face-to-face. When they write something on the Internet, they should think carefully about the possibility of embarrassing or hurting someone before posting it online.　(50 words)

〈解説〉問1　(a)　第1段落3文目のa quarter of adolescentsは「若者の4分の1」という意味である。したがって25％である。　(b)　第1段落4文目 a fifth以下は「子どもたちの5分の1が同様に大人の過剰な反応を恐れている」という意味である。したがって，それを防ぐには，両親から自分たちの好ましくない経験を「隠す」ことになる。　問2　第2段落1文目a growing gulf「大きくなり続ける溝」がヒントである。この後にbetweenが続くので，二者が比較されていることがわかる。前者は「テクノロジーとともに育った」とあるので，後者は正反対のものだとわ

かる。したがって，①は「戸惑うような，難解な」の意味が適切だとわかる。　問3　下線部②のThatは，第3段落1文目の内容である。「専門家でさえオンラインの規則や不文律を定義することが難しい」という趣旨を記述すればよい。　問4　第4段落3文目以下がヒントである。特に4文目で「しかしながら調査してみると，驚くべきことに36％の教員が，前年には一度もICT関係の研修を受けなかった」とあるので，イ「準備不足の」が適切である。　問5　第6段落最後の1文がヒントである。Onlyからhabitsまでが強調されて文頭に出たために，主語のsuch problemsと動詞部分のcan truly be addressedが倒置されている点に注意すること。この部分を解答すればよい。　問6　ここで言う「デジタル市民権」とは，いわゆるICTに対する幅広い対応力を表すものである。したがって，第7段落3文目がヒントとなる。ここでは，「教育的な手法とハイテクの安全のためのルールやオンラインを使用する時の責任について教育するプログラムが解決への道である」と述べているので，ア「技術の使用に関して，適切かつ安全に行動する責任」が正解である。イは「ソフトウェア」とあるので誤り。ウは論旨にはない。エは文字通りの「市民権」なので誤り。　問7　以下に別解を示すので，参考にしてほしい。First, I will introduce my students about ICT literacy, because it helps us to have easy communication with anyone including someone to whom we have never seen so far. However, it will be necessary to use correct and proper words to express our thoughts in order to avoid unnecessary confusions or misunderstandings. (52 words)

【中学校】

【1】問1　初めて会ってほんの少ししか話していない生徒に良い先生だと言われたから。(35字)　問2　多くの学生は成育環境のせいでやりたいことを容易に考えることができないため。(37字)　問3　学校生活に前向きに取り組むようになり学級にもより関わるようになった。(34字)　問4　background(s)　問5　A　ウ　　B　エ　　問6　ア　問7　I think good teachers stay inspired by making every effort to improve their teaching skills. They can do this by attending teaching workshops, taking a certification exam such as TOEIC or TOEFL, getting advice from other teachers and ALTs, and studying foreign teaching methods. In addition, I think taking part in club activities lets teachers and students get to know each other better.　(63 words)

〈解説〉問1　第2段落1, 2文目で「2人に会ったのはこれが初めてで, 2分と経っていないのに自分が良い先生だと言われた」という旨の記述がある。それでこのように思ったのである。この内容をまとめればよい。　問2　第3段落3文目as many以下が理由になっている。「多くの生徒たちが成育環境のせいで自分たちのやる気を伸ばすことに苦労しているから」とあるので, この趣旨をまとめればよい。　問3　第4段落最後の1文で「学校に対して以前よりも前向きになり, クラスにもより関わりをもつようになった」とあるので, この趣旨をまとめればよい。　問4　下線部③は「良い先生はどんな子どもでも, どんな1日でも信じている。人種, 宗教, 社会的経済的な地位, あるいは現在の生活状況にかかわらずに」という意味である。下線部のno matter以下がregardlessと対応している。したがって, background(s)「経歴」が適切である。　問5　A　to（　A　）challengesは第6段落4文目that experienceと同意である。続くhe gained the confidenceがその結果となるので, ウ「立ち向かう」が適切である。　B　第6段落4文目the opportunityからphysicianまでは「ERの外科医になる夢を追い求める機会」と考えればよい。したがって, エ「追求する」が適切である。　問6　第7段落1, 2文目は「良い先生は子どもたちを動機付けてさらに高い場所へ行かせる。心地よい場所から追い出す」の意味である。したがって, 「ぬるま湯の状態」と考えればよいので, ア「何のストレスも感じない場所」が適切である。　問7　以下に別解を示すので, 参考にしてほしい。I think a good teacher is always concentrating to study by him/herself and ready to provide lectures based on his / her experiences. In order to be such a good teacher, the teacher should always try to challenge to have especially testing of listening and speaking of English, which will be supportive to keep brushing up his / her English ability. Teachers' more aggressive study will make students' aggressiveness more.　(66words)

【高等学校】

【1】問1　頭で共感の意味と作用を考え，心で他人の気持ちを感じ取り，手で実際に行動を起こす。(40字)　　問2　(a)　care
(b)　positive(その他peaceful など)　　(c)　temper　　問3　エ
問4　ウ　　問5　クラスを二つに分け，それぞれに対立する状況を与えて解決するように話し合わせ，しばらくしたらその役割を入れ替えて逆の立場に立たせる。(65字)　　　問6　ハイチに学校を作るために募金すること。(19字)　　　問7　I will try to show students my positive attitude toward life and encourage them to be confident during school and after. When students are positive and proud of themselves, they will also develop empathy with their friends. I will cover the walls of the classroom with positive messages and posters with inspiring pictures and words. I believe this will greatly help.　(61 words)

〈解説〉問1　第1段落4文目の内容を，頭と心と手についてまとめればよい。　　問2　下線部②を直訳すれば「子どもたちの感情のバケツを満たせ」である。この具体的な説明が，第2段落2文目のWhenからfor themまでである。第2段落2文目のtheir parent, 〜 has more empathy for themをwe care about childrenと言い換えている。また，同段落4文目のfeel more loved and more secureの部分をbecome full of positive / peaceful feelingsと言い換えている。問題文最後のlose one's temperは「腹を立てる」の意味である。　問3　第3段落2文目trying to以下と，4文目以下の発言内容がヒントである。特に，後半の「あなたがどのようにこれを見ているか」の部分が重要である。ア「適性。才能」，イ「気まま。道楽」，ウ「成熟」，エ「物の見方」。　問4　第4段落2文目のwe以下の「他人が感じていることは正確にはわからない」がヒントである。この趣旨に沿えば，ウの「あなたはこのように感じていると私は想像するが，合っているか」が適切である。　問5　第5段落3文目以降に具

体的な方法について記述している。いわゆる簡単なディベートの方法が示されている。　問6　第7段落4文目and they以下が具体例である。問7　以下に別解を示すので，参考にしてほしい。When I am assigned to take a class, I first watch students individually to try to know them with watching carefully. Second, I will put a phrase saying, "Complete the class target" on the wall at teacher's side. Third, I will take a leading position in the class to realize the class target steadily, having supportive talking with them. (59 words)

2016年度　実施問題

【中高共通】

【1】聞き取りテスト

　これから1〜10の英語を1回ずつ放送します。それぞれの英語のあとに，その内容について質問を一つします。その質問に対する答として適切なものをア〜エの中から一つずつ選び，その記号で答えなさい。

1　W : I am going to San Francisco.

　　M : When are you leaving?

　　W : Oh, I will leave Kagoshima on June 13th and come back five days later.

　　Question (M) : When will the woman return?

　　ア　June 13th.　　イ　June 18th.　　ウ　June 30th.　　エ　July 5th.

2　W : So, where does it hurt?

　　M : It's my arm — especially here.

　　W : Did you play any sports today?

　　M : No, but I did help my mother move some furniture yesterday.

　　Question (W) : What probably happened to the man?

　　ア　He injured his arm playing sports.

　　イ　He injured his arm moving some furniture.

　　ウ　He injured his back playing soccer.

　　エ　He injured his back carrying his mother.

3　W : What did you do last weekend?

　　M : I moved to a new apartment.

　　W : Really?　　Could I have your new address?

M : Sure. It's 4910 Stanley Street, apartment number 305.

Question (W) : What is the man's new address?

ア　1419 Stanley Street, apartment # 503.

イ　4910 Stanley Street, apartment # 503.

ウ　1419 Stanley Street, apartment # 305.

エ　4910 Stanley Street, apartment # 305.

4　W : Hello. May I speak to Mr. Michael Lee, please?

M : I'm sorry, but he's out right now. Would you like to leave a message?

W : Yes, thank you. My name is Elizabeth Brown. I am a librarian at the city library. I found his wallet in the reading room.

M : Oh, that's great!　Michael was really worried about it.

Question (W) : Which statement is true?

ア　Michael left his wallet in the library.

イ　Elizabeth studied with Michael in the library.

ウ　Michael works at the library.

エ　Elizabeth is a close friend of Michael's.

5　M : Excuse me. I ordered the fried chicken and the pumpkin soup about 30 minutes ago, but I'm still waiting.

W : Oh, I'm sorry. I'll go and ask the chef what's taking so long.

M : Actually, I'd like to cancel my order. I have an important meeting in 10 minutes.

W : I understand. I'm very sorry about that, sir.

Question (M) : What will the man probably do?

ア　He'll wait for his food.　　イ　He'll cancel his meeting.

ウ　He'll talk to the chef.　　エ　He'll leave the restaurant.

6　W : Excuse me, but how much is this jacket?

M : It is three hundred dollars in a set with this skirt.

W : Oh, I see. I just need a jacket, so I'll look for another one.

Question (M) : What is the woman going to do?

ア　She is going to buy the jacket and skirt.

イ　She is going to keep looking at the jacket.

ウ　She is going to look for a different jacket.

エ　She is going to ask for a discount.

7　M :　How are we going to seat 15 people?

W : It's no big deal. We just have to get another table from the next room.

M : Oh, you're right. We should be able to fit 3 people at each table.

W : Let's go and get a table.

Question (M) : How many tables do they need in total?

ア　Ono table.　　イ　Three tables.　　ウ　Four tables.

エ　Five tables.

8　M : My budget is unexpectedly tight right now. I was going to buy a new bag tomorrow, but my microwave oven broke down this morning, and it's too old to repair. I also need a new computer for my chemistry thesis. I can't afford everything now.

W : So, you have to decide which to buy.

M : Well, I can't fail chemistry this year.

Question (W) : What will the man probably buy first?

ア　A bag.　　イ　A camera.　　ウ　A microwave oven.

エ　A computer.

9　Your attention, please. We have a lost little girl with us at the information desk. Her name is Emily Jones. She is four years old. She said she came to this shopping mall with her mother and her brother, Tom. Emily was found crying near the toy shop on the third floor. Would Mrs. Jones please come to the information desk on the first floor?

Question (M) : What happened?

ア　Mr. Jones lost sight of his daughter.

イ　Emily Jones got lost at the shopping mall.

ウ　Emily's brother made her cry at the toy shop.

エ　Emily Jones lost her toy at the shopping mall.

10　OK. I will give you two kinds of medicine. The yellow tablets will stop the headache, and the red pills are to help you sleep. But you have to remember that you should take one yellow tablet three times a day after eating and take only one red pill once at night before you go to bed.

Question (W) : Which statement is true?

ア　Four yellow tablets should be taken daily.

イ　One red pill should be taken daily.

ウ　Both medicines should be taken before a meal.

エ　Both medicines will stop a stomachache.

(☆☆☆◎◎◎)

【2】次の各英文の(　　　)に入る最も適切なものを下のア～エの中から一つずつ選び，記号で答えよ。

1　Please call me back if (　　　) convenient for you to talk now.

ア　it is not　　イ　you are not　　ウ　we are not

エ　it will not be

2　If you like this fruit pie, (　　　) make one yourself?　I'll give you the recipe.

ア　how come you　　イ　why don't you　　ウ　how about

エ　what do you say to

3　I don't think we can come up with a solution to the problem, however long we spend (　　　) it.

ア　discussing about　　イ　to talk about　　ウ　to discuss

エ　discussing

4 Angela was sent home from school to change after she appeared wearing a tank top, which was a clear (　　) of the dress code.

　ア　recession　　イ　obligation　　ウ　violation　　エ　obedience

5 Discourse competence is knowing how to interpret the larger context and how to construct longer stretches of language so that the parts make up a (　　) whole.

　ア　specific　　イ　coherent　　ウ　coincidental　　エ　illogical

(☆☆☆◎◎◎)

【3】あなたは，英語の授業が英語で行われたことでどのようなことが期待されると思うか，80語程度の英語で書け。なお，使用した語数を記入すること。

(☆☆☆◎◎◎)

【4】次の英文を読んで，後の問に答えよ。

　As a mathematics educator, I have taught six-year-olds in a Year 1 Mathematics Intervention program, senior secondary students studying Year 12 mathematics subjects and adults studying to be early childhood, primary and secondary teachers. Among these students, I have worked with many suffering from mathematics anxiety. Some of them went out of a lecture theatre in a hurry when numbers were displayed on a screen.

　Researchers have found that the way mathematics is taught contributes to mathematics anxiety, particularly when there is an emphasis on (　A　). Timed tests and 'drill type' games cause stress for many students in mathematics classrooms. When working with tertiary students training to be primary teachers the level of anxiety was increased when they had to complete timed tests as a hurdle requirement in their first year mathematics subject.

　"Maths anxiety is a problem for educators because it can prevent students from demonstrating their maths capabilities. In the long term, it can lead to students avoiding situations that involve maths, which means they may shut the door on some important opportunities," Dr Sarah Buckley, Research Fellow at the Australian Council for Educational Research says.

Whether working with children or adults I have found that one of the most important things that I can do as a parent, teacher, tutor, or lecturer is to develop a good relationship with the student experiencing mathematics anxiety. I needed to provide support and encouragement by demonstrating what these students could already do and what they needed to do next. The ①onus on me as the mathematics teacher is to demonstrate that I have confidence in their ability to eventually succeed with mathematical tasks at their level.

As a parent, teacher, and lecturer I always try to demonstrate my passion for mathematical activities, that I do not know all the answers, that I sometimes make mistakes and have to try different solution methods, that I value alternative ways of solving problems and that I can always learn something new. I still get excited when a student can show me an alternative way of solving a mathematical task that I had not tried previously.

One of the aims stated in *The Australian Curriculum : Mathematics* is for students to : 'recognise connections between the areas of mathematics and other disciplines and appreciate mathematics as an accessible and enjoyable discipline to study' (ACARA, 2014). We need to ensure students can recognise the mathematics in their everyday lives and in the other subjects they are studying.

Swan (2004) lists six ways that teachers can engage their students' interest in mathematics. These include using literature that focuses on mathematical content to engage students, using mathemagic that links to the development of meaningful mathematics, games that have a clear purpose and specific mathematical content, investigations that focus on interesting problems or using mathematical trivia and making links between the mathematics students complete in the classroom and their everyday life. However, a context that is real life or everyday for a teacher may not be relevant to the students they are teaching.

A paper entitled *Strategies for reducing math anxiety* (2011) lists several techniques for teachers to use to lessen their students' mathematical anxiety. Techniques include strategies such as : developing strong mathematical content knowledge and positive attitudes towards mathematics; encouraging their students to use critical thinking and active learning; placing more emphasis on understanding rather than (A); using concrete materials and technology; and providing support and encouragement for all students.

Parents should have realistic expectations of their children and providing ongoing support and encouragement, while students should ②incorporate practice into their daily routine, and focus on their earlier mathematical successes rather than failures.

Buckley says, "It is vital that students understand that 'being good at maths' is not simply something that people are born with — practice will lead to improvement," so both parents and teachers should provide ongoing encouragement for them to study according to the way they learn best.

問1　数学に不安を抱える筆者の教え子にはどのような行動が見られたか，本文に即して30字程度の日本語で書け。

問2　数学教師として筆者が今でも興奮するのはどのような時か，本文に即して35字以内の日本語で書け。

問3　*The Australian Curriculam*によると，生徒が数学を学ぶ目的の一つは何か，本文に即して40字程度の日本語で書け。

問4　下線部①，②の意味に最も近い語を，ア〜エの中から一つずつ選び，記号で答えよ。

　　ア　distract.　　イ　introduce　　ウ　responsibility　　エ　support

問5　本文中の(A)に共通して入る最も適切なものをア〜エの中から一つ選び，記号で答えよ。

　　ア　critical thinking of assumption and verification

　　イ　logical thinking of rules and procedures

　　ウ　practical learning of assumption and verification

　　エ　rote learning of rules and procedures

問6　英語学習に不安があるために授業に積極的に参加できない生徒に対して，あなたはどのような策を講じるか，40語程度の英語で書け。なお，使用した語数を記入すること。

(☆☆☆○○○)

【中学校】

【１】次の英文を読んで，後の問に答えよ。

　As individuals, and no doubt as teachers, when we are impatient we become edgy and unkind and treat those around us with disrespect. However, ①this should not be, for as teachers we are called to be kind and caring to our students. Our words and actions should be those that can build up the student's self-esteem, rather than tear him or her down.

　A teacher should always be ready to offer an encouraging word to the student; one that will positively propel him or her into greatness. If we as teachers tear down our students with unkindness in the school and classroom, what will happen to them in a world that is already cold and callous? 　a　 No, we much teach them kindness by our own deeds and words, so that at the end of the day, as they go out into the world, they can （　A　） what is good and true.

　Some may say that we since live in such an imperfect world, how can the teacher do all of this?　I believe that teachers change lives by reaching students one by one. Within the heart of the teacher lies a great power that in many instances can make or break a student. Yes, it is a challenging task, but with some love, a kind and joyful heart, a peaceful effort and a touch of kindness, the teacher can indeed positively mold the lives of his or her students.　b　

　Sometimes our students are just waiting for a kind word. 　c　 Even when we are calledd to be stern with our students we should endeavour to do

180

so in kindness. I have often heard the phrase...*It's not what you say that counts at times, but rather how you say it.* Teachers, be mindful of this in your daily walk with your students. Remember, ②we communicate all of this in our response when our students say, "*Good morning teacher.*"

Missy was a very disruptive child in her grade four class. It seemed as if no matter what the teacher did, Missy would find a way to make some sort of mischief. The teacher had tried talking to her parents as well as the Principal, but all to no avail; for, Missy continued to display (B) behaviour.

It was not until the next school year, when Missy went into the grade five class with Ms.Green that things began to change. Ms.Green had heard all the stories of Missy as she came up the grade levels. So she was well aware of Missy's behavioural problem.

On the first day that the students came to the class, Ms.Green laid down her classroom rules. ③Missy only smiled. As the school term progressed, Missy tried all of her tactics with Ms.Green. Each time, Ms.Green gently rebuked her. She would let Missy know what she did was wrong and punished her accordingly. Ms.Green, despite Missy's bad behaviour, after each punishment, always had a kind word for her.

④Missy was puzzled by this calm gentle response from Ms.Green, for she was used to teachers shouting at her and her parents yelling. Sometimes their shouts provoked her to further display unpleasing behaviour. So this kind behaviour from Ms.Green was new to her.

Slowly, but surely Missy began to change. Missy noticed it, her parents noticed it, Ms.Green noticed it, and even other teachers and students at the school noticed it. It was so noticeable that one day in a staffmeeting, a teacher asked Ms.Green how she had transformed Missy into a well behaved student. Ms.Green simply said that she showed Missy kindness and that in a gentle spirit she rebuked her. She reminded her colleagues that sometimes it's not what you say or do, but rather, how you say or do it.

問1　本文中の(A)，(B)に入る最も適切な語をア～オの中から

一つずつ選び，記号で答えよ。

　ア　admirable　　イ　pattern　　ウ　proper　　エ　despise

　オ　poor

問2　下線部①が指す内容を本文に即して45字以内の日本語で書け。

問3　次の英文が入る最も適切な箇所を　 a 　～　 c 　の中から一つ選び，記号で答えよ。

　　In so doing, teachers further enrich their own lives and the teaching profession.

問4　次の英文が下線部②とほぼ同じ内容を表すように(　ア　)，(　イ　)に適切な英語1語をそれぞれ書け。

　　The students can tell how much their teachers (　ア　) about them from the (　イ　) their teachers respond to their greetings.

問5　下線部③におけるミッシーの心情として最も適切なものをア～ウの中から一つ選び，記号で答えよ。

　ア　I don't know what to do as Ms.Green's rules are strict.

　イ　Ms.Green appears to be so nice that I'll be a good girl.

　ウ　Whatever Ms.Green may do, it won't make any difference to me.

問6　下線部④の理由を60字程度の日本語で書け。

問7　本文の事例を参考にして，あなたに影響を与えた出来事や経験について50語程度の英語で書け。なお，使用した語数を記入すること。

(☆☆☆◎◎◎)

【高等学校】

【1】次の英文を読んで，後の問に答えよ。

　Marlene and her husband, Steve, were houseparents and lived in the home along with the approximately eight teenage girls who were placed there. She had been walking by, carrying yet another load of laundry upstairs, when she noticed that no one was in the dining room. An empty room in this hectic house is ①a rare oasis in a vast desert. The needs of the group house and its young female residents were endless. At the end of each day, Marlene was often both physically and emotionally exhausted.

This day had been as difficult as any of the others. Marlene felt as threadbare as the chair cushion beneath her. She glanced down at the dining room table and a look of shock ran across her face, followed by a dim smile. *Marlene is a witch!* had been carved deeply into the surface of this most visible piece of furniture. Marlene traced her index finger along the letters gouged into the table. She thought about the hundreds of girls she had nurtured, comforted, supported, defended, and loved during her five years there. She thought about how mean the girls had been to her the first year, and how nearly every night she had cried herself to sleep alongside Steve in their cramped little sofa bed.

The squeals of teenage girls from the room upstairs snapped Marlene back. She surmised from the excited noise above that the culprit had just informed the other girls of ②her public act of defiance. "Ellen, you and the other girls get down here," Marlene shouted. "Right now!" After nearly a minute, sixteen feet crept tentatively down the steps. The girls stood around, looking awkward and ill at ease. Marlene studied the eight girls silently for a moment. Every one of them was there against her will. Most of them had experienced things no human being should ever endure — things that could take a lifetime to heal.

Tears began to well in Marlene's eyes as she exhaled a deep sigh. Her tender heart was near breaking. It took this rebellious act for her to step back and remember, once again, (③) the girls truly were. Whoever did this was lashing out at Marlene because she, herself, was in severe pain. Marlene cleared her throat, and in her best attempt at sounding stern said, "I wanted you all to know that I've seen the little art project permanently etched into our dining room table." "Ooooooooo," said a couple of the girls in unison as if rehearsed and on cue. The other girls giggled nervously. "Anyway," Marlene continued. "As I said, I've seen it and I don't think it's fair." Marlene paused for effect.

"It's not fair that I be called a witch for running this house as I do. After all," Marlene continued, a big smile bursting across her face, "Steve makes as many decisions around here as I do." This wasn't what the girls had expected. "So," Marlene concluded, "if I'm a witch, then Steve is a witch, too." The smile she beamed into each of their faces showed (A). *I will love you no matter what!* She affirmed resolutely in her mind. "Steve's a witch," a girl quietly said. Another girl giggled and several repeated the comment. Someone suggested carving Steve's name into the table alongside Marlene's. At this, everyone laughed. Marlene shouted a playful and overly dramatic, "No!" and everyone laughed again. ④<u>The girls who walked back up the stairs that evening were not the same girls who had walked down.</u>

Marlene admits that she hated her job at the group home in the early years. She was always surrounded by so much pain and anger, and everything she tried was met with(B). "One day I decided to give these girls the one thing they all needed and none of them had ever had — unconditional love. I just opened my heart to the immense pain they had suffered and that continued to haunt them every moment. And suddenly they began to change. They became more helpful and considerate."

When Marlene's attitude shifted, ⑤<u>it affected the girl's behavior and the whole culture of the house</u>. Whenever a girl left the house and another moved in, the other girls quickly brought the new one up to speed as to appropriate behavior and the importance of helping out. And it was all because Marlene put into practice the power that will transform anything and anyone — *love*.

問1　次の英語が下線部①とほぼ同じ意味を表すように，空所に入る
　　適切な英語1語を書け。

　　　a special place where she can(　　　)for a while in her very busy life

問2　下線部②の具体的内容を本文に即して25字程度の日本語で書け。

問3　本文中の空所(　③　)に入る最も適切なものをア～エの中から一
　　つ選び，記号で答えよ。

ア　how fragile and wounded　　イ　how active and positive

ウ　how sneaky and evil　　　　エ　how wise and sensible

問4　次の英文が下線部④に至った経緯を表すように，(a)～(c)に与えられた文字で始まる英語1語をそれぞれ書け。

When the girls were called to the dining room, they expected that they would be (a)(p　　) for the act one of them did. However, Marlene took advantage of the opportunity and eased a tense situation with (b)(h　　). This attitude of hers helped the girls to build a better (c)(r　　) with her.

問5　下線部⑤は具体的にはどのようなことか，本文に即して50字程度の日本語で書け。

問6　本文中の(　A　)，(　B　)に入る最も適切な語をア～エの中から一つずつ選び，記号で答えよ。

ア　achievement　　イ　compassion　　ウ　cooperation

エ　rebellion

問7　あなたは反抗的な態度をとる生徒にどのような点に留意して指導するか，50語程度の英語で書け。なお，使用した語数を記入すること。

(☆☆☆○○○)

解答・解説

【中高共通】

【1】1　イ　　2　イ　　3　エ　　4　ア　　5　エ　　6　ウ　　7　エ
　　8　エ　　9　イ　　10　イ

〈解説〉リスニングテストでは，問題文中の数値，順序，地名，色などの情報は質問の対象になりやすいので，特に注意して聞く必要がある。問題用紙に選択肢が書かれている場合は，目を通しておくと質問内容がある程度予測でき，集中するポイントを絞ることもできる。

1　質問は「女性はいつ戻ってくるか」。女性は「6月13日に鹿児島を発って5日後に戻ってくる」と言っているので，6月18日である。

2　質問は「男性に何が起こったと思われるか」。probablyは「たぶん。おそらく」なので，ここでは上記のように意味をとればよいだろう。男性は女性の「今日なにかスポーツをしていたか」という質問に否定の回答をしたうえで，「前の日に母の手伝いで家具を動かしていた」と答えている。その時に腕を負傷したものと推測される。　3　質問は「男性の新しい住所はどのようであるか」。番地部分や部屋番号の聞き取りに注意を要する。一般的には，数字を1つずつ読み上げる。また，数字の0はオーと読まれることがあるのでこの点にも気をつけること。　4　質問は「どの記述が正しいか」。ここでのstatementは選択肢のことである。市立図書館の司書であるElizabeth Brownは館内で利用者のMichael Leeが落とした財布を拾い，Michaelの連絡先に電話をした。Michaelは不在であったが，電話を受けた人物は，彼が財布を落として困っていたことを知っていたのでElizabethからの連絡にほっとした，というのが会話文の流れである。　5　質問は「男性はこれから何をすると思われるか」。注文した料理が30分経っても出てこなかった男性は，「10分後に大事な会議があるから」としてその注文をキャンセルした。選択肢のうちこの流れから推測される次の行動は，レストランを出ること以外には考えられない。　6　質問は「女性は何をするつもりか」。女性は1着のジャケットの値段を男性(店員)に尋ねた。スカートとセットの値段で示されたが，女性はジャケットだけが欲しいのである。よって，値段を聞いたジャケットの購入に直接結び付く行動ではなく，違うものを探しにいくことが予想される。

7　質問は「机は全部でいくつ必要か」。机1脚につき3人が座れ，15席を用意するので，机は5脚必要である。　8　質問は「男性は最初に何を買うと思われるか」。男性は最後の発言で「今年は化学(の単位)は落とせない」と言っているので，化学の論文を作成するために必要なコンピュータを最初に買うと思われる。　9　質問は「何が起こったか」。英文はショッピングモールでの迷子のお知らせである。迷子はEmily

Jonesという4歳の女児。母親と兄のTomと一緒に来ていたが，3階の玩具店の前で泣いているところを保護されたという内容。　10　質問は「どの記述が正しいか」。英文は薬局などでの薬の説明である。処方された薬は，頭痛をとる黄色の錠剤(1日3回食後に服用)と，睡眠をたすける赤色の丸薬(1日1回就寝前に服用)である。

【2】1　ア　　2　イ　　3　エ　　4　ウ　　5　イ

〈解説〉1　if節の内容が「もし〜ならば」という単純な仮定を表す場合には，未来のことを言っていても現在形で表す。ただし，if節の内容が主節に対する結果を表す場合や主語の意思を表す場合には，ifの副詞節にwillが用いられる場合もあるので注意。　2　why don't you＋動詞原形で「〜したらいかがですか(ぜひ〜しなさい)」という意味で，「ご自分で作ってみられたらいかがですか」で意味が通る。アのhow comeは「なぜ，どうして」の意味で「How come you to do 〜?」で「どうして〜するのか」という意味。ウのhow about，エのwhat do you say toも「どうですか」の意味になるが，いずれも名詞(および名詞句，動名詞)を取り，動詞の原形であるmakeが続いている本問にはあてはまらない。　3　discussは他動詞で前置詞aboutは不要。how long we spend doing 〜や how much time we spend doing 〜は「〜するためにどれだけの時間を費やすか／費やしても」で，〜ingをとるので，イウは不可。(ただし，イがtalking aboutであれば可)。howeverで強調しているので「いかに長時間検討したところで〜ない」という意味になっている。

4　clear violation of the dress codeで「明らかな服装規定違反」。アは「景気後退」，イは「責務」，エは「服従」の意味。　5　「(それらの部分が，)首尾一貫する全体(を形成するように)」で，a coherent whole。discourse competenceは「談話能力」。アは「特定の」，ウは「偶然一致する」，エは「非論理的な」の意味。

【3】In English classes taught in English, students are expected to have many chances to listen to English. They are exposed to English so often that they will come to be familiar with an atmosphere where they have to use English. Besides, they can have many chances to express themselves in English. When they can make themselves understood in English to their friends or teachers, they will feel successful and happy. That will lead them to be more motivated to improve their English ability.　(83 words)

〈解説〉解答例では「英語による英語授業」の利点として「英語を聞き，話す機会」をあげ，そのことで生徒が「英語を話さなければならない環境に慣れ，英語での自己表現で達成感を得，モチベーションが上がる」としているが，他に「教師が常に英語で話すことにより，会話の自然なリズムが身に付く」，「日常的な会話の中で教科書に掲載されている以外の表現や語彙に触れることができる」など様々な意見があろう。自由な意見を論理的にかつ正確に書けばよい。字数制限に慣れることも必要なので，なるべく毎日短い文を様々なテーマに沿って書くといった練習が望まれる。なお，公式の採点基準としては，内容の適切さ，論の展開の適切さ，語彙・文法の適切さ，分量が示されている。

【4】問1　数字がスクリーンに写し出されると急いで教室から出ていくという行動(32字)　問2　筆者がこれまでにやったことのない解き方で生徒が問題を解いて見せる時。(34字)　問3　数学と他の学問の領域との関連性を認識し，数学は学びやすく楽しい学問であると理解すること。(44字)　問4　①　ウ　②　イ　問5　エ

問6　I would stop asking such students to answer questions in front of others because they are probably afraid of making mistakes and getting embarrassed. Instead, I would give them enough opportunity to express themselves in pairs or in small groups.　(40 words)

〈解説〉問1　第1段落に，筆者がいろいろな年齢層の生徒に数学を教えてきた経緯が書かれており，同じ段落の最後に，その経験の例として，教室から出て行ってしまった生徒のエピソードが書かれている。

問2 「興奮する」は(get) excitedなどで表される。第5段落最後の1文のI still get excited when a student can show me an alternative way of solving a mathematical task that I had not tried previously.を問題の指示に沿ってまとめればよい。　問3　第6段落がOne of the aims stated in *The Australian Curriculum*で始まっているので，コロン以下をまとめればよい。　問4　選択肢は，ア「散らす。転じる」，イ「導入する」，ウ「責務」，エ「支持する」の意味。　①　定冠詞theがついており，名詞と判断できるので，ウが選択できるだろう。確認として，「数学教師としての私のonusは，彼ら(生徒)が彼らのレベルでの数学の課題を最終的にやり遂げることができるだろうとの信頼を私が持っている，ということを明らかに示すことである」という文脈から，「なすべきこと」という意味で文脈上間違いないと判断できる。　②　「生徒たちは彼らの毎日の日常の作業の中に，練習をincorporateすべきである」から，「取り入れる，組み込む」という意味が浮かぶだろう。

問5　第2段落では(A)に続く文で例として「時間制限のあるテストやドリルタイプのゲーム」とあり，第8段落ではplacing more emphasis on understanding rather than (A)「(A)よりもむしろ理解により重きをおいて」という文脈になっている。ここから，生徒の自発的な思考や検討，実験ではなく，機械的に公式を暗記したり大量の計算をこなして数式に慣れたりするような作業を指していると推察できる。rote learningは「暗記」。　問6　「あなたはどのような策を講じるか」という問題なので，ある程度自由に自分の考えを述べることができる。解答例では「クラス全員の前で間違えることを恐れる生徒にはペアワークなど，より小さいグループでの発表作業をさせる」とあるが，他に「間違いを指摘するのではなく，ヒントを与えて正解を引き出す」，「記憶できていない単語などは授業中に覚えてしまえるような作業を行いながら，少しずつ自信を与える」なども可能だろう。いろいろなケースについて日頃から考え，実際の授業に対するイメージをつくっておくことが大事である。

【中学校】

【１】問１　A　イ　　　B　オ　　　問２　人はいらいらすると，我慢できずに不親切になり，周りの人に失礼に振る舞ってしまうこと。(42字)
問３　b　　　問４　ア　care/worry　　イ　way　　　問５　ウ
問６　ミッシーは悪いことをした時，教師や親に大声で叱られることに慣れていたが，グリーン先生に穏やかに優しく対応されたから。(58字)　　　問７　When I was small, I painted on the wall of my house. I was scolded by my mother. After that, she said gently, "I like your paintings. Use this when you want to paint," and handed me a big sketchbook. I swore that I would never paint on the wall again.　(51 words)

〈解説〉問１　A　空欄の前に助動詞canがあり，空欄の後に名詞節があって目的語となっているので他動詞を探す。形容詞のア，ウ，オは不適。「手本とする，真似る」のイがあてはまる。エは「軽蔑する。ひどく嫌う」。　B　「教師は両親を呼び出して話をしたが無駄だった。というのは，ミッシーは(B)な行動をとり続けた」とう文脈なので，オのpoorが適切。poor behaviourで「行儀の悪い態度」の意味。　問２　thisは近くのものごとを指す指示代名詞であり，その内容はすでに述べられていることが多いので，前の文を遡って確認する。本問の場合は前に出てくるのは1文だけなので，その文を字数制限に従ってまとめればよい。　問３　aはIf 〜 what will happen …?「もし教師が学校で不親切な態度をとったなら，冷淡な校外の世界で彼らに何が起こるでしょうか」と，質問というよりは反語になっており，「そうであってはなりません」を意味するNoが続いている。cは前の文の主語がour studentsであり，In so doingの主語teachersと一致しない。bの前の文の主語はthe teacherであり，それを受けて，「そのようにして教師は」と，複数で一般化して続けており，この箇所であてはまる。　問４　下線部②のall of thisは，直前の文中の「時として，大事なのは何を言うか，ではなく，それをどのように言うかである。教師は生徒との日常の歩みの中で，このことを忘れないようにしなくてはならない」との記述を受けているので，「生徒は自分の挨拶に対する教師の答え方で，教

師が自分をどれだけ気にかけているかを判断できる」となるような語を考える。 問5 下線部がMissy smiled.であったなら，イの「とてもよい先生らしいのでいい子でいよう」もあり得なくはないが，onlyがあることで，smiledの肯定的な意味合いが割り引かれており，微笑の裏に何らかの意図があると読み取れる。アの「どうしたらいいかわからない」は，肯定的にせよ否定的にせよsmiledという行為にはそぐわない。「先生がどうしようと，関係ないわ」とするウが最もあてはまる。 問6 下線部④に続く部分の "from Ms. Green, for she was …" のforは理由を表す接続詞なので，for以下が下線部④の理由と考えてまとめればよい。 問7 「本文の事例を参考に」とあるので，「何を言うか，よりも，それをどのように伝えるかが大事である」というテーマを中心に書く。「あなたに影響を与えた出来事や経験」なので，叱った例よりは，叱られた経験の方が，年齢的にあてはまるだろう。こういった問題では，あてはまる事例を考えつく想像力と同時に，思いついた事をすぐに英文にする表現力が必要となる。英文をすぐまとめる力をつけるには，毎日習慣的に書いて馴れることが一番の早道である。

【高等学校】

【1】問1 rest/relax 問2 食堂のテーブルにマーリーンの悪口を彫ったこと。(23字) 問3 ア 問4 (a) punished (b) humor (c) relationship 問5 新しい子が入ってくると，他の少女たちが適切な行動や助け合いの大切さについて教えるようになったこと。(49字) 問6 A イ B エ 問7 First, I'll try to find out what has caused him/her to act like this, because it will help me decide what approach I should take. Second, no matter what response I get from him/her, I'll keep showing my interest in him/her to demonstrate that I'm ready to listen to what s/he is worried about. (54 words)

〈解説〉問1 下線部①は「広大な砂漠の中に滅多にないオアシス」なので，「彼女が多忙な日常のなかでしばらくの間ゆっくりできる(休める)特別の場所」という意味の文になるような語を探す。 問2 下線部

②を含む文は「彼女(Marlene)は，階上からの興奮したざわめきから，犯人がたった今[下線部②]について他の女の子に知らせたところだと推測した。」というもの。下線部②のher public act of defianceは「彼女(犯人)の公然たる挑戦的行為」，すなわちテーブルに文字を彫り付けたことを指していると判断できる。　問3　(　③　)を含む文は，「彼女(Marlene)が一歩離れ，少女たちが実は(　③　)ということをもう一度思い出すためには，この反抗的な行為が必要だったのだ」。It takes ～人 to …は通常「…をするために，～(時間)がかかる」という文脈で使われるが，このように「～という行為を要する，必要とする」という文脈でも用いられる。この文に続き，「誰であれ，これを行った少女は彼女自身がひどい痛みを抱えていたからこそMarleneに打ちかかったのだった」とあり，「少女たちが実はどんなに脆く，傷ついているかを」とするアがあてはまると判断できる。　問4　第1段落と第2段落では，Marlineが日常に追われて疲れた様子，そして施設の仕事を始めた最初の年には意地の悪い少女たちの世話に疲れ，泣き暮らしていた様子が書かれている。しかしまた，「5年間で愛情をこめて世話をしたたくさんの少女たちのことを思った」とも書かれている。ここから，Marlineがつらい思いを経て，少女たちと敵対するのではなく，彼女らを癒し，互いによい関係を築いてきたことが想像できる。問題箇所はそんなMarleneの少女たちとの接し方を具体的に述べたものである。「食堂に降りてきた少女たちは罰せられると予測していたが，Marleneはこのきっかけを利用し，緊張した状況をユーモアでほぐした。この接し方は，少女たちが彼女とよりよい関係を作ることを助けるものだった。」　問5　下線部⑤にすぐ続く文 "Whenever a girl left the house and another moved in, …" 以下に，その具体的説明が書かれているので，そこをまとめる。　問6　A　Marleneが少女たちに向けた笑顔がどのようだったかを表す語が入る。続く文にI will love you no matter what!「何があってもあなたたちを愛しているわ」とあるので，「思いやり」のイが適切。　B　「彼女(Marlene)は常に，苦痛や怒りに取り囲まれ，やってみたことはすべて反逆という結果をもたらした」でエ。同文中

の「苦痛」「怒り」，そして「反逆」は，施設の少女たちがMarleneにぶ
つけた感情や行為について言っている。　問7　問題の英文の内容に
沿って書くようにと特に条件づけされているわけではないが，長文問
題中の英作文である限り，内容を何かしら反映した内容であるべきだ
ろう。解答例では「相手の返答がどのようなものであっても，きちん
と関心を示し，聞く用意があることを示す」とあるが，このように長
文の主旨を取り入れていればよいわけである。英語教育について，ま
た生徒との接し方など実際の教職について英文で書く問題は出題され
ることが多いので，日頃から自分なりの考え方をしっかり持つよう，
考えておくことが大事である。なお，公式の採点基準としては，内容
の適切さ，論の展開の適切さ，分量，語彙・文法の適切さが示されて
いる。

2015年度　　**実施問題**

【中高共通】

【1】聞き取りテスト

　　これから1〜10の英語を1回ずつ放送します。それぞれの英語のあと
に，その内容について質問を一つします。その質問に対する答として
適切なものをア〜エの中から一つずつ選び，その記号で答えなさい。

1　W: Can I help you?

　　M: Thank you, but I'm just looking.

　　W: You're welcome to browse. I'll be here if you need anything.

　　M: OK.

　　Question (W): Where does the conversation most likely take place?

　　ア　In a hospital.　　　　　　イ　At a station.

　　ウ　In a shop.　　　　　　　　エ　At a business meeting.

2　W: The bus to the station only comes once an hour. What should we do?

　　M: When's the next one?

　　W: In about 50 minutes.

　　M: How about walking there? The weather is nice, and we'll be there in
　　　　half an hour.

　　Question (W): What does the man suggest?

　　ア　Taking a train.　　　　　　イ　Driving.

　　ウ　Going by bicycle.　　　　　エ　Going on foot.

3　W: Let's go to see this new movie tonight!

　　M: Tonight? It's opening night and Saturday, so it'll be crowded.

　　W: OK. How about going in the middle of the week?

M: Sounds good.

Question (W): What will they probably do?

ア　They will cancel the appointment.

イ　They will go to the movies on Wednesday night.

ウ　They will go to the movies tonight.

エ　They will go to the movies on Sunday night.

4　M: We're going to be late for the game. Hurry up!

W: Wait! An e-mail just came from a friend. It looks like the game will be delayed 30 minutes.

M: That means it's going to begin at 7:30?

W: Right. We have 40 minutes left.

Question (M): What time is it now?

ア　6:20.　　イ　6:50.　　ウ　7:20.　　エ　8:10.

5　M: Can you believe it's Friday already?

W: Yes, finally!

M: Really? This week seemed to go by in a blur.

W: Oh, not for me.

Question (M): Which sentence is true?

ア　She forgot what day it was.

イ　She thought time flies while having fun.

ウ　She felt it was a long week.

エ　She complained a lot about her boss.

6　M: Hurry up! Get on the train.

W: I'm trying, but it's too crowded.

M: The doors are closing!

W: I'll see you at the next station!

Question (M): What happened?

ア　The woman got on the train.　　イ　The train came in late.

ウ　The man got off the train.　　エ　The woman missed the train.

7　M: Hello, I'm calling to find out what time the show is on tonight.

W: I'm very sorry, but the last show started an hour ago. Our shows run Monday to Friday at 4:00 p.m. and 7:30 p.m. And tomorrow, we have only one show at 8:00 p.m.

M: Should I reserve a ticket from your website, or can I buy it at the box office?

W: It's likely the tickets will sell out, so you should purchase them on our website in advance.

M: OK, I will.

Question (W): What will the man probably do after this conversation?

ア　He will watch the show at once.

イ　He will order the ticket online.

ウ　He will go to the bank.

エ　He will check the schedule of the show.

8　Tomorrow we will clean up the beach. If you can join us, please bring gloves and rubber boots. There is no need to bring plastic bags and buckets. We will provide them for you.

Question (M): What should you bring if you can join the clean-up?

ア　Plastic bags and rubber boots.　　イ　Gloves and rubber boots.

ウ　Plastic bags and buckets.　　エ　Nothing.

9　The Kagoshima Mentors Association is looking for volunteers to mentor youth who are at risk of dropping out of school. Some examples of mentoring activities are library visits, academic help and playing sports. Volunteer mentors must spend 2 or 3 hours a week with their assigned students. Call us for more information regarding this program.

Question (W): Which sentence is true?

ア Volunteers are supposed to help young people who are dropping out of school.

イ Volunteers are supposed to go to the theater twice a month.

ウ Volunteers are supposed to spend about a week with their assigned students.

エ Volunteers are supposed to see the website about this program.

10 Thank you for calling Satsuma Bank. We apologize, but our office is currently closed for the national holiday. We will open again next Monday. For information about business hours, please press 1. If you have a question about your account, please press 2 to leave a message, and a representative will contact you when our bank reopens on Monday. If you need information about credit cards, please call 0120-111-2222. Thank you for calling Satsuma Bank and have a happy holiday.

Question (M): What should the caller do to ask about credit cards?

ア Press 1.　　　　　　　イ Press 2.

ウ Leave a message.　　　エ Call another number.

以上で英語の聞き取りテストを終わります。次の問題に進みなさい。

(☆☆☆◎◎◎)

【2】次の各文の( )に入る適切な語をア〜エの中から一つずつ選び，記号で答えよ。

1 Many people have a ( ) idea about what a country is like. When they actually go there, however, it is often different from their imaginations.

ア concealed　イ preconceived　ウ logical　エ flexible

2 I was going to rent a car last weekend, but then I realized that my driver's license was invalid. I will get it ( ) this week.

ア expired　イ refined　ウ found　エ renewed

3　Small children have teeth which usually fall out between the age of five and twelve, after (　　) they get their permanent teeth.

　　ア　what　　イ　when　　ウ　which　　エ　that

4　Nancy was badly injured in the accident. If only she had left here ten minutes earlier, she (　　) involved in it.

　　ア　would not have　　イ　will not have been　　ウ　could not be

　　エ　would not have been

5　(　　) learning is an educational approach which aims to organize lessons into academic and social learning experiences. In that process, students must work in groups to complete tasks collectively.

　　ア　Comprehensive　　イ　Extensive　　ウ　Competitive

　　エ　Cooperative

(☆☆◎◎◎◎◎)

【3】次の英語を読んで，英語教師にとって大切だとあなたが思うことを，80語程度で書け。なお，使用した語数を記入すること。

If you give me rice, I'll eat today.

If you teach me how to grow rice, I'll eat every day.　　　*Mahatma Gandhi*

(☆☆☆☆☆◎◎◎)

【4】次の Reflective Thinking (反省的思考)に関する英文を読んで，後の問に答えよ。

　　Early in the 20th century, the great American educator John Dewey suggested that one main aim of education is to help people acquire habits of reflection so they can engage in intelligent thought and action rather than routine thought and action. Dewey's work was situated in the post-Great Depression U.S. society, and he felt the need for a thinking citizenry in a democratic society. For him, ①this was the larger purpose of reflective inquiry. Dewey first outlined what reflective inquiry was not: it is not just considering things that interest us, which unfortunately seems to be ②a wide

198

<u>interpretation of reflective thinking today</u>. Dewey viewed reflective inquiry as "active, persistent, and careful consideration of any belief or supposed form of knowledge in the light of the grounds that support it and the further conclusions to which it tends that constitutes reflective thought."

Within education, Dewey observed that teachers who do not bother to think intelligently about their work become slaves to routine, and he noted that one of the main challenges of learning was learning how to think intelligently: "While we cannot learn or be taught to think, we do have to learn how to think well, especially how to acquire the general habits of reflecting." Some may say that routine is necessary, but it all depends how each student reacts or does not react. So Dewey is correct to suggest that teachers should be on guard against blindly following routine, because if we do that, then we will certainly be teaching "classes" rather than (A).

For Dewey, the cause of reflective thinking comes out of the feeling of doubt or conflict connected to teaching. He mapped out five main phases of reflective thought that he considered not in a particular order but rather as fluid:

1. *Suggestion*: A doubtful situation is understood to be problematic, and some vague suggestions are considered as possible solutions.

2. *Intellectualization*: The difficulty or perplexity of the problem that has been felt (directly experienced) is intellectualized into a problem to be solved.

3. *Guiding Idea*: One suggestion after another is used as a leading idea, or hypothesis; the initial suggestion can be used as a working hypothesis to initiate and guide observation and other operations in the collection of factual material.

4. (B): This links present and past ideas and helps elaborate the supposition that reflective inquiry has reached, or the mental elaboration of the idea or supposition as an idea or supposition.

5. *Hypothesis Testing*: The refined idea is reached, and the testing of this

refined hypothesis takes place; the testing can be by overt action or in thought (imaginative action).

This was the first real systematization of reflective inquiry into teaching shown in the literature. It is structured to suggest that teachers look at their experiences, review and examine these in light of what evidence they can collect from their practice, and then plan what action they want to take as a result.

Dewey encouraged teachers (and all citizens really) to make ③informed decisions about their teaching, and that these decisions be based on systematic and conscious reflections rather than fleeting thoughts about teaching. He maintained that when teachers combined these systematic reflections with their actual teaching experiences, then they could become more aware, and this would lead to professional development and growth as a teacher.

In Dewey's work on reflective inquiry, he noted that in order to engage in reflective practice, teachers need to have at least three attributes of reflective individuals that remain important today: open-mindedness, responsibility, and wholeheartedness. Open-mindedness is a desire to listen to more than one side of an issue and to give attention to alternative views. Responsibility means careful consideration of the consequences to which an action leads; in other words, what is the impact of reflection on the learners? Wholeheartedness implies that teachers can overcome fears and uncertainties to critically evaluate their practice in order to make meaningful change. Dewey added a fourth attitude that needed to be cultivated in order to engage in reflective practice: directness. Directness implies a belief that something is worth doing, which nicely sums up why teachers should engage in reflective practice: because it is worth doing. The main idea of what we do is that we teach （　Ａ　） rather than lessons.

（出典：TESOL Journal 3.1, March 2012 一部改作）

問1　下線部①が指す内容を本文に即して20字程度の日本語で書け。

問2　下線部②の具体的内容を本文に即して20字程度の日本語で書け。

問3　本文中の(　A　)に共通して入る最も適切な英語を1語書け。

問4　本文中の(　B　)に入る最も適切な語をア～エの中から一つ選び，記号で答えよ。

　　ア　*Questioning*　　イ　*Conditioning*　　ウ　*Reasoning*

　　エ　*Observing*

問5　下線部③はどのようなものであるべきか，本文に即して40字程度の日本語で書け。

問6　本文の第4段落(This was the first real systematization...)の内容を踏まえ，なぜ以下のような状況が起こると考えられるか，また，それに対してあなたは教師としてどのような手立てを講じるか，60語程度の英語で書け。なお，使用した語数を記入すること。

　　〔状況〕Your students seem to enjoy your classes and work very hard in class, but they don't do well in the examination.

　　　　　　　　　　　　　　　　　　　　　　　　　　　　(☆☆☆◎◎◎)

【5】次の英文を読んで，後の問に答えよ。

　Mark was a great kid from a bad neighborhood. A scholarship fund provided his tuition to Catholic High, where he played an important part in the sports program. He showed considerable talent not only for football but for baseball. In his junior year, many college coaches and pro scouts came to see him play football and / or baseball.

　Mark, however, struggled in the classroom, due to a more than (　A　) home environment. Mark's mom died from a drug overdose while he was in high school. He left to live with an elderly grandmother.

　The area where Mark's grandmother lived was dangerous, and he was soon the victim of a drive-by shooting. The school community jumped to his aid. A student's dad who was a surgeon accepted Mark as his patient. He removed the bullet and then made arrangements for therapy so that Mark's muscles could be retrained. Another family, whose son Kevin also attended Catholic High and played sports, fixed a bedroom for Mark. Kevin and Mark became best friends, and Kevin's dad took a personal interest in Mark, even attending parent / teacher conferences with him.

(　B　) the attention from pro scouts, Mark had wanted to attend college. Interest from several universities was high, but Mark's scores on his college entrance exams were low. Somehow, some way, he had to make better marks on his American College Test (ACT). Several teachers, including me, discussed Mark's needs. We agreed that he required help far beyond what we could offer him within our class periods. After-school teaching wasn't possible because of football and / or baseball practice. ①<u>Some felt Mark should give up sports and concentrate on "schooling."</u> But, in reality, his opportunity to attend college was linked to sports. To miss practice would prevent Mark from performing at his best on the field. It would cause the opposite result from the one that he wanted to achieve. A fellow teacher, Mrs.Jones, offered to tutor him in math at her home. I scheduled him to come to my house for all other areas of the test. No one paid us. Mrs.Jones summed it up this way: "Pay day doesn't always come on Mondays."

When we were not working with Mark to improve his skills for the ACT, the coach and Kevin's dad took him to various colleges to talk with both baseball and football program coaches. He settled on the one college that offered him scholarships to play both sports. We were all delighted but a little (　C　). If Mark did not score the ACT minimum required by that university, he could not attend, no matter how talented he was.

The day came for Mark to take the ACT. I picked him up and took him for breakfast, then delivered him to the testing center, along with pencils, candy bars, and apples supplied by his other teachers.

It takes months to receive the results of college entrance exams—so long, in fact, that I lost my sense of when to begin expecting Mark's scores. One afternoon after school, while grading papers in my room, I heard quite a lot of noise outside the hall. It sounded like a freight train coming down the hall. Then suddenly, ②the freight train burst through my door.

Mark lifted me out of the seat behind my desk, spun me around in the air, and jubilantly yelled over and over, "I'm going to college! I'm going to college! I'm going to college!"

"I guess you got your scores?" I asked once he set me down.

"Well, yeah! And guess what? It is one point more than I need to be accepted. One point extra! Thank you, thank you, thank you! Now, where's Mrs.Jones? I have to tell her too!" The freight train was off and running again.

Until that moment, I had never quite understood, ③*Pay day doesn't always come on Mondays*. But the meaning became clear the instant Mark ran into the room to announce his news. No amount of money could ever replace my spin in the air at the hands of a boy who finally had a chance at a better life.

Sometimes we educators get stuck in a rut, feeling we are limited by the walls of our rooms. And sometimes we are. But there are those times when a special circumstance dictates a different path, one that requires the involvement of a community. As the saying goes, ④it takes a village to raise a child. There's some wisdom in it, for sure.

(出典：Eloise Elaine Schneider 2010 *A Cup of Comfort for a Better World* 一部改作)

問1　本文中の(A)～(C)に入る最も適切な語をア～カの中から一つずつ選び，記号で答えよ。ただし，文頭に来る語も小文字で記してある。

ア　concerned　　イ　ordinary　　ウ　disappointed　　エ　difficult
オ　despite　　　カ　unlike

問2　下線部①に対する反論としてどのようなものがあるか，本文に即して60字程度の日本語で書け。

問3　下線部②の指すものを20字以内の日本語で書け。

203

問4　下線部③に関して，次の英文が筆者がマークとの関わりを通して学んだことを表すように，（　a　）～（　c　）に入る最も適切な語をア～カの中から一つずつ選び，記号で答えよ。

We gave Mark a lot of time and energy to help him pass the entrance examination, but no one was given a financial reward. However, all of our efforts had (　a　) off when I heard the good news and words of (　b　) from him. I realized that these experiences were priceless; for us teachers, to (　c　) to our students' success and share the joy of their success with them was far more valuable than money.

ア　appreciation　　イ　contribute　　ウ　apology　　エ　put
オ　belong　　カ　paid

問5　(1)　下線部④はどういうことか，本文に即して20字程度の日本語で説明せよ。

(2)　あなたは下線部④に対してどのように考えるか，その理由も添えて40語程度の英語で書け。なお，使用した語数を記入すること。

(☆☆☆◎◎◎)

【高等学校】

【1】次の英文を読んで，後の問に答えよ。

I teach in a tough environment, and within that hostile environment I teach a challenging course: science. On the other hand, tough environments are good for my other line of work, which is coaching. Tough kids make good wrestlers, but it's still a hostile environment. ①Tough environments and challenging classes sometimes don't go together as well as tough environments and tough sports. Effective teachers, however, can make even the toughest learning situations a great place for students to prepare themselves for success.

The key to helping students from tough environments succeed lies in creating (　A　) with them. For example, Justin, a young man in my advanced placement chemistry class and a starter on the wrestling team, confided to me that while he slept, his drug-addicted mother had been taking money he hid in his socks to help pay for her drug habits. Justin wanted to go into the armed services, but he also wanted to go to college right away. I knew what a tremendous student he was and, being the academician I am, I was hoping for the college route. I worked with Justin and the uncle who was taking care of him to make college a credible option for him. He performed well on the ACT (American College Test), received a full scholarship from the University of Illinois, and received his degree in nuclear engineering.

Working with young adults like these often means [②]. I took one of my wrestlers, who was also a baseball player and a chemistry student, mountain climbing in Colorado for two summers because I recognized his love for the outdoors. I have also established a book scholarship at Elmhurst College for students who attend Elmhurst after graduating from the high school where I teach.

Following up on kids in a tough environment also means early wakeup calls. I call my athletes at the crack of dawn to make sure they are on their way to school. I make every attempt to convey to students and the community that I really do care about them, and that I am not there just to teach chemistry, but to help them succeed.

Providing structure is also another important ingredient to overcoming (B). All teachers have to deal with interruptions, accepting new students into their environment at any point and dealing with tardy students on a daily basis. Establishing a structure helps your students learn to adhere to a logical set of rules. Believe it or not, they actually appreciate the discipline. Students know they cannot interrupt a demonstration once it has begun; they know where to pick up their assignment; and if they break the rules, they know that they have lost five points from their participation grade.

Structure also builds mutual understanding and respect. To make it work, I make time to explain to students why I am disciplining them for certain behaviors. ③<u>Maintaining structure is like traversing a swift river; you cannot be absolute, but must allow room for creative decisions that will get you safely to the other side.</u> Discipline must always be positive in nature, recognize certain limits, and not be so repressive that it drives students back to the streets. When disciplinary actions are needed, we try to learn from them.

How does someone like me compete with Tiger Woods? How do some of my students compete in baseball, wrestling, or chemistry with students in surrounding communities who enter high school more academically prepared? As the famous golfer Ben Hogan once said, "The harder I work, the luckier I get."

Through hard work, my students begin to see the learning curve really isn't a curve at all—it's a vertical line. With hard work, my students begin to believe that they can become champions both on and off the playing field, and in the classroom. Even if my students don't go on to further their education, I want them to leave my class with fond memories, to know how chemistry affects their lives, and with the feeling they can, as Maya Angelou says, "④<u>Let nothing dim the light that shines from within</u>." Sometimes my students face formidable hardships and they know it. Together, we help each other navigate our tough environment; together, we help each other succeed.

Teaching is one of the greatest professions in the world; ⑤<u>teachers have the greatest gifts of all to give: knowledge, confidence, opportunities, and happiness.</u>

（出典：Joseph W. Underwood 2009 *Today I made a difference* 一部改作）

問1　下線部①を本文に即して60字程度の日本語でわかりやすく説明せよ。

問2　本文中の[　②　]に入る最も適切なものをア～エの中から一つ選び，記号で答えよ。

　ア　giving our students as much free time as possible

イ　going above what many teachers are willing to do

ウ　workihg with other teachers at any momemt

エ　praising our students for their accomplishments

問3　下線部③は, 躾(しつけ)・規律に対する筆者のどのような考え方を表しているか, 本文に即して40字程度の日本語で書け。

問4　本文中の(A), (B)に入る最も適切な語をア～オの中から一つずつ選び, 記号で答えよ。

ア　atmospheres　　イ　obstacles　　ウ　temptations

エ　disasters　　　　オ　relationships

問5　次の英文が下線部④に対する筆者の思いを表すように, (a), (b)に入る最も適切な語をア～オの中から一つずつ選び, 記号で答えよ。

　　Some students come from negative backgrounds for learning and tend to be less (a) about learning. As a result they cannot go on studying persistently, losing trust in themselves. Teachers, however, can urge such students not to allow their environment to diminish the positive energy inside of them, and (b) them to take on any challenge.

ア　order　　イ　motivated　　ウ　warn　　エ　encourage

オ　pessimistic

問6　下線部⑤に関して, あなたが考える「教師が生徒に与える the greatest gift」は何か。下線部の例から一つ選び, 以下の(　)に記入し, その理由を40語程度の英語で書け。なお, 使用した語数を記入すること。

　　I believe one of the greatest gifts is (　　).

(☆☆☆◎◎◎◎)

解答・解説

【中高共通】

【1】1　ウ　　2　エ　　3　イ　　4　イ　　5　ウ　　6　エ　　7　イ
　　8　イ　　9　ア　　10　エ

〈解説〉聞き取りテストで解答の選択肢があらかじめ示されているとき
は，放送が始まる前に必ず目を通しておくこと。放送が1回だけ流れ
る場合は，どこに集中して聞き取ればよいのかを判断する上でも大切
である。放送内容の中に出てくる数値や人名などの名詞は聞き取りの
ポイントとなることが多い。聞き取れない箇所があっても慌てずに，
その前後関係から判断して意味をとるように心がけ，以降の放送内容
が頭に入らなくなるという事態を避ける。聞き逃しがないよう日頃か
ら放送による聞き取りテストの練習を重ね，落ち着いて本番に臨むよ
うにしたい。

【2】1　イ　　2　エ　　3　ウ　　4　エ　　5　エ

〈解説〉1　「多くの人が，ある国がどんな風であるか(　　)の考えを持っ
　　ているが，実際に行くと想像と違っていることが多い」という文脈。
　　正答のイの原形preconceiveは，conceive「想像する，思う，身ごもる」
　　に「あらかじめ，～以前の」の意を表す接頭辞pre-をつけ，「あらかじ
　　め想像する」の意味となる。preconceived ideaで「既成概念」。
　　2　1文目で「免許が失効していた」と言っているので，renewed「更新
　　する」が正解。　　3　(　　)の2語前に「5歳から12歳までの間に」とあ
　　るのでwhenが入りそうだが，after whenという表現は英語では使われな
　　い。ここでの関係代名詞は「5歳から12歳までの間に歯が抜ける」と
　　いう事象全体を指していると考えて，after whichとするのが正解。
　　4　全体の文意から，(　　)の前後は「巻き込まれていなかっただろう」
　　となるので，willの過去形＋have＋beの過去分詞形を使う。　　5　2文目
　　で「グループで協力して課題を完成させなければならない」と書かれ

ているので，cooperative「協力的な」がふさわしい。

【3】 What is important for English teachers is to show their students how to learn English. Teachers cannot improve students' attitudes toward studying English by only saying, "Study English hard!" or by only teaching them English theory. Students may be able to memorize English vocabulary and grammar, but it is doubtful whether they can keep studying English without teachers. If teachers succeed in teaching them how to learn English, however, students can become autonomous learners and continue studying English according to their needs. (82 words)

〈解説〉「米をもらったら，今日食べて終わりだが，米を育てる方法を教えてもらったら，一生食べて暮らせる」という，インドの政治指導者ガンジーの言葉。これに基づいて，英語教師は何を教えることが大切かを考え，英語で解答する。「問題に対する答え」や「英単語や文法の知識」を与えるだけではなく，「自ら英語を学ぶ方法を教えること」や「自分で英語の能力を伸ばす方法」「実際の会話の中から英語を学んでいくこと」などを教えることが大切，という文意になるだろう。なお，公式に示されている採点基準は，①内容の適切さ，②論の展開の適切さ，③分量，④語彙・文法の適切さ，である。

【4】 問1　民主主義社会において考える市民を育てること。
問2　自分の興味を引く事柄について考えること。
問3　students / learners　　　問4　ウ　　問5　教え方に関する思いつきに基づくのではなく，体系的で意識的な振り返りに基づく決定。
問6　I would think it was because my examination was not good enough to check their learning. I'd reflect on what I did in class and what I asked my students to do. If there were any gap between my practices in class and testing, I'd try to fix it by trying another approach in the exam. (56 words)

〈解説〉問1　「本文に即して」ということで，下線部①のthisが本文で指している内容に言及しつつ解答する必要がある。指示語の指している

内容は，前の部分を見るとわかる。ここでは，the need for a thinking citizenry in a democratic societyを指しているので，それを日本語にして制限字数以内でまとめる。　問2　considering things that interest usは実際には反省的思考には含まれていないのだが，unfortunately seems to be a wide interpretation of reflective thinking today「今日，不幸にも，反省的思考の幅広い解釈に含まれると考えられている」とある。したがって，下線部②の具体的内容とはconsidering things that interest usである。問3　1つ目の(　A　)のある第2段落の後半部分を見てみると，「いつも決まった活動をすることは必要かもしれないが，すべては各個人の生徒がそれに反応するかどうかにかかっている。したがって，Deweyが『教師はいつも決まった活動をやみくもにすることを避けなければならない。なぜなら，そうすることは(　A　)の代わりに"クラス"を教えていることになるからだ』と述べたのは正しかったと言える」という意味で，「生徒個人」と「クラス全体」の対比がなされていることがわかる。2つ目の(　A　)を含む第6段落最後の文でも，classesをlessonsに言い換えて同様の主旨を述べている。　問4　(　B　)以下の文は，「現在と過去のアイディアを関連付け，反省的疑問が到達した提案をより精度の高いものにすること」という内容。反省的思考によって導かれたアイディアを，過去の経験などに基づいて再考する，という意味なので，「アイディアを理にかなったものにする」ということ。ア「問うこと」，イ「条件付け」，ウ「論理付け」，エ「観察」という選択肢の中ではウが最適。　問5　「教育内容について，背景知識に基づく決定」ということで，下線部③に続くthese decisions以下でこの詳しい意味を説明している。　問6　第4段落は「実際に教えた内容から得られる証拠に基づいて，問題を考察，再考，分析し，その上でどういった対処をするか決定する」という内容。これを踏まえて，なぜ「授業中は大変まじめな生徒が，試験では良い結果を出せない」という状況が起こると考えられるかを説明し，その対処法を述べる。たとえば，「授業内容と試験内容が一致していなかった」や，「復習を促す教え方ができていなかった」などが考えられる。なお，公式に示さ

れている採点基準は，①内容の適切さ，②論の展開の適切さ，③分量，④語彙・文法の適切さ，である。

【5】問1　A　エ　　B　オ　　C　ア　　問2　マークが大学に合格するかどうかはスポーツと大いに関係があり，練習不足で最高のプレーができなければ，大学に合格できないという反論。

問3　合格の喜びで興奮しているマーク　　問4　a　カ　　b　ア　c　イ　　問5　(1)　子どもの育成には，地域の協力が必要だということ。　　(2)　I think this is true. Even if children have a difficult home environment, people in the community, such as teachers and other families, can help to raise them. Community members in various fields can teach children a variety of skills and give them support. (44 words)

〈解説〉問1　A　第2段落2文目の「マークの母親はマークが高校生の時に，薬の過剰摂取により亡くなってしまった」という文脈から，（　A　）の前後はmore than difficult home environment「大変だという表現以上の家庭環境」とするのが適切。　　B　「プロのスカウトが関心を示していた（　B　），マークは大学に進学することを望んだ」ということで，despite「〜にも関わらず」がふさわしい。　　C　「私達は嬉しかったが，少し（　C　）でもあった」という文脈から，concerned「心配している」が適切。　　問2　下線部①の直後に，Butから始まる反論内容が書かれているので，それを日本語にして要約する。「スポーツの練習をしなければ試合で良い結果を出すことができず，大学に合格できない」という要旨。　　問3　下線部②は「貨物列車」という表現で，合格の知らせを受け取ったマークが興奮して廊下を走ってきた様子を表している。　　問4　下線部③は「給料日はいつも月曜に来るとは限らない」という表現で，「自分のしたことに対する成果がすぐに現れる，期待した時期に現れるとは限らない」というたとえである。　　a　paid off「意義があった」という表現。　　b　「マークからの良い知らせと，お礼の言葉」でappreciationが適切。　　c　contribute to 〜で「〜に貢献する」の意味。　　問5　(1)　直訳すると「子どもを育てるには村全体が

必要だ」という表現で，同段落の内容から，「教師だけではなく地域全体で子どもを育てることが大切」という意味であることがわかる。
(2)　「子どもを育てるには，教師だけではなく地域全体の関わりが必要」という意見に対しての考えを英作文する。議論の適切さに加えて，文法に誤りがないように気をつける。なお，公式に示されている採点基準は，①内容の適切さ，②文法・語法の適切さ，③分量の適切さ，である。

【高等学校】

【１】問1　指導が困難な生徒が激しいスポーツでは大いに力を発揮することがあるが，理科のような難しい教科には意欲的に取り組めないこと。　問2　イ　　問3　躾は柔軟であるべきで，生徒を再び学校から遠ざけるほど抑圧的であってはならない。　問4　A　オ
B　イ　　問5　a　イ　　b　エ　　問6　I believe one of the greatest gifts is (confidence). A student tends to compare himself with other students and feels he can't keep up with them. This sense of inferiority can be the greatest obstacle for his growth in every aspect. Teachers can help him to have experiences through which he will take pride in himself. (47 words)

〈解説〉問1　「本文に即して」ということで，下線部①の直訳ではなく，それが本文で指している内容に言及しつつ解答する必要がある。下線部①の前の部分を読むとわかるように，ここでのtough environmentsは「指導が難しい環境」，challenging classesは筆者の教えている教科である「理科」，そしてtough sportsは「レスリングなどの激しい競技」を指している。　問2　アは「生徒にできるだけ多くの自由時間を与えること」，イは「普通の教師がやること以上のことをする」，ウは「いつも他の教師と一緒に働くこと」，エは「生徒の達成したことを褒める」という意味。第3段落1文目は「これらの青年達と一緒に働くということは，しばしば[　②　]を意味する」という内容であり，そのあとに「生徒を山登りに連れて行った」や「生徒のために奨学金制度を設立した」という例があがっていることから，イが正解であるとわかる。

問3　下線部③は，「しつけの制度を保つことは，流れの速い川を渡る
ようなものである。つまり，絶対確実という姿勢ではなく，川の向こ
う側に渡ることができるだけの余裕を持っていなければならない。」
という内容。第6段落全体を読むと，これはすなわち「躾はその意味
が生徒に伝わるものでなければならないが，生徒を抑圧するほど厳し
すぎてはいけない」という筆者の考えをたとえた表現であることがわ
かる。　問4　A　「難しい環境で育ってきた子ども達の手助けをする
鍵は，彼らとの（　A　）を持つことだ」という文脈なので，オの「関係」
が正解。　B　「はっきりした仕組みを作るということは，（　B　）を克
服する上でのもう一つの重要な要素である」という文脈。ここでは
「難しい環境で育ってきた子ども達」について話しているので，イの
「障害，障壁」が適切。　問5　a　lessの後に来ることができるのは形
容詞のみ。選択肢の中では形容詞はイのmotivated「やる気がある」か，
オのpessimistic「悲観的な」の2つのみで，「生徒の一部は学習に意欲
的でない環境で育ってきており，（　a　）の状態になりにくい」という
文脈からイが正解。　b　この空欄に入ることができるのは動詞の原
形のみ。ア，ウ，エが考えられるが，「生徒にどんな挑戦でも受けて
立つように（　b　）」という文脈から，エのencourage「励ます」がふさ
わしい。　問6　教師が生徒に与えることができる最大の贈り物は，
knowledge「知識」，confidence「自信」，opportunities「機会」，
happiness「幸福」のいずれであるとあなたは考えるか，一つ選んで答
える。理由を書くときに，論理展開がきちんと成り立っているように
気をつける。なお，公式に示されている採点基準は，①内容の適切さ，
②論の展開の適切さ，③分量，④語彙・文法の適切さ，である。

2014年度　実施問題

【中高共通】

【１】聞き取りテスト

　　これから1～10の英語を1回ずつ放送します。それぞれの英語のあとに，その内容について質問を一つします。その質問に対する答として適切なものをア～エの中から一つずつ選び，その記号で答えなさい。

1　W：Are you ready to order?

　　M：Yes. I'll have today's special.

　　W：OK. Anything to drink?

　　M：Orange juice, please. I'd like to have it first. After that I'll have the food, please.

　　Question (M)：When will the woman bring the drink?

　　ア　After the meal.　　イ　Before the meal.　　ウ　With the meal.

　　エ　After the dessert.

2　M：Oh, my God! My computer has gone down! I can't send my report to our boss by e-mail.

　　W：Oh, that's too bad. Why don't you send a fax instead?

　　M：That's a good idea. Do you know his number?

　　W：Of course.

　　Question (W)：How will the man send his report?

　　ア　By fax.　　イ　By e-mail.　　ウ　By mail.　　エ　By hand.

3　W：John, you look pale. What's the matter?

　　M：I have a headache. Do you mind if I leave the class early?

　　W：Oh, not at all. You had better see a doctor.

　　M：Yes, I will.

　　Question (W)：Why will John leave early?

　　ア　Because he has a dental appointment.

　　イ　Because he has to care for his sick mother.

ウ　Because he has an interview for a job.

エ　Because he is not feeling well.

4　M : Excuse me, but what time will the next train for Boston leave?

　　W : It will leave at 11:45.

　　M : How long will it take to get to Boston?

　　W : Half an hour.

　　Question (M) : What time will the train arrive in Boston?

　　ア　At 11:45.　　イ　At 12:15.　　ウ　At 12:30.　　エ　At 12:45.

5　M : Excuse me. I like these shoes, but they're a little too big for me. Do
　　　　you have smaller ones?

　　W : Yes, but they're black instead of gray.

　　M : I think black will look OK. May I try them on?

　　W : Sure. I'll go and get them.

　　Question (M) : What will the woman do next?

　　ア　She will try on some shoes.

　　イ　She will bring the shoes to the man.

　　ウ　She will order the shoes.

　　エ　She will buy the shoes for the man.

6　M : Excuse me. I'm looking for the new book about Steve Jobs. Can you
　　　　tell me where it is?

　　W : I'm sorry, but it's been lent out. It's very popular. If you give me
　　　　your name and phone number, I can call you as soon as it is returned.

　　M : OK, thank you. I can't wait to read it.

　　Question (W) : Where is this conversation most likely to take place?

　　ア　In a computer shop.　　イ　In a bookstore.　　ウ　In a hospital.

　　エ　In a library.

7　M : Hello, Customer Service.

　　W : Hello, my name is Susan Green. Last Wednesday I ordered a ring on
　　　　the Internet, but you sent me earrings.

　　M : We are terribly sorry about the mistake, ma'am. You ordered the one with a large pearl, right?

W : Yes, and it has two diamonds on each side.

Question (M) : Why did the woman call customer service?

ア　Because she wanted to order another ring.

イ　Because she wanted to have a ring repaired.

ウ　Because a ring and earrings were broken.

エ　Because earrings were sent to her instead of a ring.

8　M : Today, let me talk about coffee. Coffee is so popular in America. People often drink it at work and most companies allow their workers to have coffee breaks. You may think tea is more popular in Britain, but they often drink coffee at the end of a meal.

Question (W) : Which statement is true?

ア　People in America drink a lot of tea at home every day.

イ　People in America can't drink coffee during work.

ウ　People in Britain enjoy coffee at the end of a meal.

エ　People in Britain rarely have tea breaks in their office.

9　W : Thank you for visiting Sky Amusement Park. Please be aware that Space Roller Coaster is an exciting high-speed ride. Children under 6 years old and people over 60 cannot go on this ride. If you have a heart problem, we advise you not to go on this ride.

Question (M) : Who is not allowed to go on this attraction?

ア　A 5-year-old child.

イ　A person who easily gets excited.

ウ　A person who is hungry.

エ　A person weighing over 60 kg.

10　M : Good morning, and welcome to our ice cream factory. I'm happy to be able to show you around today. First, you'll watch a short video on the history of our factory. After that, you'll visit the special freezer area. And finally, you'll have a chance to taste some of our new ice cream flavors. Please enjoy.

Question (W) : What will the visitors do first?

ア They will taste a new ice cream flavor.

イ They will check the freezers.

ウ They will see a video.

エ They will take pictures.

以上で英語の聞き取りテストを終わります。次の問題に進みなさい。

(☆☆◎◎◎)

【2】次の各文の(　　)に入る適切なものをア～エの中から一つずつ選び，記号で答えよ。

1 Despite some (　　), Mr. Miura succeeded in climbing Mt. Everest at the age of 80.

ア excursions　　イ explorations　　ウ imaginations

エ obstacles

2 According to the Courses of Study, English teachers should have students (　　) four skills: listening, speaking, reading, and writing.

ア divide　　イ integrate　　ウ interrupt　　エ collect

3 When I told Chiho what had happened, she (　　).

ア seemed surprising　　イ seemed to have surprised

ウ seemed surprise　　エ seemed surprised

4 (　　) is a long novel written by Margaret Mitchell. This novel tells you something about the Civil War.

ア *East of Eden*　　　　イ *Uncle Tom's Cabin*

ウ *Gone With the Wind*　　エ *The Old Man and the Sea*

5 (　　) markers, which include words or phrases such as *however, in addition*, and *therefore*, are used to indicate relations between sentences in a piece of writing.

ア Bilingual　　イ Discourse　　ウ Grammatical

エ Strategic

(☆☆◎◎◎)

【３】次の言葉は，教育者ウィリアム・ウォードの言葉である。この言葉を参考にして，良い教師と偉大な教師は何が違うのか，具体例を挙げて80語程度の英語で書け。なお，使用した語数を記入すること。

　凡庸な教師は指示をする。<u>良い教師</u>は説明をする。優れた教師は範となる。しかし<u>偉大な教師</u>は内なる心に火をつける。

(☆☆☆◯◯◯)

【４】次の英文を読んで，後の問に答えよ。

Perhaps the majority of language teachers today, when asked to identify the methodology they employ in their classrooms, mention "communicative" as the methodology of choice. However, when pressed to give a detailed account of what they mean by "communicative," explanations vary widely. Does communicative language teaching (CLT) mean teaching conversation, an absence of grammar in a course, or an emphasis on open-ended discussion activities as the main features of a course? What do you understand by communicative language teaching?

[　　A　　]

Communicative language teaching sets as its goal the teaching of *communicative competence*. What does this term mean? Perhaps we can clarify this term by first comparing it with the concept of *grammatical competence*. Grammatical competence refers to the knowledge we have of a language that accounts for our ability to produce sentences in a language. It refers to knowledge of the building blocks of sentences (e.g., tenses, phrases, clauses, sentence patterns) and how sentences are formed. Grammatical competence is the focus of many grammar practice books, which typically present a rule of grammar on one page, and provide exercises to practice using the rule on the other page. The unit of analysis and practice is typically the sentence. While grammatical competence is an important dimension of language learning, it is clearly not all that is involved in learning a language since one can master the rules of sentence formation in a language and still

218

not be very successful at being able to use the language for meaningful communication. ①The latter capacity is understood by the term communicative competence.

Communicative competence includes the following aspects of language knowledge:

- Knowing how to use language for a range of different purposes and functions
- Knowing how to vary our use of language according to the setting and the participants
- Knowing how to produce and understand different types of texts
- Knowing how to maintain communication despite having limitations in one's language knowledge

[B   ]

Our understanding of the processes of second language learning has changed considerably in the last 30 years and CLT is partly a response to these changes in understanding. Earlier approaches to language learning focused primarily on the mastery of grammatical competence. ②Lanuguage learning was seen as a process of mechanical habit formation. Good habits were formed by having students produce correct sentences, memorize dialogs and perform drills. The chances of making mistakes were minimized. Learning was very much seen as under the control of the teacher.

[C   ]

Recently, language learning has been seen from a very different perspective. It is seen as resulting from processes such as:

- Creating meaningful and purposeful interaction through language
- Negotiation of meaning as the learner and his or her interlocutor arrive at understanding
- Learning through attending to the feedback learners get when they use the language

With CLT began a movement away from traditional lesson formats where

219

the focus was on mastery of different items of grammar and practice, and toward the use of pair work activities, role plays, group work activities and so on.

[　　D　　]

The type of classroom activities proposed in CLT also implied ③<u>new roles in the classroom for teachers</u> and learners. Learners now had to participate in classroom activities that were based on a cooperative rather than individualistic approach to learning. Students had to become comfortable with listening to their peers in group work or pair work tasks, rather than relying on the teacher for a model. They were expected to take on a greater degree of responsibility for their own learning. Teachers now had to assume the roles of facilitator and monitor. Rather than being a model for correct speech and writing and one with the primary responsibility of making students produce plenty of error-free sentences, the teacher had to develop a different approach to learners' errors and to his or her own role in facilitating language learning.

問1　下線部①とはどのような能力か，本文に即して30字程度の日本語で書け。

問2　下線部②の考えに基づいて教師はどのような手立てを講じたか，本文に即して30字程度の日本語で書け。

問3　下線部③を端的に表す英語6語を本文から抜き出して書け。

問4　次の段落を入れるのに最も適切な箇所を[　A　]〜[　D　]の中から一つ選び，記号で答えよ。

Communicative language teaching can be understood as a set of principles about the goals of language teaching, how learners learn a language, the kinds of classroom activities that best facilitate learning, and the roles of teachers and learners in the classroom. Let us examine each of these issues in turn.

問5　次の英文のうちCLTの考え方にあてはまるものをア〜オの中から二つ選び，記号で答えよ。

ア　Grammar is no longer important in language teaching.

220

イ　Teachers are concerned with only developing speaking skills.

ウ　Classroom activities should be meaningful and involve real communication.

エ　Accuracy is the top priority in language teaching.

オ　Learners should be more responsible for their own learning.

問6　次の質問に60語程度の英語で答えよ。なお，使用した語数を記入すること。

In order to encourage your students to use English, which of the three classroom activities mentioned above would you use? Choose one and explain why.

(☆☆☆◎◎◎)

【中学校】

【1】次の英文を読んで，後の問に答えよ。

Why do we always have to blend in? What makes us want to be just like everyone else? When our goal in life is simply to be accepted by others, we forget who we are as individuals. ①That was me in the seventh grade. I was young, impressionable, and lost. What was most important to me was to get along with my friends and to win their acceptance. I did what they did, said what they said, and adopted their interests as my own. The last thing I wanted to be seen as was different.

One day my English teacher asked me to stay after class. Terrified, I approached her desk once the bell had rung. "What did I do, Mrs. Madden?" I asked nervously.

Mrs. Madden, who was probably in her fifties and had a strikingly youthful and kind face, replied, "It's not what you did—it's what you haven't done." I was (A). "When I was reading the essay you wrote for our last assignment," she continued, "I kept thinking to myself, *This kid could be a writer someday. He has talent, but it's all bottled up inside.* If you ask me, you're just scared to let it all out."

I was so surprised. "I don't know what to say."

"Of course you don't," she said, smiling. "Like most students your age, you spend so much time trying to fit in that you lose your sense of identity in the process. It's hard to express yourself when you don't know who you are. You're different, you're unique, and you have a special gift for expressing your thoughts very clearly. You just don't realize it yet! That's why I want you to join the creative writing club I run after school. It'll help you find your voice."

I took Mrs. Madden's recommendation and showed up at the next meeting. I had no idea what to expect. When I walked into the room, ② it was a bit of a shock. Kids were all over the place: some were sitting in beanbag chairs; others were lying on the floor. One of them even had a pillow and had taken off his shoes! All of them were busy writing in journals as "Carry On My Wayward Son" by Kansas, one of my favorite songs at the time, played loudly in the background. Mrs. Madden greeted me, then handed me a journal and told me to start writing.

"About what?" I asked her.

"About whatever you want," she said. "Find a place in the room and try closing your eyes. It will come to you."

③At first I felt stupid and self-conscious sitting there on the floor with an empty journal in my hand and my eyes shut. *What if my friends looked in through the window and saw me?* "Relax," I heard Mrs. Madden say to me from across the room. I tried focusing on the music, and that helped calm me down. Then for some reason I started thinking about my Uncle Joe, whose funeral I had just attended over the weekend. He was someone that I loved very much and was really going to miss. That was it! Suddenly I had a (B) of thoughts about what a great guy Uncle Joe had been, and I began writing. When I left the room an hour later, I had written my first poem.

From that point on, when very few of my friends thought writing poetry and short stories was cool, I religiously attended Mrs. Madden's creative writing club. She taught me writing techniques, the art of creative expression, and most of all the importance of discovering who I was and having the courage to be that person without any regrets. I can still hear her telling me, "Find your authentic voice." That is exactly what I did.

Instead of trying to fit in, be different from everyone else. Find your hidden talents. Live (C) to your core beliefs. Express your viewpoint even if it is unpopular. Follow your heart and pursue whatever taps your passion. Find your own voice and unleash your full potential.

問1 下線部①の具体的内容を本文に即して35字程度の日本語で書け。

問2 下線部②の理由を日本語で簡潔に書け。

問3 下線部③の理由を本文に即して55字程度の日本語で書け。

問4 本文中の(A)～(C)に入る最も適切な語をア～オの中から一つずつ選び，記号で答えよ。

　　ア confused　　イ flood　　ウ lack　　エ strange　　オ true

問5 次の英文が本文の内容に合うように，(a)～(c)に入る最も適切な語をア～オの中から一つずつ選び，記号で答えよ。

　　When the author was a seventh grade student, Mrs. Madden was sure that he was a student of (a). By saying "Find your authentic voice," she made him (b) of his identity and drew out his talent. Thanks to her advice, he has been (c) in expressing himself.

　　ア afraid　　イ aware　　ウ promise　　エ successful
　　オ excuse

問6 本文の事例を参考に，あなたにとって忘れられない言葉を，理由を添えて30語程度の英語で書け。なお，使用した語数を記入すること。

(☆☆☆◎◎◎)

【高等学校】

【１】次の英文を読んで，後の問に答えよ。

I grew up thinking my mother was a sucker. She answered every request, whether it was from one of my siblings, our neighbors, or the endless number of charities who routinely mailed donation requests to her. Then there was the time my mother cut our lunch plans short to buy a couple of hamburgers for a homeless guy in downtown San Francisco.

My mom and I were standing with other pedestrians at a traffic signal. An untidy man sat at the corner begging for money. He couldn't speak clearly and had a bottle hidden in a paper bag next to him. His dirty clothes hung limply over his lean figure, and the disagreeable smell made me hold my breath. We all pretended to ignore him—everyone but my mother.

Looking him straight in the eye, Mom asked him, "If I give you money, then are you going to go and buy alcohol?" Right in front of all those people, she asked this. The man couldn't quite meet my mother's eyes when he answered, "No, ma'am. I don't drink. Just need a little food, that's all." Mom looked around and noticed a McDonald's sign above us. "You want a burger?" she asked.

I wanted to drag my mother away from the curious eyes of all those onlookers. The man would turn down her offer. He wanted money, after all, not cheap burgers. He stalled, looked uncomfortable—maybe because he was surprised she hadn't ignored him or just tossed him a coin like most people. ①Instead, my mother had spoken to him, asked a question, and was waiting for his answer.

"Okay. I wouldn't mind a burger," he replied nervously. ②So my mother marched inside to order the food, with me following along behind. Another mother might well have done the same: Shown her child that helping other people was important. But, honestly, what difference would my mother possibly make in this man's life? My mother giving food to someone so despised amounted to a small act of kindness. Her suggesting he'd rather drink than eat, though, meant she recognized his weakness, that he was a human being who made mistakes, like everyone else. Only, my mother wasn't about to feed an addiction, to further a wrong.

Following my mother into the McDonald's restaurant that day in San Francisco, I told her the man probably wasn't hungry, that whatever she was going to buy him would hardly make a dent in his day. "It's good to help," she said simply. It was the same answer she'd given me before, each time I'd told her that ten bucks would hardly make a difference to one charity or another, so why (A) writing check after check?

"It's good to help."

She didn't say anything about her past, when she had lived in misery herself during World War II. When she was eight, her family was trying to cross the border in the dark, to (B) the soldiers who'd come in and taken over her house and her town in Eastern Europe. My grandmother put their lives on the line because she was determined to lead her six children from certain hell toward a chance at a better future. Only, for six years after that night, they found themselves in ③another kind of misery. They lived in a single building with other families, all refugees, which offered no privacy, not enough space, and little comfort. The food was bad and paltry, barely enough for all of them. So they searched for bits of food other people had thrown away.

During those years, an American lady used to send her money and boxes of clothing. My mother would reply with letters of thanks, telling the lady about her life in the camp. Then my mother's family received word that they would get visas to leave the camp and go to the United States. My mother never heard from the lady again. But my mother never forgot her or her kindness.

As I watched my mother hand the man at the corner a bag of cheeseburgers, I realized she saw herself in him, in each person she gave to. Her past motivated her to do what she did day to day, giving what she could to charities, to loved ones, and to strangers like the homeless man on the streets of San Francisco. Her motto was "[④]" It reflected how she saw the

225

world: Some have less; some have more. And, sometimes, the merest stroke of luck separates the haves from the have-nots. It's up to those who have to help those who have not. And even a little bit can help.

"Be thankful, Elizabeth," she could have told me that day. But she didn't. My mother was a woman of (　C　), not of admonition. In fact, I didn't recognize until much later that what she did that day in San Francisco made a difference. ⑤It made a difference in me.

問1　下線部①について筆者が考える母親の真意を本文に即して40字程度の日本語で書け。

問2　下線部②の時に筆者が取った行動を本文に即して50字程度の日本語で書け。

問3　下線部③の具体例を本文に即して日本語で二つ書け。

問4　本文中の[　④　]に入る最も適切な英文を本文から抜き出して書け。

問5　本文中の(　A　)～(　C　)に入る最も適切な語をア～オの中から一つずつ選び，記号で答えよ。

　　ア　action　　イ　curiosity　　ウ　escape　　エ　keep　　オ　train

問6　次の英文が下線部⑤の内容を表すものになるように，(a)～(c)に与えられた文字で始まる英語1語をそれぞれ入れよ。

I always thought that my mother was a person who was easily deceived, for she never (a)(r　　) to help others. On that day in San Francisco, however, I realized why she had behaved so kindly toward people in (b)(n　　) of help. Her behavior came from her experience of having survived a difficult time during World War Ⅱ and showed her (c)(v　　) of life.

(☆☆☆○○○)

解答・解説

【中高共通】

【1】1　イ　2　ア　3　エ　4　イ　5　イ　6　エ　7　エ
8　ウ　9　ア　10　ウ

〈解説〉音声は一度しか流れないが，設問の選択肢はあらかじめ読んでお
くことができ，内容も初級の日常会話レベルなので特別な対策は必要
ないだろう。聞き取りを特に苦手としている人は，TOEICの対策CDで
聞き取り問題に慣れておく，ラジオの英会話番組などで音声による英
語に慣れておく，などの準備をしておくとよい。

【2】1　エ　2　イ　3　エ　4　ウ　5　イ

〈解説〉1　despite は「～にもかかわらず」。後の文に「成功した」
(succeeded)とあるので，「障害にもかかわらず」とする obstacles が適
切。　2　中学校学習指導要領　外国語の「目標」に「聞くこと，話
すこと，読むこと，書くことなどのコミュニケーション能力の基礎を
養う。」とあるが，have students ～で「生徒に～をさせる」という文脈
なので，「4つのスキルを取り入れさせる，統合させる」とする
integrate が適切。　3　「何が起きたか伝えると，Chiho は驚いたようだ
った」の意で　seemed surprised となる。イの完了形だと，主節の時制
以前にすでに知っていて驚いていた，という意味になり，文前半と対
応しない。　4　「風と共に去りぬ」は Margaret Mitchel の有名な小説。
他選択肢の作者はそれぞれ，ア：John Steinbeck，イ：Harriet Elizabeth
Beecher Stowe，エ：Earnest Hemingwayである。　5　discourse marker は
「指標語」「談話標識」などと訳されるが，いわゆる「つなぎ言葉」。
however, in addition などの例が引かれているので判断できよう。

【3】 When students ask why they have to study English, good English teachers may talk about the importance of studying English. They may say English is essential in this global age or that it is a necessary subject for entrance exams.

　Great English teachers, however, will try to make them notice the joy or usefulness of studying English. Great teachers will praise students and are very good at motivating them to study harder. They will make students independent learners. (78 words)

〈解説〉問題文を読んで心に浮かぶ具体例は人それぞれであろう。「内なる心に火をつける」はほぼ定訳となっているが，元の言葉は The great teacher inspires. である。inspire には「動機を与える，やる気にさせる」などの意味があるので，それに沿った例を使って書ければよい。いろいろなテーマでショートエッセイを書くには，まずは日ごろの練習がものを言うので，身近なテーマを使って80語から120語程度でまとめる練習をしておきたい。

【4】 問1　意味のあるコミュニケーションのために言語を使うことができる能力。　問2　生徒に正確な文章を作らせ，対話を覚えさせ，何度も練習をさせた。　問3　the roles of facilitator and monitor
問4　A　　問5　ウ，オ　　問6　I am going to use pair work activities, because even a student who is too shy to perform in front of a lot of people can express his or her opinion. In addition, by working together with a partner, the students can share ideas, learn from each other and solve what wouldn't be possible with just one person. (58 words)

〈解説〉問1　前の文の since 以下に「文構造のルールをマスターすることはできるが，それでもなお意味のあるコミュニケーションのために言語をうまく使うことはできない」とあるので，その後半を引けばよい。　問2　下線部②に続く文に，具体的な方法論が述べられているので，その個所を引けばよい。　問3　下線部は「教室での教師の新しい役割」。下線部に続き and learners とあり，続く文で教師，生徒両方の役割について説明していることが分かる。たどって行くと，生徒

についてのコメントに続いて，Teachers で始まる文がある。「教師は世話役兼監視役を引き受けなければならなかった」　問4　与えられた段落は，まず communicative language teaching の定義として考えられるものを挙げており，最後に段落中で触れた項目について「これらを検証していこう」と結んでいるので，空欄直前に「communicative language teaching によって何を理解しているだろう？」と疑問を投げ，空欄後に段落中の項目の解説に入っているAの個所が適切である。

問5　文中CLTについて，文法よりもペアワーク活動，ロールプレイ，グループ活動に，より焦点があてられる，とあるが，「文法は重要でない」「スピーキング能力のみ促進させればよい」とは述べていないので，ア，イは不可。エの Accuracy について本文では詳述されていないが，最後の文に「間違いのない文を生徒に作成させることにではなく，新しいアプローチを工夫しなくてはならない」とあり，エは不適切と判断できる。　問6　本文中に，pair work activities，role plays，group work activities の3つが挙げられているが，解答にはそのどれを選んでもよい。自由に思う通り書けばよいわけであるが，communicative language teaching という文趣旨を踏まえ，その考え方に沿って書くべきなのは言うまでもない。指導法に関しての意見はいろいろな問題で問われると考えられるが，指導要領におけるコミュニケーション重視の傾向を踏まえつつ，いろいろな場面を想定して自分の意見を構築しておくことが必要である。

【中学校】

【1】問1　周囲に受け入れられることを人生の目標とし，自分の個性を見失っていること。　問2　子どもたちが好きな場所で好きな格好で，自由に書いていたから。　問3　目を閉じて白紙の用紙を持って床に座っていることが滑稽で，他の生徒に自分の姿を見られたらどうしようと思ったから。　問4　A　ア　B　イ　C　オ
問5　a　ウ　b　イ　c　エ　問6　I've never forgotten the advice my baseball coach game me: Don't give up on yourself. It always reminds me

how important it is to believe in myself and try harder. (30 words)

〈解説〉問1　下線部の文頭の That は代名詞であり，it と異なり文全体や述べられている状況全体を受けることも多いので，冒頭から読んで行く。最初の二つの質問は抜いて，その質問に答えている部分をまとめればよい。　　問2　下線部は「それはちょっとした衝撃だった」。続く文に，その「衝撃だった」時の状況が詳述されているので，それを書けばよいが，問題に「簡潔に」とあるのでだらだらと引用するのではなく，要旨をまとめて書くことがポイントである。　　問3　直接の解答としては，下線部を含む文の次の文，イタリック体の What if 以下だけでもよいが，問題に55字程度，と指定があるので，その前の文にある状況描写も交えて詳しく書く。　　問4　各選択肢の意味は，ア「混乱した」，イ「洪水」，ウ「不足」，エ「奇妙な」，オ「真の」。Aは先生の「あなたがしなかったことに関することよ」という言葉が謎めいていたので，ア，Bは叔父の事を思い出し，突然いろいろな考えが「洪水のように」溢れてきたことを述べており，イ，C は live true to で「〜に忠実に生きる」という意味の成句。「あなたの核となる信念に忠実に生きよ」　　問5　a　前置詞の後は名詞が基本なので，形容詞のアイエは除外する。of promiseで「前途有望な」，of excuse で「言い訳(の手段)としての」という意味で，前者が適切。「Madden 先生は，彼が前途有望な生徒だと確信した」　　b　(make ＋ 人 ＋ 形容詞)のかたちで，「人を〜の状態にする」という意味。形式としてあてはまるのはアかイで，前者は「恐れさせる」，後者は「気づかせる」となり，後者が適切。「彼女は彼に自分が何であるかに気づかせ，彼の才能を引き出した」　　c　be successful in 〜 で，「〜に成功する」。「彼女の助言のおかげで，彼は自分を表現することに成功した」

問6　どのような体験を書いてもよく，表現も自由であるが，本文の内容を踏まえ，自分のためになったことや参考になったことについて書くのが順当だろう。内容と理由づけの整合性や文法的な正しさに気をつけて書く。どのようなテーマでも即時にアイデアを絞ってまとめられるようにするためには，毎日少しずつでもいろいろなテーマで英

文を書くことが最も効果的である。

【高等学校】

【1】問1　お金を渡すと酒を買うと分かっており，アルコール依存を悪化させないという強い気持ち。　問2　その男性は空腹ではないし，彼に何を買ってあげても彼の生活に何の良い影響も及ぼさないと言って母親を諭した。　問3　・他の難民家族と一つの建物に住み，プライバシーも十分な空間も，安らぎもなかった。　・食べ物はまずく，家族がかろうじて食べる量しかなく，他人が捨てた食べ物を探し求めることもあった。　問4　It's good to help.　問5　A　エ　B　ウ　C　ア　問6　(a)　refused　(b)　need　(c)　view(s)

〈解説〉問1　続く段落，Her suggesting 以下で，筆者が母の行動について述べている。「彼女が，彼は食べるより酒を飲みたいのではないか，と示唆したことは，彼女が彼の弱さに，そして彼も過ちをおかす人間なのだということに気付いたことを意味した。ただ母は，中毒者を増長させ，過ちを助長しようとはしなかった」　ここから，浮浪者が飲むつもりならお金を出さないし，それを相手にも伝えようとする母の意志を筆者が感じたことが推察できる。　問2　第6段落 I told her 以下に，筆者が母に告げた内容が書かれている。　問3　下線部に続く文に，具体的な内容が書かれている。　問4　第6段落に "It's good to help," she said simply. It was the same answer she'd given me before, each time I'd told her that ten bucks would hardly make a difference to one charity or another, … とあり，It's good to help. が，母が繰り返し筆者に伝えてきた motto だと分かる。　問5　A　「小切手につぐ小切手」から，母が継続的に小切手を切っていたことが分かるので，keep を入れて，「なぜ小切手を切り[続ける]のか」とする。　B　ここでの escape は他動詞で，「～を避ける」の意味。　C　admonition は警告や勧告。a woman of action で「母は口で言うより行動する人だった」となる。問6　(a)　「母が他の人たちを助けることを決して[拒む]ことをしなかったので，私は，彼女は騙されやすい人だと思っていた」　(b)　in

231

need of help で「助けを必要としている」の意味の形容詞句。

(c)　「彼女の行動は第2次世界大戦で困難な時期を生き抜いてきた体験に基づいており，彼女の人生に対する[見方]を示すものだった」

2013年度　実施問題

【中高共通】

【1】聞き取りテスト

　これから1〜10の英語を1回ずつ放送します。それぞれの英語のあとに，その内容について質問を一つします。その質問に対する答として適切なものをア〜エの中から一つずつ選び，その記号で答えなさい。

1　W : Hello. I'm here to visit my friend, Tom Green. He had an operation on his knee yesterday. Which room is he in?

　　M : Let me check. Here it is. He's in Room 205 on the second floor.

　　W : Thank you.

　　Question (M) : Where is this conversation most likely to take place?

　　ア　In an office building.　　　イ　In a school.

　　ウ　In a hospital.　　　　　　エ　In a hotel.

2　M : Excuse me. I think I left my dictionary in the library.

　　W : I just locked the doors now, but I can check for you.

　　M : Thank you so much. I need my dictionary to prepare for tomorrow's lessons.

　　W : OK, wait here. I'll go and check.

　　Question (M) : What will the woman do?

　　ア　Look for the man's dictionary.

　　イ　Let the man study in the library.

　　ウ　Let the man go into the library.

　　エ　Lend the man her dictionary.

3　M : How do you like your new apartment?

　　W : Well, I think it's better than the last one because it's cheaper and closer to the office. But, sometimes I can't sleep well because the guy next door often invites his friends and they are noisy.

M : Why don't you consult with the building manager?

Question (W) : What is she complaining about?

　ア　The rent.　　イ　The location.　　ウ　The size.

　エ　The neighbor.

4　W : Hello. I'd like to book a room, please.

　M : All right, for when?

　W : This coming weekend, Saturday night and Sunday night.

　M : Well...OK, we have rooms available then.

　Question (W) : What is the man's occupation?

　ア　A bookstore manager.　　イ　A librarian.　　ウ　A hotel clerk.

　エ　A deliveryman.

5　M : May I help you?

　W : Oh,this jacket has become much cheaper. It was ten thousand yen last week, wasn't it?

　M : Yes, ma'am. We are holding a special sale at 40% off this week. It's a final sale.

　W : Oh, I didn't know that. I'll take it.

　Question (M) : How much will the woman pay?

　ア　4,000 yen.　　イ　6,000 yen.　　ウ　10,000 yen.

　エ　14,000 yen.

6　W : Excuse me, Mr.Smith.

　M : Today's class has already finished. What happened?

　W : I'm sorry. I overslept this morning.

　M : Well, make sure you will be on time next week.

　Question (W) : What problem did the student have?

　ア　The student couldn't finish his homework.

　イ　The student couldn't make it to the class.

　ウ　The student couldn't prepare for the lesson.

　エ　The student couldn't find the classroom.

7　M : Hello. This is the Ohara Festival Volunteer Services. How may I help you?

W : Hello. This is Margaret Parker. I have an appointment with Mr,Tanaka at three o'clock. But I'm calling to change my volunteer interview schedule.

M : Certainly, please hold on.

Question (W) : Why does the woman want to speak with Mr.Tanaka?

ア　Because she wants to quit her volunteer position.

イ　Because she wants to discuss the problem with him.

ウ　Because she wants to reschedule her volunteer interview.

エ　Because she wants to know the details about the volunteer work.

8　M : Attention, students. This is the principal. A typhoon is approching Kagoshima, so school will finish at twelve o'clock today. Be careful on your way home. If school is canceled tomorrow morning because of the typhoon, there will be an announcement on the radio at 6 a.m.

Question (W) : Which statement is true?

ア　School will end earlier today.

イ　School will be closed at noon tomorrow.

ウ　A typhoon hit Kagoshima just now.

エ　The radio was broken because of a typhoon.

9　M : This is the captain speaking. We will soon be landing at Hong Kong International Airport. The local time is 8:15 p.m. We apologize for the delay due to heavy air traffic. If you have missed a connecting flight, please go to the transfer desk. We'll give you information about your next available flight.

Question (W) : What caused the airplane to be delayed?

ア　Poor in-flight service.　　　イ　Bad weather.

ウ　Heavy air traffic.　　　エ　Connecting flight information.

10　W : Good morning, this is the weather report. The island was covered with snow overnight and another winter storm is on its way. We expect that it will start snowing again by noon. Temperatures are likely to change early next week though. Normal weather for November should return by Sunday and temperatures will once again rise above zero.

Question (M) : What will likely happen next Sunday?

ア　It will continue snowing.　　　イ　A winter storm will hit.

ウ　Temperatures will normalize.　　エ　It will get colder.

(☆☆☆◎◎)

【2】次の各文の(　　)に入る適切な英語をア〜エの中から一つずつ選び，記号で答えよ。

1　In Japan, there is much prospect of another rise in consumption tax to meet the social welfare needs of its (　　) society.

ア　traditional　　イ　primitive　　ウ　ancient　　エ　aging

2　(　　) is the type of language produced by second-and foreign-language learners who are in the process of learning a language.

ア　Metalanguage　　イ　Interlanguage　　ウ　Isolating language

エ　Native language

3　Mark Twain, who was an American novelist, wrote (　　) in the nineteenth century.

ア　*The Adventures of Tom Sawyer*　　イ　*For Whom the Bell Tolls*

ウ　*To the Lighthouse*　　　　　　　エ　*Robinson Crusoe*

4　Extensive reading means reading in quantity and in order to gain (　　).

ア　a partial understanding of which is read

イ　a general understanding of what is read

ウ　a partial understanding of which is reading

エ　a general understanding of what is reading

5　The Ministry of Education, Culture, Sports, Science and Technology suggests that (　　) to see the world from a global standpoint.

ア　much Japanese students should go abroad

イ　many Japanese students go to abroad

ウ　more Japanese students go abroad

エ　few Japanese students had better go to abroad

(☆☆☆◯◯◯)

【3】今回の学習指導要領改訂に伴い，中学校及び高等学校で指導すべき語数が増加した。このことにより期待できる生徒の姿について，具体例を示しながらあなたの考えを70語程度の英語で述べよ。なお，使用した語数を記入すること。

(☆☆☆☆◯◯◯◯)

【4】次の英文を読んで，後の各問に答えよ。

　　Professional test development and management is a highly complex matter. Anyone who is involved in the preparation of important tests should have some basic understanding of two concepts, validity and （　A　）, and the relationship between them.

　　An achievement test can be considered to have <u>validity</u> if it contains only forms and uses the learners have practiced in the course, and it employs only exercises and tasks that correspond to the general objectives and methodology of the course.

　　The first type of validity, called content validity, means that the grammar, vocabulary, and functional content of a test should be carefully selected on the basis of the course syllabus. This is only logical and fair. If the learners have not practiced the Passive Voice, they should not be tested on it. If they have not practiced the vocabulary of cooking, they should not be tested on it. The language content of the test should go outside the syllabus only when it is not significant in the exercise or task : for example, in a reading comprehension test, where the learners may actually have been encouraged to ignore incidental language they do not know or to guess its meaning from context. The second type of validity, called construct validity, means that the exercises and tasks in a test should be similar to those used in the course and correspond

237

to the general approach of the course. If the learners have never practiced translating on the course, they should not have to translate a passage in the test. If the main aim of the course has clearly been to use grammar in natural discourse such as conversations, the grammar should not be tested only through grammar manipulation exercises. If a test conforms to these principles, it will probably be seen as fair by the teachers and the learners. If it does not, it will probably be considered unfair, and justifiably so.

[　B　]

The reliability of a test also depends partly on how far it can be marked objectively. Multiple choice exercises, where the learner has to select the best answer from a choice of three or four, are purely objective by nature. One-word fill-in exercises — completion of a text with one word in each space — are purely objective when only one word is possible. But when many different words are possible, they are fairly subjective, requiring teachers to use their personal judgement. Composition marking is by nature highly subjective.

The reliability of a test also depends on its length and on how it is administered. A long test is usually more reliable than a short one. Any test provides a sample of a learner's English, and a small sample of something is less reliable than a large one.

The administration of a test may affect its reliability. For example, reliability is reduced if : [　C　].

There is often a conflict between validity and reliability. The most reliable types of question are multiple-choice. The learners produce no English themselves, but only recognize correct language. Their answers can actually be marked by a computer, with no need for any subjective human judgement. The least reliable types of task include activities, such as the letter-writing and the interview role-play. These have to be marked subjectively by human beings.

The solution reached by many teachers and institutions is a compromise. Some exercises in the tests are of an objective, recognition type, for example, multiple-choice. These can cover a range of grammar and vocabulary as well as listening and reading comprehension. Other exercises and tasks are of a more subjective type, involving production and the communicative use of English. To reduce subjectivity, marking guides can be provided, which include the possible answers for fill-in and completion exercises, and criteria for marking compositions and interviews. This compromise also makes tests more practical.

問1　本文中の(　A　)に入る適切な英語1語を本文から抜き出して書け。

問2　次の表は下線部に関して説明したものである。(　a　)に日本語，(　b　)に英語を記入し，表を完成させよ。

種　　類	説　　明
content validity	(　a　)
(　b　)	テストの問題やタスクが授業で行われたものと類似したものであり，コース全体の教え方と一致していること。

問3　次は本文中の[　B　]に入る段落である。本文の内容に即して，(　a　)〜(　c　)に入る適切な語をあとの語群から一つずつ選び，記号で答えよ。

　　Reliability is a matter of how far we can believe or trust the results of a test. A specific test exercise or task is normally reliable when :

— the (　a　) are clear and unambiguous for all the learners

— the exercise or task has (　b　) over how learners respond to some extent, for example, it should be clear in 'fill the gap' exercises whether a single word or a phrase is required

— there are no (　c　) in the test, for example, if the learners have to 'select the best answer — a,b,c or d,' there should not actually be two or more acceptable answers.

　　　語群　ア　analyses　　イ　burdens　　ウ　controls　　エ　errors
　　　　　　オ　instructions

問4　本文の内容に即して次の文の(　a　)，(　b　)に最も適切な英語1語を本文から抜き出してそれぞれ書け。

The reliability of tests rests on how clearly teachers can mark; multiple-choice tests are (　a　) while composition tests are (　b　) to some extent.

問5　本文中の[　C　]に当てはまらないものをア～ウから一つ選び,記号で答えよ。

ア　one group is given much more time than another

イ　one group is helped by the teacher and another is not

ウ　one group is more in number than another

問6　次のようなテストを実施する場合，どのような採点基準を設定したらよいか。本文の内容を踏まえ，あなたが考える基準をあとの表の(　a　)，(　b　)に日本語で書け。

【テスト内容】対象：中学3年生

問題：「中学生が携帯電話を持つことに賛成か，反対か，あなたの意見を3文の英文で書け。」

項　目	点数配分	採　点　基　準
Content	5点	(a)
Fluency	3点	(b)
Accuracy	2点	誤りの個数が0個であれば2点　／　6個までは1点　／　7個以上は0点

(☆☆☆☆◎◎◎◎)

【中学校】

【1】次のGillian Lynne(ジリアン・リン)に関する英文を読んで，後の各問に答えよ。

Gillian was eight years old. Her schoolwork was a disaster, at least as far as her teachers were concerned. She turned in assignments late, her handwriting was terrible, and she tested poorly. Not only that, she was a disruption to the entire class, one minute fidgeting noisily, the next staring out of the window, and the next doing something to disturb the other children around her. Gillian wasn't particularly concerned about any of this. She was used to being corrected by authority figures and really didn't see herself as a difficult child, but the school was very concerned. At last the school wrote to her parents. [　A　]

Gillian's parents received the letter from the school with great concern and sprang to ①action. Gillian's mother put her daughter in her best dress and shoes, tied her hair in ponytails, and took her to a psychologist for an assessment, fearing the worst.

Gillian was invited into a large oak-paneled room with leather-bound books on the shelves. Standing in the room next to a large desk was an imposing man in a tweed jacket. He took Gillian to the far end of the room and sat her down on a huge leather sofa. Gillian's feet didn't quite touch the floor, and the setting made her wary. Nervous about the negative impression she would make, she sat on her hands so that she would sit still.

The psychologist went back to his desk, and for the next twenty minutes, he asked Gillian's mother about the difficulties Gillian was having at school and the problems the school said she was causing. While he didn't direct any of his questions at Gillian, he watched her carefully the entire time. ②This made Gillian extremely uneasy and confused. Even at this tender age, she knew that this man would have a significant role in her life. She genuinely didn't feel that she had any real problems, but everyone else seemed to believe that she did. Given the way her mother answered the questions, it was possible that even *she* felt this way. [　B　]

Eventually, Gillian's mother and the psychologist stopped talking. The man rose from his desk, walked to the sofa, and sat next to the little girl. "Gillian, you've been very patient, and I thank you for that," he said. "But I'm afraid you'll have to be patient for a little longer. I need to speak to your mother privately now. We're going to go out of the room for a few minutes. Don't worry; we won't be very long." Gillian nodded apprehensively, and ③the two adults went out leaving her sitting there on her own. But before the psychologist left the room, he leaned across his desk and turned on the radio.

As soon as they were in the corridor outside the room, the doctor said to Gillian's mother, "Just stand here for a moment, and watch what she does." There was a window into the room, and they stood to one side of it, where Gillian couldn't see them. Nearly immediately, Gillian was on her feet, moving around the room to the music. The two adults stood watching quietly for a few minutes, transfixed by the girl's grace. Anyone would have noticed there was something natural, even primal, about Gillian's movements. Anyone would have caught the expression of utter pleasure on hef face.

At last, the psychologist turned to Gillian's mother and said, "You know, Mrs. Lynne, Gillian isn't a problem child. She is a dancer. Take her to a dance school." [　C　]

Gillian's mother did exactly what the psychologist suggested. Gillian later said, "I can't tell you how wonderful it was. I walked into the room, and it was full of people like me. People who couldn't sit still. People who had to move to think."

She started going to the dance school every week, and she practiced at home every day. Eventually, she auditioned for the Royal Ballet School in London, and they accepted her. She went on to join the Royal Ballet Company itself, becoming a soloist and performing all over the world. When that part of her career ended, she formed her own musical theater company and produced a series of highly successful shows in London and New York. Eventually, she met Andrew Lloyd Webber and created with him some of the most successful musical theater productions in history, including *Cats* and *The Phantom of the Opera*.

Little Gillian became known the world as Gillian Lynne, one of the most accomplished choreographers of our time, someone who has brought pleasure to millions. This happened because someone looked deep into her eyes, someone who had seen children like her before and knew how to read the signs. Someone else might have put her on medication and told her to calm down. This story tells us that a child needs to be who he or she really is.

問1　下線部①の具体的内容を30字程度の日本語で書け。

問2　下線部②の理由を60字程度の日本語で書け。

問3　下線部③の後に室内で起きたことを50字程度の日本語で書け。

問4　次の英文を入れる最も適切な箇所を，本文中の[　A　]〜[　C　]

より一つ選び，記号で答えよ。

Maybe, Gillian thought, they were right.

問5　筆者の主張を踏まえ，教師としてどのようなことに配慮すべき
かを，40語程度の英語で書け。なお，使用した語数を記入すること。

(☆☆☆◎◎◎)

【高等学校】

【1】次の英文を読んで，後の各問に答えよ。

Teddy's letter came today, and now that I've read it, I will place it in my wooden chest with the other things that are important to my life. *I wanted you to be the first to know*. I smiled as I read the words he had written, and my heart swelled with a pride that I had no right to feel.

I have not seen Teddy Stallard since he was a student in my fifth-grade class, 15 years ago. It was early in my career, and I had only been teaching two years. From the first day he stepped into my classroom, I felt discomfort toward Teddy, even though a teacher is not supposed to have that feeling for a child, any child.

I had thought myself quite capable of handling my personal feelings along that line until Teddy walked into my life. There wasn't a child I particularly liked that year, but Teddy was most assuredly one I couldn't find any interest in. He seemed to pay no attention to his appearance. His hair hung low over his ears. In addition, his intellect left a lot to be desired. By the end of the first week I knew he was hopelessly behind the others. Ashamed as I am to admit it, I took perverse pleasure in using my red pen; each time I came to Teddy's papers, the cross marks were always a little larger and a little redder than necessary. "Poor work!" I would write with a flourish.

While I did not actually ridicule the boy, my attitude was obviously quite apparent to the class. He knew I didn't like him, but he didn't know why. Nor did I. All I know is that he was a little boy no one cared about, and I made no effort on his behalf.

The days rolled by. As the Christmas holidays approached, I knew that Teddy would never catch up in time to be promoted to the sixth-grade level. To justify myself, I went to his cumulative folder from time to time. He had very low grades for the first four years, but no grade failure. How he had made it, I didn't know. I closed my mind to the teachers' personal remarks :

- **First Grade** : Teddy shows promise by work and attitude, but has a bad home situation.
- **Second Grade** : Teddy could do better. Mother terminally ill. He receives little help at home.
- **Third Grade** : Teddy is a pleasant boy. Helpful, but too serious. Slow learner. Mother passed away at the end of the year.
- **Fourth Grade** : Very slow, but well behaved. Father shows no interest.

Well,they passed him four times, but he will certainly repeat fifth grade! ①*Do him good!* I said to myself.

Then the last day before the holidays arrived. Many gifts were heaped underneath our little tree, waiting for the big moment. Teachers also always get several gifts at Christmas. Each unwrapping brought squeals of delight. Teddy's gift was in the middle of the pile. Its wrapping was a brown paper bag. "For Ms.Thompson — From Teddy," it read. The students were completely silent. They all stood watching me unwrap that gift. There were two items inside; a rhinestone bracelet with several stones missing and a small bottle of cologne — half empty. I could hear the snickers and whispers, and ②I wasn't sure I could look at Teddy. "Isn't this lovely?" I asked, placing the bracelet on my wrist. I help up my wrist for all of them to admire. I dabbed the cologne behind my ears. I continued to open the gifts until I reached the bottom of the pile.

When they had all left, Teddy walked towards me. "You smell just like Mom," he said softly. "Her bracelet looks real pretty on you, too. I'm glad you liked it." He left quickly. I locked the door, sat down at my desk, and wept, resolving to make up to Teddy what I had deliberately deprived him of

— a [③] who cared.

I stayed every afternoon with Teddy until the last day of school. Sometimes we worked together. Sometimes he worked alone while I drew up lesson plans or graded papers. Slowly but surely he caught up with the rest of the class. Gradually, there was a definite upward curve in his grades. Eventually, his final averages were among the highest in the class.

I did not hear from Teddy until several years later, when his first letter appeared in my mailbox. It read, "I just wanted you to be the first to know. I will be graduating second in my class next month."

Four years later, Teddy's second letter came, which read, "I wanted you to be the first to know. I was just informed that I'll be graduating first in my class. University has not been easy, but I liked it."

And now today — Teddy's third letter came. It said, "I wanted you to be the first to know. As of today, I am *Medical Doctor Theodore J.Stallard*. How about that? I'm going to be married in July, the 27th, to be exact. I wanted to ask if you could come and sit where Mom would sit if she were here. I'll have no family there as Dad died last year."

問1　次の英文が下線部①に至るまでの筆者の気持ちを表すように，（ a ），（ b ）に最も適切な英語1語をそれぞれ入れよ。

　　　At first, Ms. Thompson had a (a) impression of Teddy because of his untidy appearance and poor school report. The teachers' personal remarks of him, however, helped her realize what reasons were (b) his struggles and she decided to back him up.

問2　下線部②の理由を本文に即して40字程度の日本語で書け。

問3　本文中の[③]に入る適切な英語1語を本文から抜き出して書け。

問4　次の英文がMs.Thompsonによって書かれたテディの5年生終了時の記録となるように，（ a ），（ b ）に最も適切な英語1語をそれぞれ入れよ。

　　　Fifth Grade : Teddy's grades (a) a lot through hard work. Yet, he is still (b) his mother.

問5　テディの3番目の手紙に，あなただったらどのような返事を書く
か。その手紙の本文を40語程度の英語で書け。なお，解答に使用し
た語数を記入すること。

Dear Teddy,
5
Sincerely yours,
Violet Thompson
手紙本文の語数：(　　　) words

(☆☆☆☆◎◎◎◎)

解答・解説

【中高共通】

【1】1　ウ　　2　ア　　3　エ　　4　ウ　　5　イ　　6　イ　　7　ウ
8　ア　　9　ウ　　10　ウ

〈解説〉リスニングテスト。内容についての質問を聞いて答えを選択する。
1　会話がどこで行われているかという質問。operation on his knee「膝
の手術」，room「部屋」といった語が聞き取れれば，この会話が病院
で行われていると想像することは容易である。よって正解はウの病院
となる。　　2　女性は何をするかという質問。最後の発話の I'll go and
check. が聞き取れれば女性が次に何をするのかがわかる。正解はアの
「男性の辞書を探す」。　　3　彼女は何について不満を言っているのか
という質問。But, sometimes I can't sleep well because the guy next door

often invites hid friends and they are noisy. とあるように，隣人の男性が友達を部屋に招待して騒いでいるということに不満を言っている。よって正解はエの「隣人について」である。　4　occupation「職業」男性の職業を聞く問題。book「予約する」，　we have rooms available then. から，ホテルの予約をしていることがわかるので，答えはウのホテルのフロント係である。　5　ten thousand yenと40％ offという語を聞き取れれば，女性は6,000円払うということがわかる。　6　生徒が I overslept this morning. と言っている。oversleep「寝坊をする」という意味である。またMr. Smithは today's class has already finished と言っているので生徒が授業に出席することが出来なかったことがわかる。

7　電話の会話である。女性は I'm calling to change my volunteer interview schedule. と言っているので，約束を変更したい旨を伝えている。よってウの「ボランティアのインタビューの予定を変更するため」が正解。

8　台風が近づいているので12時に放課となるという旨の放送である。選択肢を見ると，ア「学校は今日早く終わる」，イ「明日12時に学校は閉まる」，ウ「台風が鹿児島をちょうど今直撃している」，エ「台風のせいでラジオが壊れた」とある。放送内容に合致するのはアである。

9　航空機内の放送。　We apologize for the delay due to heavy air traffic. とあるので，航空機が遅延した理由は，ウの「航空交通の多さ」が正解。　10　天気予報の放送。Normal weather for November should return by Sunday and temperatures will once again rise above zero. とあるので，ウの「気温は正常に戻る」が正解。

【2】1　エ　　2　イ　　3　ア　　4　イ　　5　ウ

〈解説〉1　aging society「高齢化社会」，consumption tax「消費税」

2　interlanguage「中間言語」。これは，母語とも目標言語とも異なり，独自の体系を持ち，目標言語に近づきつつある言語の事を指す。英語教育における重要な語であるので，押さえておきたい。　3　文学の知識が問われる問題。The Adventures of Tom SawyerはMark Twainの著者である。その他，イの著者はErnest Hemingway，ウの著者はVirginia

Woolf, エの著者はDaniel Defoeである。　4　extensive readingとは,
「多読」のことを指す。intensive reading「精読」との違いに注意したい。
また, 選択肢イとエで迷うところだが, エは文脈に合わないので不正
解。イの「読まれていることにおける全般的な理解」が正解。
5　学習指導要領における言及。ここではsuggest that S (should) ＋原形
「Sが～することを提案する」という動詞の語法が使用されていること
に注意。go abroad「外国へ行く」というイディオムもここで押さえて
おく。

【3】 I think it good for students to learn a wider range of vocabulary in English
classes. I expect that students can make their communication more
satisfactory by developing their vocabulary. For example, when students talk
about their dreams, they can express exactly what they want to be. In
addition, students can understand better what others say, which will surely make
it easier for them to actively engage in English communication.　(70 words)

〈解説〉学習指導要領に関する問題。学習指導要領が改訂されたことによ
り, 改訂された内容に対する自分の意見や具体例を記述させる問題は
頻出である。今回は, 学習する語彙が増えたことが取り上げられてい
るが, 学習指導要領や学習指導要領の解説をよく読み, なぜ改訂され
たかを把握しておくことが重要である。また, 英語で書かれた学習指
導要領もあるので, そちらも確認し, 表現等を学んでおくとよい。英
作文の基本は, 最初に自分の意見を述べ, それに対する具体例などの
トピックを支える部分を書き, 最後に結論で締めくくるという形であ
る。この形式で書く練習と, 難しい表現を使おうとせず, 自分の使え
る簡単な表現でもよいので, 自分の意見を述べる練習をしておくとよ
い。なお, ここでの採点基準は, ①内容の適切さ, ②分量・論の展開
の適切さ, ③語彙・文法の適切さがそれぞれ10点ずつである。

【4】問1 reliability 問2 a テストの文法，語彙，機能的な内容がコースのシラバスに基づいて，慎重に選ばれていること。 b construct validity 問3 a オ b ウ c エ 問4 a objective b subjective 問5 ウ 問6 a 賛成反対のどちらかの立場に立って書いてあれば2点 / その理由が書いてあれば3点 b 3文書いてあれば3点 / 2文書いてあれば2点 / 1文しか書いていなければ1点

〈解説〉テストの妥当性と信頼性に関する長文。テスト作成の際には，この内容は重要であるので，妥当性と信頼性についてはあらかじめ勉強しておくとよい。 問1 第1段落では妥当性と(A)というトピックが述べられ，第3段落では，妥当性に関して，そして，問3と第5段落を見ると，reliability「信頼性」について書かれていることから，reliabilityが正解。 問2 2つの妥当性に関することが書かれた第3段落からの出題。 a content validity「内容的妥当性」については，第3段落の1文目に定義が書かれている。content validity, means that the grammer … の部分を日本語で説明する。 b 問題の説明に書かれている定義は，第3段落の6文目にあるconstruct validity「構造的妥当性」である。

問3 a すべての学習者にとって，明確であいまい性のないものでなければならないのは，instructions「指示」である。 b 課題やタスクは，学習者がどのように答えるかということを制御する必要があるので，controlsが正解。have control over「制御する，抑制する」

c テストの中であってはならないものはerrors「間違い」である。

問4 a multiple-choice test「多肢選択式問題」については，第5段落の1文目と2文目にかけて書かれている。この問題形式は，客観性が高いという性質を持っていることがわかる。 b composition testsについては，同じ段落の最後の文に書かれており，subjective「主観的な」問題であるという対比がされている。 問5 グループによって回答時間の制限に差があったり，教師の助けがあったりしては，信頼性が下がる要因になる。人数の差は信頼性を下げることに繋がらないので，正解はウ。 問6 a 配点が5点となっており，内容は各項目の中では一番高い。また，3文という制限があるため，この作文で重要なのは，

問題文で指定されている自分の立場を示すことと，意見であるため，それぞれが入っているかどうかを配点として考えるとよい。

b　流暢性は配点が3点であり，3文という指定があるので，それぞれ3，2，1と配点を考えると採点側もシンプルでわかりやすい。

【中学校】

【1】問1　最悪のことを心配し，ジリアンを心理学者に診断してもらうこと。(30字)　　問2　自分の人生に重要な役割を果たすと思われる人物が，自分には直接質問をせず，ずっと注意深く自分を観察しているだけだったから。(60字)　　問3　座っていたジリアンが立ちあがり，うれしそうな表情で，ごく自然にラジオの音楽に合わせて踊り始めたこと。(50字)　　問4　B　　問5　I think that teachers should first accept a child as he or she is instead of just judging the child only by his or her actions so that teachers can find out what the child really wants to be or do. (41 words)

〈解説〉問1　直後に母親が取った行動が書かれているが，30字という制限があるため，一番重要な最後の部分took her to a psychologist for an assessment, fearing the worstを取り出す。　　問2　thisの内容は第4段落に書かれている心理学者がジリアンにしたことであり，それをまとめることがポイント。また，ジリアン自身，彼が自分の人生に大きな役割を果たすと感じていたが，それがさらに彼女を不安にさせたのであり，直後に説明されたその心理学者についても付け加える必要がある。

問3　ジリアンが部屋に取り残されたあとの行動は，第6段落に書かれている。Nearly immediately…から始まる文がその内容であるが，第6段落の最後にある，彼女がどのような様子で踊っていたかということも加えるとよい。　　問4　この問題は，消去法で考えるとわかりやすい。まずAは，学校が両親にジリアンについて手紙を出したことが直前に書かれているが，ジリアンはそのことを直接は知らないので，文脈に合わない。Cは，母親と心理学者は部屋の外からジリアンを観察していたため，この会話をジリアンは聞いていないので，不適切であ

る。　問5　40語という短い指定なので1文か2文程度でよい。子ども
を見るときは，本当の姿を見る，受け入れることが大切であるという
ことを自分の言葉で説明する。ここでの採点基準は，①内容の適切さ
(6点)，②文法・語法の適切さ(4点)，③分量の適切さ(2点)である。

【高等学校】

【1】問1　a　negative　　b　behind　　問2　自分のテディへの態度が，
彼が友達から笑われる一因になっていると分かっていたから。(40字)
問3　teacher　　問4　a　improved　　b　missing
問5　Dear Teddy,

　　Congratulations on your achievements! You've become a doctor and you
are getting married. That's great! You deserve the success. I'm really proud
of you. Of course, I'm very honored to attend the wedding in your mother's
place. See you soon!

Sincerely yours,

Violet Thompson

(手紙本文の語数: 40 words)

〈解説〉問1　筆者が最初の頃はテディに対してあまりよい印象を持って
　　いなかったことが，第2，3，4段落から伺える。特に第2段落3文目の
　　I felt discomfortがポイント。悪い印象と言うことからnegative impression
　　が適当。また，テディの態度の背景を第5段落で知ることになる。彼
　　の心の葛藤の「背景，後ろ」という意味のbehindが正解。　問2　下線
　　部②の直前に，I could hear the snickers and whispersとあることから，周
　　りのテディのプレゼントに対する反応がうかがえる。snicker「くすく
　　す笑い」　問3　直前の部分に注目すると，自分がテディから故意
　　に奪ったもの，とある。また，③の後ろにはwho caredとあるので，世
　　話をする人が入る。教師である筆者が，テディに対して冷たい態度を
　　取ってきたことから世話をする教師を奪ったということで，teacherが
　　入ると考えられる。　問4　第5段落にあるテディに対する教師のコメ
　　ントを参考にする。また，彼の成績が上がったこと(a definite upward

curve in his grades)が第8段落に記されていることから，improvedが入り，筆者にテディが死んだ母親が使っていたものをプレゼントしたことから，彼はまだ母親を恋しく思っていると考えられるので，missingが適当である。　問5　まずは，テディが医者になったことと，結婚をするということに対するお祝いの言葉を書くこと。また，テディに対する筆者の思いを書く必要がある。そして，テディの結婚式に自分の母親として参加してほしいという要望に応えることが重要である。今回は，手紙の形式は解答用紙に既に印刷されているが，自分で手紙を書けるように型を身につけておくとよい。

2012年度　実施問題

【中高共通】

【1】聞き取りテスト

　　これから1〜10の英語を1回ずつ放送します。それぞれの英語のあとに，その内容について質問を一つします。その質問に対する答として適切なものをア〜エの中から一つずつ選び，記号で答えなさい。

1　W:　Excuse me, I'm getting on! Thank you.

　　M:　Which floor would you like to go to?

　　W:　I want to buy some towels.

　　M:　You'll find them on the 4th floor. I'll press the button.

　　Question (W):　Where is this conversation taking place?

　　ア　At an entrance.　　　　　イ　At an information desk.

　　ウ　In an elevator.　　　　　エ　In a restaurant.

2　M:　The weather forecast says it will be sunny and warm this weekend.

　　W:　Well then, how about driving to Kirishima? It has been three years since we went there last.

　　M:　Oh, don't you remember? Next Saturday, my soccer team is having a game.

　　W:　Now I remember. I'm sure I will go to your game.

　　Question (M):　What will the woman do next Saturday?

　　ア　She will go driving.　　　イ　She will go hiking.

　　ウ　She will play soccer in a game.

　　エ　She will watch the soccer game.

3　W:　Excuse me, how much is that sweater?

　　M:　It's nine thousand yen.

　　W:　Wow, that's too expensive for me. Would you discount it?

　　M:　Hmmm... We will sell it at 30% discount.

W:　OK. I'll take it.

Question (M):　How much will the woman pay for the sweater?

ア　9,000 yen.　　　　　　　　イ　7,830 yen.

ウ　6,300 yen.　　　　　　　　エ　2,700 yen.

4　W:　Could you tell me the way to City Hall? I might be lost.

　　M:　Go south three blocks and turn left. You'll find it opposite Seaside Hospital. It's there on your map. You had better hurry because it'll close at 5. You have only 30 minutes left. I will show you there if you would like.

　　W:　Thanks, but I can get there by myself. I hope I will be there in time.

Question (M):　What does the man propose to the woman?

ア　To go with her.　　　　　　イ　To lend her a map.

ウ　To stay there for 30 minutes.　エ　To walk to the hospital.

5　M:　Good evening, ma'am. What can I do for you?

　　W:　Would it be possible for you to change my room? Next door is very noisy. And, on my floor, young students are moving around. Their noises annoy me.

　　M:　We're very sorry. We will prepare a room on another floor as soon as possible.

　　W:　That would be nice. Thank you.

Question (M):　Why does the woman want to change her room?

ア　Because her friend's room is not on the same floor.

イ　Because it is too noisy around her room.

ウ　Because the floor has too many people on it.

エ　Because the room is too small for her things.

6　W:　Hey Bob, you are late again! Did you oversleep?

　　M:　No, I got up at 6:30. I left home at quarter to eight. It usually takes about 20 minutes by bike, but I lost another 30 minutes because of a flat tire.

　　W:　Oh, that's too bad. You'll have to fix it on your way home.

Question (M): What time did Bob arrive at school?

ア About 8:05. イ About 8:15.

ウ About 8:35. エ About 8:45.

7 M: What happened to you? I've been waiting for over an hour.

   W: Sorry, but listen to my story. I took the subway at seven, but the one running ahead of ours broke down. We had to wait until it was repaired.

   M: Why didn't you call me on your cell phone?

   W: Unfortunately it was out of service there.

Question (M): What problem did the woman have?

ア Her subway was too crowded.

イ She left her cell phone at her house.

ウ She was late for the subway she wanted to catch.

エ She wasn't able to contact him by cell phone.

8 M: What a beautiful vase! Where did you get that pottery?

   W: To tell the truth, I made it three years ago, when I was in the art club in high school.

   M: I really thought it was a work of some famous artist. Do you regularly make your own pottery?

   W: No, it was the last one.

Question (M): Which of the statements is true?

ア She doesn't have any pottery.

イ She hasn't made pottery for a few years.

ウ She is a famous artist.

エ She makes pottery in her high school.

9 W: Now, the weather: the severe hot and humid weather we've been having for a couple of days will end tonight as heavy rain and strong winds arrive from the northwest. Temperatures are expected to drop around 10 degrees by tomorrow morning. It is likely that thick clouds will bring thunder and hail. So farmers need to take great care of their crops. We will make detailed reports when more news comes in.

Question (M):　According to the forecast, what problem is going to happen?

ア　It's going to change into heavy snow.

イ　It's going to be hotter in a few days.

ウ　Temperatures will rise rapidly during night time.

エ　The crops are likely to be damaged.

10　M:　Good morning, students. We're going to the factory by bus. Sit with one of your group members. Group leaders, please make sure your members are present. When we arrive there, listen to your teacher's directions first, look around the factory in groups, and then make drafts of your reports. The deadline is next Monday.

Question (W):　What should the students do at the factory?

ア　Find seats for the group members.

イ　Prepare for the reports in groups.

ウ　Rank the reports.

エ　Sit with the group members.

(☆☆○○◎)

【2】次の各文の(　　)に入る適切な英語をア～エの中から一つずつ選び，記号で答えよ。

1　Many child welfare centers and orphanages in Japan reported (　　) donations of backpacks for schoolchildren and other items. They thanked the unknown donors.

ア　official　　イ　hidden　　ウ　arrogant　　エ　anonymous

2　(　　) means reading in quantity and in order to gain a general understanding of what is read.

ア　Scanning　　イ　Extensive reading　　ウ　Intensive reading

エ　Skimming

3　(　　) is a classic novel written by Charles Dickens in the nineteenth century.

ア　*Gone With the Wind*　　イ　*Uncle Tom's Cabin*

ウ　*A Christmas Carol*　　エ　*Alice's Adventures in Wonderland*

4　Strategic competence is the ability of a speaker to use verbal and non-verbal communication strategies (　　) a breakdown in communication.

ア　with a view to compensating for　イ　in spite of comparing with

ウ　for the purpose of causing　　エ　in addition to bringing about

5　After the introduction of Foreign language activities, elementary school students spend (　　) to English.

ア　many times getting familiar　　イ　much time getting known

ウ　a lot of time getting used　　エ　lots of times getting accustomed

(☆☆☆◎◎◎)

【3】日本の中学校・高等学校における英語教育の「不易」と「流行」について，90語程度の英語で述べよ。なお，使用した語数を記入すること。

(☆☆☆◎◎◎)

【4】次の英文を読んで，後の各問に答えよ。

'Learning to learn' is one of the most important objectives for all learning and teaching contexts for all ages. ①<u>In our fast moving world, it is simply impossible for learners to acquire all the knowledge and skills they need while they are at school.</u> It is the school's responsibility to teach learners how to learn, i.e. to equip them with strategies that they can use outside school. This process needs to start as early as possible, preferably at the beginning of schooling. Various aspects of 'learning to learn' can be introduced into the day-to-day routine of any language classroom without changing many of the usual classroom practices. I will discuss explicitly some opportunities that teachers of English for young learners can take to promote principles of 'learning to learn'.

②<u>What is the overall aim of incorporating some kind of 'learning to</u>

257

learn'? It is to raise children's awareness of the various factors that influence their language learning and to give them some time and space to think for themselves. 'Learning to learn' is a broad concept which can encompass a great variety of different activities, tasks, or discussions between children and the teacher. Some teachers might be working in contexts where 'learning to learn' is explicitly incorporated into the curriculum guidelines and both the national curriculum as well as the recommended coursebook contain specific advice on the techniques and activities used and the rationale behind them. Others might not have such explicit guidelines to work from but would be free to use their own ideas.

'Learning to learn' activities can be divided into several categories. The list below offers some ideas to begin to explore learning to learn, but is by no means complete. Teachers are invited to adapt as they see fit.

1　Social and affective strategies : to raise awareness about how learners' own emotional states and feelings as well as those of others can influence their learning. Activities in the classroom can include teacher-led discussions, usually in the mother tongue, about the social aspects of learning, such as the importance of listening to each other, turn taking in games, or controlling shyness and fear of speaking out in front of others. As part of developing awareness about affective factors, teachers can give plenty of praise and (　③　) feedback to children to raise their self-esteem and self-confidence as well as boost their motivation.

2　④Strategies related to raising awareness about what language learning is: to cover general understanding about language learning. In terms of understanding what language learning means, teachers might discuss with children how long it takes to learn a language, why it is important to practise, or why we all make mistakes.

3　Metacognitive strategies: ⑤to introduce and develop the ongoing process of reflection through planning, monitoring, and evaluating language learning. For example, teachers can encourage children to think about what they did well and why, and what they enjoyed and why. At later stages, children can think about the reasons for doing various activities and tasks and about lessons that can be learnt from each learning experience.

4 ⑥<u>Direct or cognitive strategies</u>: to develop children's ability to deal with linguistic information in an effective way, i.e. to organize, categorize, or memorize linguistic information. Activities in the classroom can include training strategies such as how to remember a list of words, how to guess the meaning of unknown words in a text, or how to link unrelated language to aid memory.

The above categories have been listed to illustrate an order in which they can be introduced. Teachers can start with emotions, feelings, and boosting self-esteem. They can then introduce metacognitive strategies which can be made applicable to any unit of learning. Finally, the cognitive strategies with older or more experienced learners can be added. This of course does not mean that this order must always be followed. Teachers are encouraged to judge for themselves what is appropriate and feasible. Some schools may be fostering learning to learn strategies in the other areas of the curriculum, which gives teachers a good chance to integrate English into an existing framework.

問1　下線部①の現状から，学校の役割を本文に即して日本語で書け。

問2　下線部②に対する答を本文に即して日本語で書け。

問3　本文中の(　③　)に入る適切な語を次から一つ選び，記号で答えよ。

　　ア　additive　　イ　mechanical　　ウ　positive　　エ　vertical

問4　下線部④を学習者に身に付けさせるための具体的な手立てを本文に即して日本語で書け。

問5　下線部⑤の具体的内容を本文に即して日本語で書け。

問6　下線部⑥の具体例として適切なものを次から一つ選び，記号で答えよ。

　　ア　Students refer to prefixes or suffixes when they come across the words they don't know.

イ　Students have discussions about the need to be patient when learning a new language.

ウ　Students share some ideas with other people who see things in different ways.

問7　英語の学習方法がわからずに悩んでいる生徒に一つだけアドバイスをするとしたら，あなたはどのようなアドバイスをするか。理由を添えて30語程度の英語で書け。なお，使用した語数を記入すること。

(☆☆☆◎◎◎)

【中学校】

【1】次の英文を読んで，後の各問に答えよ。

It may be difficult for teenagers who have exceptionally talented siblings to focus on their own creative expression, particularly in the same area of endeavor, and to be satisfied with themselves without comparing themselves to their siblings. As parents, we can affirm each child's uniqueness and encourage creative expression as a value in itself. However, if there is an obvious star in the family, ①we can't pretend otherwise. We often downplay the talented teen in a vain attempt to protect the other sibling from hurt feelings or feelings of insecurity.

Audrey's sister had an absolutely beautiful singing voice. She got all the solos in the school chorus and the lead in the school play. Audrey, who was two years younger, also had a nice voice, but it was nothing special. She got pretty tired of all the attention she got for her singing. When Audrey began high school, she decided not to audition for the chorus.

"Why don't you go out for chorus?" Mom encouraged her. "I'm sure you'll get in."

"②I'm not interested," Audrey declared emphatically. Mom found no possibility of further discussion.

Mom realized that Audrey needed to find something completely her own, something her older sister wasn't involved in. But Mom couldn't really help her. This was something Audrey had to do for herself.

It can be painful for a parent to watch as a teenager struggles to find her own style of creative expression, a way of establishing who she is in her world. All we can do is be supportive as our teens seek to find their way through the maze. Mom encouraged Audrey in all the activities she explored and never pressured her to be "the best," but always expressed support, telling her just to have fun and "see if you like it."

After a few (A) starts—with the debate team, the student council, and on the yearbook — Audrey joined the newspaper staff. She began writing articles, but they didn't always get published, and when they did, they were so heavily edited that she hardly recognized them as hers. But Audrey loved working on the paper anyway, and her mom was glad she had found something she could call her own. One day the editor noticed her doodles on her notebooks and asked if she could draw a cartoon for the paper. That was the opportunity Audrey had been waiting for, without knowing it. The cartoons were the perfect outlet for her creative scribbling and her wry sense of humor. Audrey began to draw cartoons for the paper on a regular basis. She loved doing them, and they were very well received by her peers. Most important of all, she had found her niche and was no longer just the younger sister.

Mom was wise to understand that Audrey had to find her own opportunities for self-expression, quite apart from those of her older sister. Thanks to ③her encouragement, Audrey was quite happy on the newspaper staff, even when her articles weren't published the way she had written them. She didn't care about that, because she had found ④a place where she could be herself and carve out her own domain, free from the shadow of her sister.

Developing her ability in cartooning was an extra (B) for Audrey. The key was that her mom understood her need to find her own avenue of self-expression and that she didn't pressure Audrey in any way. Sometimes when one teenager is highly successful in a certain area, the parents may assume that the other sibling needs to succeed at the same level in order to feel okay about themselves. Audrey didn't need to be a singing star. She just wanted to have fun and share who she was with others.

When Audrey was a senior, Mom found the perfect way to celebrate her daughter's contribution to the school newspaper with as much enthusiasm as she had celebrated her older daughter's vocal achievements. She collected all of Audrey's cartoons and put them into a scrapbook for her as a graduation gift. ⑤Audrey didn't say much when she opened the package, but she didn't have to—the look of pride and gratitude on her face said it all.

問1　下線部①の具体的内容を本文に即して60字程度の日本語で書け。

問2　オードリーが下線部②のように答えた理由を本文に即して70字程度の日本語で書け。

問3　下線部③の具体的内容を本文に即して70字程度の日本語で書け。

問4　下線部④の内容を表す1語を本文中から抜き出して書け。

問5　本文中の(Ａ), (Ｂ)に入る適切な語を次から一つずつ選び, 記号で答えよ。

　　ア　bonus　　イ　false　　ウ　job　　エ　true

問6　下線部⑤におけるオードリーの気持ちを40語程度の英語で書け。なお, 使用した語数を記入すること。

(☆☆☆◎◎◎)

【高等学校】

【1】次の英文を読んで, 後の各問に答えよ。

On my first day in McKee High School, I sit at my desk in an empty classroom. In a minute the bell will ring, and the students will rush in. What will they say if they see me at the desk? "Hey, look. He's hiding." They know everything about teachers. If you sit at the desk they think you're scared. You're using the desk as a wall. You should get out there and stand. If you make ①<u>such a mistake</u> on your first day, your students will remember it for months.

Here they are. The door hits the wall with a loud noise. Why can't they just walk into the room, say, "Good morning," and sit? One says, "Hey," in a playfully violent way, and another one says, "Hey," in reply. They insult each other, ignore the late bell, and are in no hurry to sit down. Look, there's a new teacher up there and new teachers don't know anything. So? Bell? Teacher? Who is he? Who cares?

The problem of the sandwich started when a boy named Petey asked the class, "Does anyone want a sandwich?"

"Are you joking?" laughed a boy named Andy. "Your mother must hate you, giving you cold-meat sandwiches like that." Petey threw his brown-paper sandwich bag at Andy, and the class cheered excitedly. The bag landed on the floor between the blackboard and Andy's desk.

I came from behind my desk and made the first sound of my teaching career: "Hey." They ignored me. I moved toward Petey and made my first teacher statement: "Stop throwing sandwiches." Petey and the class looked shocked. This teacher, this new teacher, just stopped a good fight. New teachers should look the other way or send for the principal. Benny called out from the back of the room. "Hey, teacher man, he already threw the sandwich." The class laughed. One boy covered his mouth and said, "Stupid." I wanted to knock him out of his seat, but of course I couldn't.

②<u>The class waited. What would this new teacher do?</u>

Professors of education at New York University never taught you what to do about flying-sandwich situations. Should I say, "Hey, Petey, come here and pick up that sandwich?" Should I pick it up myself and throw it into the wastepaper basket? No. They had to recognize I was boss and I was strong. I wasn't going to accept this kind of behavior.

I picked up the sandwich, took it out of its bag, and ate it. It was my first act of classroom management.

Thirty-four boys and girls stared at me in shocked silence. I could see the admiration in their eyes. They'd never seen a teacher pick up a sandwich from the floor and eat it in front of the class before. Sandwich man.

When I'd finished, I made a ball of the paper bag and threw it into the wastepaper basket. The class cheered. "Wow," they said. "Did you see that? He eats the sandwich. He makes the basket. Wow."

I felt in total (　A　) of the classroom. I could do nothing wrong. Fine, except I didn't know what to do next. I was there to teach English, and wondered how to move from a sandwich situation to spelling or grammar.

My students smiled until they saw the principal's face in the door window. He opened the door and said, "A word, Mr. McCourt?" Petey whispered, "Hey, Mister. Don't worry about the sandwich." The class said, "Yeah, yeah," to show me [　③　].

Outside the classroom, he said, "I'm sure you understand, Mr. McCourt, that teachers shouldn't eat their lunch at nine o'clock in the morning in their classrooms in front of these boys and girls. It gives children the wrong idea. What would happen if all the teachers began to eat their lunches in class, especially in the morning? We have enough trouble trying to stop the kids eating in class." I wanted to tell him the truth about the sandwich and how well I'd managed the situation. I wanted to say that it wasn't my sandwich. But if I did, it might be the end of my teaching career. So I said nothing. The principal said he was there to help me because I seemed to need help. "I agree you have acquired their great interest," he said. "But can you do it in a different way? Try teaching. That's why you're here. Teaching. Now that's all. Remember, no eating in class for teacher or students." I said, "Yes, sir," and he waved me back to the classroom.

The class said, "What did he say?" "He said I shouldn't eat my lunch in the classroom at nine o'clock in the morning." "That's (　B　). You weren't eating lunch." Petey said, "I'll tell my mom you liked her sandwich." "All right, Petey, but don't tell her you threw it away." "No, no. She'd kill me."

"Tell her it was the most delicious sandwich I ever had in my life." "OK."

問1　下線部①の具体的内容を本文に即して40字程度の日本語で書け。

問2　次の英文が下線部②における筆者の心情を表したものになるように，(a)，(b)に入る適切な英語1語を書け。

　　　Though the writer knew the student were (a) him at classroom management, he was at a loss how to show he wouldn't (b) them to behave like that.

問3　本文中の[③]に入る適切な英語を次から一つ選び，記号で答えよ。

　ア　they were curious about the principal's punishment for me

　イ　they were on my side even if I had trouble with the principal

　ウ　they were hopeful that I would tell the principal what Petey had done

　エ　they were wondering who to support, Petey or me

問4　次の英文が本文の内容を表したものになるように，(a)〜(c)に入る適切な英語1語を書け。

　　　The principal thought that the writer had eaten his own lunch in front of the students to attract their (a). He wanted to correct the principal's (b), but he kept silent. He thought he might not develop a better (c) with the students if he told the whole story.

問5　本文中の(A)，(B)に入る適切な語を次から一つずつ選び，記号で答えよ。

　ア　control　　イ　despair　　ウ　reasonable　　エ　unfair

問6　What's your first priority in classroom management and why? Write your opinion in about 40 English words. Record your word count in the brackets.

(☆☆☆☆○○○)

解答・解説

【中高共通】

【1】1　ウ　　2　エ　　3　ウ　　4　ア　　5　イ　　6　ウ　　7　エ
8　イ　　9　エ　　10　イ
〈解説〉放送が流れるのは1回だけなので，会話が流れる前に選択肢にざっと目を通しておき，選択肢に関連する情報を耳で追いながら会話を聞いていくと良い。会話と質問の内容自体は難しいものではないが，こういった設問のパターンに慣れていないと慌てて聞き逃すことも有り得るので，TOEICリスニングテスト対策CD等で集中力を養っておくことが望ましい。

【2】1　エ　　2　イ　　3　ウ　　4　ア　　5　ウ
〈解説〉1　児童施設に対するランドセルのプレゼントの話題は，2010年の末にニュースを賑わしたのでピンと来る人も多いだろう。ウ「尊大な」は人の態度を言い表す形容詞なので適切とは言えないが，ア「公的な寄贈」，イ「秘密献金」は文法的にはあてはまる。解答の決め手は後の文の「彼らは知られざる寄贈者に感謝した。」で，エの「匿名の」が適切。　2　問題文は「多くを読み全般的な理解を得ること」の意。選択肢の日本語訳としては，アとエは「速読」，イは「多読」，ウは「精読」で，イがあてはまる。ちなみにアのスキャニングは特定の情報について拾うための速読であり，エのスキミングはざっと目を通して全体的内容を把握するための速読，という違いがある。
3　ディケンズの著作を知っていれば解ける問題。アはMargaret Mitchellの『風とともに去りぬ』，イはMrs. Stoweの『アンクル・トムの小屋』，ウはCharles Dickensの『クリスマス・キャロル』，エはLewis Carrollの『不思議の国のアリス』である。名作の筆者を問う設問は時々あるので，有名な作品は常識としても押さえておきたい。　4　問題文の空欄までは「方略的ストラテジーは，言語的・非言語的コミュニケーシ

ョン戦略を使用する，話し手の能力」で，空欄以下との関係を正しく
示すフレーズとして「(コミュニケーションの失敗を)補償するための」
とするアがあてはまる。イは「(失敗と)比べながらも」，ウは「(失敗
を)ひきおこす目的の」，エは「(失敗の)原因になることに加え」とあ
り，「能力」の定義としては不可解である。　5　spendは時間やお金を
費やすという意味であり，timeを「回数」の意味で使っているアとエ
は動詞と対応しない。また，空欄の後がtoであり，イだと「小学生は
英国人に知られるため多大な時間を費やす」となり意味の上で不可解。
「外国語活動の導入の後，小学生は英語に慣れるよう多大な時間を費
やす。」とするウがあてはまる。

【3】Looking back at English language teaching in Japanese schools, accuracy
has long been emphasized. Learners have been required to use the language in
proper ways based on its grammar. Thanks to this practice, it has been said
that Japanese people generally read and write English properly.

On the other hand, there is a new trend. Many teachers now put emphasis
on communicability in teaching English. In classrooms, learners are
encouraged to actually use the language in various activities even if their
English is not perfect. Many learners gradually learn to communicate in
English. (93語)

〈解説〉「不易」は変わらないこと，「流行」は時代時代で変化することを
言うので，我が国の英語教育におけるそれら2つの面について書けば
良い。どちらか一方についての考察が欠けたり，文法的誤りがある場
合は減点対象となるので注意すること。英語教育の変遷についての設
問は時として出題されるのでしっかり把握しておきたい。また，英作
文は制限語数が50語，100語，200語程度で出題されるので，その長さ
でまとめられるよう書き慣れておくことが望ましい。

【4】問1　学習者に学校外においても役に立つ学習方法を身に付けさせ
るなど，学び方を教えること。　問2　生徒に，自分の言語学習に影

響する様々な要素についての意識を高めさせることと，それらの要素について，自分で考える時間や余裕を与えること。　問3　ウ

問4　「ある言語を学ぶのにどのくらいの時間がかかるか」，「なぜ練習が大切なのか」，「なぜ我々はみんな間違うのか」といったことについて教師と生徒が話し合うこと。　問5　生徒に，どんな活動が，なぜうまく行ったのかを考えさせたり，どんな活動が楽しく，なぜ楽しいのかを考えさせること。そうすることで，後になると，生徒はいろいろな活動をする理由や，それぞれの学習活動から得られるものについて自分で考えるようになること。　問6　ア　　問7　I will advise the student to read English textbooks aloud every day. By doing this, the student will be able to improve his/her pronunciation, read faster, and learn words, phrases and sentence patterns.　(33語)

〈解説〉問1　下線部①「急速に動いて行く私達の世界では，学習者がすべての知識・技術を学校にいる間に習得することは不可能である」が問題提起として「それについてどうすべきか」との考えを導くと考えられるので，続く文にヒントを探す。設問では直後の文が "It is the school's responsibility(以下に述べることは学校の責任である)" で始まっているので，how to以下を解答としてまとめれば良い。　問2　下線部②も①と同様，問題提起をし，それに対する筆者の考えを述べるという構造になっているので，続く文を日本語にまとめれば良い。

問3　接続詞andから，③はplenty of praise(多くの褒め言葉)と並列的な意味を持つと考えられるので，「好意的な反応(positive feedback)」を選択する。他の選択肢はいずれも「褒め言葉」に並ぶ肯定的な意味合いを含まないので，ここにはあてはまらない。　問4　下線部を含む文に「言語学習とは何であるかについての意識を高めることに関連した戦略は，言語学習についての一般的理解を対象とする。」とあり，続く文に，より具体的な内容が示されている。　問5　下線部に続いてfor example(例えば)とあるので，そこに具体的内容が示されると考えて良い。「身に付けさせるための具体的な手立て」という問題なので，teachers can encourage children to(教師は生徒に以下のことを促すことが

可能である)以下を解答として整える。　問6　Direct or cognitive strategies (認知ストラテジー)の説明として,「言語情報を効果的に扱う,すなわち言語情報を整理,分類,記憶する能力を開発すること」とあるが,イ「新しい言語を学習する際の忍耐の必要性についての討議」や,ウ「異なる考え方をする他の生徒の考えを共有する」等は「言語情報の整理,分類,記憶」にはあてはまらない。アは「生徒たちが未知の単語に出会ったとき,接頭辞や接尾辞に注意を向ける」という意味。問7　「学習方法」というテーマに沿って具体的に自分の考えを述べること,その根拠を論理的に説明すること,の2点を踏まえて解答を作成する。日頃から英文を書き慣れておき,文法的誤りなく30語,50語,100語等の文字制限でうまく時間内にまとめる技術を養っておこう。

【中学校】

【1】問1　兄弟が傷ついたり気持ちが不安定になったりしないように,しばしば才能のある子どもを控えめに扱おうとするが,無駄に終わること。　問2　オードリーには学校のコーラスでソロを担当するほど歌が上手い姉がいるが,自分はそれほど上手くなく,自分と姉とを比べられることにうんざりしていたから。　問3　オードリーが何に挑戦しても激励し,一番になれというプレッシャーはかけなかったが,好きなことを楽しんで取り組むように声をかけ,常に支えてくれた。問4　niche　問5　(A)イ　(B)ア　問6　Audrey was more confident in herself than ever before because she could find her own way of expressing herself. She was thankful that her mother always supported her whatever she tried and never gave her too much pressure to do it well.　(42語)

〈解説〉問1　We can't pretend otherwise.の文字通りの意味は「そうではない振りをすることはできない。」となる。otherwiseは何かを基準にした上での「そうではない,他の」という意味であり,その基準となる描写が前後のどこかにある筈なので,それを探す。設問の場合は直後に具体的な説明が書かれているので,それを日本語にすれば良い。問2　問題箇所の直前の第2段落に,この言葉が発せられるまでのいき

269

さつが記されている。　問3　Thanks to her encouragement(彼女の勇気づけのおかげで)という表現は最初のステートメントというより，それまでに語られてきたことをまとめるニュアンスがある。したがって，オードリーがコーラスのオーディションを拒否した最初のエピソードの後の段落からざっと目を通し，具体的な描写を探す。　問4　下線部④は「彼女が自分のままで居ることができ，自分だけの領域を作り出せる場」という意味なので，「得意分野，領域」を意味するnicheがあてはまる。　問5　（　A　）を含む段落には，Audreyが本当に楽しんで没頭できる世界を発見する過程が書かれている。最初の文にはそれ以前に彼女が取り組んだいろいろな分野が列挙されており，それらが最終的ゴールではなかったことが示されているので，冒頭は「出だしの失敗をいくつか経た後」と考えられる。　（　B　）を含む段落の直前に，Audreyが学校新聞に関るという自分の世界を発見した経緯が書かれている。extraは「余分の，追加の」という意味であり，自分の領域を得たことに加えて何か別のものを得たと考えられる。不定冠詞のanがあることから，可算名詞のア，ウに可能性があるが，学校生活についての文なのでjobはあてはまらない。オマケとして発見した新たな能力のことを「余分のボーナス」と表現している。　問6　下線部⑤に続く文に「彼女は何も言う必要がなかった。彼女の顔に浮かんだプライドと感謝の表情がすべてを物語っていた。」とあり，それが解答になるわけだが，条件として40語程度とあるので，"pride and gratitude"の内容を具体的に説明することが必要である。ここでは「自分の場所を発見して得た自信」と「プレッシャーをかけずに支援してくれた母への感謝」がポイントとなる。

【高等学校】

【1】問1　初日に，自分の席に着いたままでいたら，生徒を恐れているという印象を与えてしまうこと。　問2　(a) testing　(b) allow
問3　イ　問4　(a) attention　(b) misunderstanding
(c) relationship　問5　(A) ア　(B) エ　問6　My first priority
in classroom management is to get trust from students. I think we teachers
sometimes have to be strict with students. When we discipline them, they
won't listen to us without any trust in us.　(37 words)

〈解説〉問1　「そのような間違い(such a mistake)」とあるので，前にその内容が書かれていると判断する。さかのぼって読んで見ると，If you
sit at the desk they think you're scared.(デスクに着いていると，彼らはあなたが怯えていると考える)とあるので，その部分を解答として整える。
問2　(a)　下線部は「クラス(の生徒達)はじっと待った。この新任の先生はどう出るかな？」といった意味。この部分は前の段落の最後，生徒を殴り倒したいがそうはできない状況の補足説明となっている。つまり，挑発に乗って力に訴えれば信頼は得られないし，かと言って悪い態度を放置すればクラスの管理はできないというジレンマである。そこで，「クラスの管理能力を試されている(testing)のは知りつつも，生徒のそのような行いを許さない(wouldn't allow)ことをどう示せばよいか途方に暮れている」という心情となる。　問3　Peteyの "Don't
worry"，他の生徒たちの "Yeah, yeah" というささやきから，筆者への肯定的な態度が読み取れる。一方，他の選択肢の「校長による罰則」，「校長への告げ口」，「どちらをサポートするかの迷い」と言った要素を示唆する箇所は本文にない。　問4　(a)　校長の言葉に「あなたが生徒の関心を多いに集めたことは認めます(I agree you have acquired 〜.)」とある。　(b)　校長とのやり取りについて「私は真実を話し，その状況にどんなにうまく対処したか話したかった」とあり，すなわち「誤解を解きたかった」となる。　(c)　文中「しかしそれを話すことは自分の教師としてのキャリアを終わらせるかもしれない」とあり，「校長に生徒の行いを告げ口することが，生徒との良い関係を築く妨げに

なるかもしれない」との心情を表現している。　問5　(A)　total control of the classroomで「クラスの完全な掌握」。思いがけない行動に出たことで主導権を握った様子を表している。　(B)　筆者が自分の弁当をはやばやと食べた，と校長が誤解したことに対して「それは不当だ」と言っている。　問6　クラス管理における最優先事項について受験者に自分の考えを英語で書かせる問題。解答は「生徒の信頼を得ること」とあるが，これはあくまでも一例であり，自分が教師として教室で何を優先していくか自由に解答して良い。英文記述の問題の文字制限は40語，50語，100語その他いろいろなケースがあるので，何語でどれくらい盛り込めるかを日頃から把握しておくこと。

2011年度　実施問題

【中高共通】

【1】聞き取りテスト

　これから1～10の英語を1回ずつ放送します。それぞれの英語のあとに，その内容について質問を一つします。その質問に対する答として最も適当なものをア～エの中から一つずつ選び，その記号で答えなさい。

1　ア　Her homeland.　　　　　　イ　Her return flight.
　　ウ　The length of her stay.　　エ　The reason for her trip.

2　ア　At a police station.　　　　イ　At a school library.
　　ウ　At a stadium.　　　　　　エ　At a theater.

3　ア　A dentist.　　　　　　　　イ　A nurse.
　　ウ　A receptionist.　　　　　　エ　A teacher.

4　ア　In her brown bag.　　　　　イ　In her office.
　　ウ　In her pocket.　　　　　　エ　In her red bag.

5　ア　Eight years old.　　　　　　イ　Fifteen years old.
　　ウ　Twenty-two years old.　　　エ　Twenty-five years old.

6　ア　He brought her lunch.　　　イ　He gave her a present.
　　ウ　He offered assistance.　　　エ　He put off a deadline.

7　ア　Its design.　　　　　　　　イ　Its material.
　　ウ　Its price.　　　　　　　　エ　Its size.

8　ア　It's 3 : 00.　　　　　　　　イ　It's 3 : 10.
　　ウ　It's 3 : 20.　　　　　　　エ　It's 3 : 30.

9　ア　He forgot about the test.　　イ　He practiced playing soccer.
　　ウ　He didn't like chemistry.　　エ　He didn't study enough.

10　ア　To explain road construction.　イ　To give traffic information.
　　ウ　To offer weather information.　エ　To sell a new type of car.

（☆☆☆◎◎◎）

273

【2】次の各文の(　　)に入る最も適当な英語をア〜エの中から一つずつ選び，その記号で答えよ。

1　Japan and San Marino in Europe have the world's longest life (　　) at 83 years, according to the World Health Organization.

　　ア　expansion　　イ　expectancy　　ウ　expenditure
　　エ　exponent

2　Under a parliamentary system of government, a (　　) parliament is a legislature in which no political party has an absolute majority of seats.

　　ア　halfway　　イ　hidden　　ウ　humble　　エ　hung

3　A lingua franca is a shared language of communication used by people (　　).

　　ア　whose main languages are different
　　イ　whose profession relates to apparel
　　ウ　who have no knowledge of economics
　　エ　who research into SLA in Europe

4　(　　) eating lunch before many students entered the teachers' room to ask me questions.

　　ア　Hardly did I finish　　　　イ　Hardly had I finished
　　ウ　No sooner did I finish　　　エ　No sooner had I finished

5　(　　), elementary school teachers are preparing for complete introduction of Foreign Language Activities.

　　ア　Having released the new Courses of Study
　　イ　The new Courses of Study having been released
　　ウ　Having the new Courses of Study released
　　エ　The new Courses of Study were released

(☆☆☆◎◎)

【3】次の文を読んで，あなたが思ったことや考えたことを90語程度の英語で書け。なお，使用した語数を記入すること。

　「一生懸命指導しましたけれど，お宅のお子さん，どうもうまくおできになりません。」私は，そういうことは，教師として言うべきでは

ない。教師が一個の職業だというんなら言ってはいけないと思います。

『教えるということ』大村はま(共文社)より

(☆☆☆◎◎◎)

【4】次の英文を読んで，後の各問に答えよ。

Anyone who has taught knows the importance of student motivation. The best technology, curriculum, and assessments don't make a difference if the students don't want to learn. Great technology and curriculum may help by connecting with student interests, but if the students are more motivated to put their energy into something outside of learning, they will.

From the moment we're born, we're motivated to learn. Almost without exception, every student is motivated to learn something. Unfortunately, many students are more motivated to learn things other than what we're trying to teach them. ①The problem is not that many students aren't motivated to learn, it's that they're not motivated to learn what we're teaching or in the way that they're being expected to learn.

If we're asking the question, "What can we do to motivate our students?" we're asking the wrong question. No one can motivate someone else, and yet, for years we've tried to motivate students. We've tried just about ②every trick that can be imagined. We've tried awards, points, notes to parents, prizes, grades, names on boards, honors, and scholarships. Over the years, we've discovered that these extrinsic motivators can be powerful and work for short periods of time. Unfortunately, they soon become either not enough, or demotivators for many students, or both.

I give you ③two movies to show the importance of motivation. In the movie *Brave Heart*, we can see the power of intrinsic motivation. No matter what the potential reward or punishment, the Scotsmen could not be pulled from their quest for freedom. In the movie *Stand and Deliver*, we learned the power of student motivation. In this story, Jaime, a teacher, convinced his students of two things — that they could learn and that what he had to teach was important.

The struggle is not in how to motivate students to learn. The struggle is in creating lessons and classroom environments that focus and attract students' intrinsic motivation. Fortunately a lot has been learned about how to create lessons and classroom situations that are "motivating." They can be designed to adhere to pre-determined standards. These standards for lessons and classrooms increase the probability students will value the learning enough so that they will choose to focus their energies on learning what is being taught.

There are principles and standards that are essential for establishing and maintaining a highly motivating classroom.

Two principles maximize student motivation for learning in a classroom. The first principle is operating from understanding. If we are to be successful in increasing the levels of student motivation in our classroom, teachers must make decisions based on a total understanding of our students' needs. The second principle is managing context not students. Focus not on how to make students do or want to do something ; instead, focus on creating situations in which students will want to do what needs to be done. The musical lyric "... ④a spoonful of sugar makes the medicine go down" is very helpful in clarifying the principle "manage context, not students." It is not suggesting that sugar be offered as a bribe ; the implied suggestion is to change the situation (context) so the child is more likely to choose to do what is desired. Note that the lyric does not suggest "watering down" the medicine, bribing the child, promising future benefits, or threatening punishment. If the lyric had been written about school and not medicine, it might have been something like, "a motivating teacher helps the students to learn."

Six standards enhance student motivation for learning in a classroom.

Valuable　: If the students believe what they are being asked to do or learn is more valuable than the other options they consider available, they will (A) in the learning.

Involving : People need to feel involved or included in groups in which they are a part.

Successful : People tend to continue or repeat those things in which they are successful. Feelings of success can come from successfully mastering something or from regular evidence of (B) with a complex endeavor.

Safe : Students must feel safe from any physical danger and fear of significant embarrassment.

Caring : People have a basic need to feet loved, valued, and to have a sense of belonging.

Enabling : Students learn in different ways. If learning needs are not met, students will most likely not meet with success and their motivation for learning will (C).

問1　下線部①を本文に即して30字程度の日本語で具体的に説明せよ。

問2　下線部②の問題点は何か。本文に即して35字程度の日本語で書け。

問3　下線部③の映画から教師が教室で心がけるべきことは何か。本文に即して30字程度の日本語で書け。

問4　下線部④を具体的に示している箇所を抜き出し，英語で書け。

問5　本文中の(A)～(C)に入る最も適当な語を次から一つずつ選び，その記号で答えよ。

　　ア　diminish　　イ　engage　　ウ　increase　　エ　lie
　　オ　occupy　　カ　practice　　キ　progress

問6　次の英文が本文の内容に合うように，(a)～(c)に最も適当な英語を1語ずつ本文から抜き出して書け。

　　Though (a) motivators are powerful, they can become demotivators in the long-run. To encourage our students to study, we should improve our lessons and classroom atmosphere instead of telling them that they are guaranteed their (b). Six standards help students have the feelings which tend to be present when people are in states of (c) motivation.

（☆☆☆☆◎◎◎◎）

【中学校】

【１】次の英文を読んで，後の各問に答えよ。

I know my students. Masses of awkward seventh graders swarm the halls of my rural middle school each day. I watch them from my classroom door and smile at the fact that I can call each one by name.

①I know their secrets, their stories. Jay can pitch like a tenth grader, but I know he doesn't really even like baseball that much (he plays because his dad wants him to). The kids think Keith is just the class clown, but I know of his dreams to become an astronaut. I know my students because I am their writing teacher. They trust me with their stories and so I am given the privilege of having a secret bond with each and every one of them.

I teach my students about the power of words, and I try to let them find release and expression through writing. We learn to trust each other in writing class because we learn how hard it is to write openly and honestly, and we learn that sharing your words takes courage. I see courage every day in my classroom, and I am always amazed at the words that come from my students' hearts.

One such example of courage took place during ②author's chair, a sharing session at the end of our writer's workshop in which students volunteer to share what they have written. We had a new student to the school, Paul. Paul was small and, with his dimpled cheeks and baby face, he looked younger than his classmates. In fact, when Paul was first introduced to the class two weeks earlier, one student said, "You're not in the seventh grade. You're a baby."

To that, Paul quickly responded, "I'm Paul Billslington, and I am in the seventh grade."

Despite his obvious courage, Paul had been with us for only a short while and was still trying to fit in, so ③I was a little surprised when he volunteered to read during author's chair. I had one of those teacher moments, when I smiled and nodded for him to read, while inside I said a silent prayer that the

other students would not tease the new kid after he read. The room fell
(　A　), and Paul began to read.

"If I had one wish, it would be to meet my dad..." He started out loud and
clear and held the attention of my usually restless seventh graders as he read
on for what seemed like fifteen minutes. He told of how he had never known
his father, who had left the family when Paul was a baby. He shared the
intimate details of his struggles to be the only man in the house at such a
young age, of having to mow the lawn and fix broken pipes. He revealed to us
the thoughts that raced through his mind constantly about where his father
might be and why he might have left.

My eyes scanned the room for snickering faces of seventh-grade kids who I
knew were prone to jump at a weakness and try to crack a joke, but there were
no snickers. There were no rolling eyes or gestures insinuating boredom or
pending attacks. All of my seventh-grade students were listening, really
listening. Their eyes were on Paul, and they were absorbing his words like
sponges. My heart was (　B　).

Paul continued on, telling of nightmares of never knowing a man so
important to him, yet so unreal. I could hear his voice growing shaky as he
read such passionate and honest words, and I saw a tear roll down one of his
dimpled cheeks. I looked to the audience. There were tears on Jessica's face
and on the faces of a few others seated quietly, intently listening.

They are letting him do this, I thought. They are allowing him to share
something he perhaps has never shared before, and they have no intention of
judging him or teasing him. I felt a lump in my own throat.

Paul finished, struggling now to read his last sentence. "If I had one wish, it
would be to meet my dad, so I wouldn't..." His tears were rolling, and so were
ours, "... so I wouldn't have to close my eyes in bed every night just
wondering what he looks like."

Without any cue from me, the class stood up and applauded. Paul smiled
from ear to ear as they all rushed him with hugs. I was (　C　).

　　This is why I teach. I teach because I am allowed to learn the stories behind the faces. I teach because I can watch kids grow and laugh and learn and love. I teach because of students like Paul.

問1　下線部①の理由を，本文に即して70字程度の日本語で説明せよ。

問2　下線部②をとおして生徒に知ってもらいたいと筆者が考えていることは何か，本文に即して20字程度の日本語で答えよ。

問3　下線部③の理由を表した次の英文の(　a　)〜(　d　)に入る英語をそれぞれ1語で答えよ。

　　Paul did not have a chance to get (　a　) to the class. Paul was (　b　) to the school only a few weeks ago. Also, as he didn't look like a seventh grader because of his (　c　), he even had been made (　d　) of by a student.

問4　Paulの話を生徒はどのような態度で聞いたか。次の英文の(　a　)，(　b　)に入る語を本文中から1語ずつ抜き出して書け。

　　There was no sign of (　a　) him. Students were just listening to the speech without judging him, and seemed to (　b　) Paul's words.

問5　本文中(　A　)〜(　C　)に入る最も適当な語を次のア〜カから一つずつ選び，その記号で答えよ。

　　ア　flat　　イ　floored　　ウ　full　　エ　shaped　　オ　silent
　　カ　sober

問6　筆者の授業のあり方についてのあなたの考えを30語程度の英語で書け。なお，使用した語数も書くこと。

(☆☆☆☆◎◎◎◎)

【高等学校】

【 1 】 次の英文を読んで，後の各問に答えよ。

Joe and Sally asked if I would spend some time with Nancy, their 15-year-old, mentally challenged daughter. Nancy had been placed in a special needs class in a public high school and was reading at a third-grade level. The kids at school bullied her and called her "dummy" and "retard." These words were severe enough to hurt her. The stress had caused Nancy to have headaches and stomachaches, and to bite her nails until they bled. Though she hadn't experienced any trouble of that kind in elementary school, blossoming into womanhood in high school and being rejected proved very difficult and painful for her.

"We think," Sally said to me, "that you might be able to help her understand why she is the way she is and find some peace with it. Would you please try to help?" I agreed, and the family drove four hours to my home the following weekend. I allowed Nancy some time to get comfortable with me before we started. When Nancy seemed relaxed enough, I began to speak. "Nancy, why do you think the kids in school are bullying you?" "Uh, I don't know," Nancy replied. She stared down at the table-top and twisted her fingers. "Why do you think you chew your fingernails?" I continued. Again she replied, "Uh, I don't know," and avoided eye contact. Her answers to my third and fourth questions garnered the same apathetic response. ①<u>I was at a loss as to how to handle her.</u> In desperation, I asked myself the magical question I always ask when I don't know what to do : *What would LOVE do?*

I suddenly felt myself shudder and shift and began to feel really nasty and ugly. "No wonder everybody calls you a dummy and a retard," I mocked. "You keep saying, 'Uh, I don't know,' to every question. If I kept hearing that all the time, I'd call you a dummy and a retard too." Part of me was shocked to hear what had issued from my mouth. Was this the answer I received to my question of what would LOVE do? I let it continue. I babbled on and on for at least a minute, mocking her, repeating what the kids in school had said to her.

②<u>Oh my God! What was happening?</u> I felt a strange mixture of panic on the outside, and stole a furtive glance at Nancy's parents to see how they were affected by this, yet inside I felt a deep stillness. I had never spoken to anybody in such a callous and demeaning way, especially to someone with special needs. I could sense that her parents were shocked.

Though my words and behavior shocked me, and though I was aware of her parents' concerns and could feel Nancy withdraw, I knew I had to trust that what was happening was supposed to happen and I let this process continue. "Please, God, help me to help your child," I prayed. I let go of any attempt to control what was happening. "Do you believe God is inside you?" I asked firmly. "Uh-huh" she whispered. "Good!" I snapped. "From this moment on I don't want to hear another word from you!" I suddenly felt my body shudder and shift and become my usual calm self again. I said softly, "I want you to let God use your tongue, your breath, your mind. I want you to let God do all the talking." "Okay," she replied shyly. ③<u>For 15 minutes, she spoke confidently, with no hesitation, clearly enunciating every word.</u> She told us why she chose her parents, and why they were perfect for her life's expression.

When I asked the next question we were not ready for her reply. "Why did your soul choose a body that would look and act retarded?" She paused and smiled. "That's so simple," she whispered, "I came to teach LOVE. It would be easy for you to love me if I looked like you and walked like you and talked like you. But will you still love me when I drool, when I chew my nails until they bleed? Will you still love me when you have to change my diaper? I came to teach LOVE." A sacred hush filled the room. I couldn't speak. Her true beauty and grace and the courage of her soul took my breath away. Tears filled my eyes. Many hugs and more tears were exchanged before Sally and Joe took Nancy and left for home.

Nancy had remembered ④<u>her mission</u> and had allowed God's Voice to speak through her. Joe and Sally saw the perfection of their child and realized how they were to serve her. Two months afterward I received a card from

Sally informing me Nancy was going for her first professional manicure because "God doesn't want me to chew my fingernails anymore." She added that Nancy hardly said "Uh, I don't know" anymore, and had been invited to join a girl's club.

問1　ハイスクール入学後のナンシーにとって苦痛や困難になっていることを二つ，本文に即してそれぞれ日本語で書け。

問2　下線部①の理由を本文に即して40字程度の日本語で書け。

問3　次の英文は下線部②のように心の中で叫んだ時の筆者の心境を説明している。英文中の(　a　)〜(　c　)に最も適当な英語を1語ずつ本文から抜き出して書け。

　　I myself was (　a　) that I had said things that would (　b　) Nancy, but I felt something (　c　) in my mind.

問4　下線部③のように状況が変わった理由を本文に即して40字程度の日本語で書け。

問5　次の英文は下線部④の内容を説明している。英文中の(　a　)〜(　c　)に最も適当な英語を1語ずつ書け。

　　Though it is not (　a　) for us to love those whose appearances or behaviors are (　b　) to ours, but it is to love people like Nancy. If we can (　c　) Nancy as she is and love her, our love is true. The existence of Nancy teaches us the essence of love.

問6　あなたが生徒にカウンセリングをするとすれば，どのような工夫をするか。本文に出てくる事例を参考にして40語程度の英語で書け。なお，使用した語数も書くこと。

(☆☆☆○○○○○)

解答・解説

【中高共通】

【1】1　ウ　　2　イ　　3　ウ　　4　ア　　5　ウ　　6　ウ　　7　ア
　　8　イ　　9　エ　　10　イ

〈解説〉1　How long are you going to stay in Japan? 日本での滞在期間を尋
ねている。　　2　books, shelf, readingなどのキーワードを選択的に聴
き取る必要がある。学校図書館が正解。　　3　トピックがreservationに
関することから，女性の職業は受付であることがわかる。　　4　昨日
はbrown bagを身に着けていたことを指摘されていることからアとな
る。　　5　15＋7＝22となる。　　6　女性は仕事を手伝うことを申し出
ている。　　7　cool pattern という指摘を聴き取る。　　8　ten past threeが
正しい。　　9　ケビンが遅くまでサッカーの試合を見ていたことから，
勉強不足だとわかる。　　10　交通情報に関するトピック。

【2】1　イ　　2　エ　　3　ア　　4　イ　　5　イ

〈解説〉1　life expectancy：平均余命　　2　hung parliament：絶対多数政
党のない議会　　3　lingua francaの定義が問われる。　　4　否定の副詞
hardly ＋ 大過去の用法に注意。　　5　現在完了受動態及び分詞構文の
用法を整理しておきたい。

【3】（解答例）　This reminds teachers to be proud of themselves as a
professional. "Though I have been trying so hard, nothing changes…" is just
an excuse by teachers to protect themselves by attributing some bad result to
students. This kind of excuse would never work in other kinds of professions.
Teachers should never forget that teaching students to learn to do what they
can't yet do is their job. I would like to be a professional and I will always
keep studying to improve myself as a teacher. (87語)

〈解説〉教師の信念について自論を展開するよう求められている。評価基

準としては，内容の適切さ，論の展開および分量，語彙・文法の適切さの3点が挙げられている。求められる内容としては高度ではないので，教師としての職業観をおさえた上で，難易度の高い語彙や文型は避け，簡易な表現を用いて着実に自分なりの文章を組み立てればよい。

【4】問1 （解答例） 教師が教える内容や期待する学び方では，生徒は学ぶ意欲を持てないこと。 問2 （解答例） すぐに効果が薄れるか，逆にやる気を失わせるか，またはその両方であること。

問3 （解答例） 生徒の内的動機付けとなるような授業や環境を創造すること。 問4 to change the situation (context) so the child is more likely to choose to do what is desired. 問5 A イ B キ C ア

問6 a extrinsic b future (success) c intrinsic

〈解説〉問1 10行目it's that以降 問2 18行目Unfortunately以降

問3 第4段落と第5段落で生徒の内的動機付けの重要性について述べられている。 問4 下線部を直訳すると「スプーン1杯の砂糖」だが，これが暗示していること (implied suggestion) として45行目に示されている 問5 A engage in ～ 「～に従事する」 B たくさん努力して「向上」すること C 学習のニーズが満たされないと，生徒の学ぶ意欲は「減少する」 問6 a 第3段落参照 b 第7段落参照 c 第4，5段落参照

【中学校】

【1】問1 （解答例） 生徒は作文の先生である筆者を信頼して自分自身のことについて書き，そのため筆者は彼ら一人一人と秘密のきずなをもつ特権を与えられていたから。 問2 （解答例） ことばを分かちあうことは勇気がいるということ。 問3 a…used (accustomed)
b…transferred c…appearance d…fun 問4 a…teasing
b…share 問5 A オ B ウ C イ

問6 （解答例） I agree with the author. Students tend to talk only with their friends. If students have chance to share their words, they will come to know each other and broaden their friendships.　(32語)

〈解説〉問1　第2段落の最終文参照　　問2　先行段落から第6段落にかけてcourageについて書かれている　　問3　a　get used to ～「～に慣れる」，b　Paulはnew studentとあるように「転校生」である，c　Paulはsmallでbaby faceという「外見」から幼く見えた，d　make fun of ～「～をからかう」　　問4　a，bともに第10段落参照　　問5　A　Paulが読むことに対し，教室は「静まりかえった」，B　Paulに心が「満たされた」，C　Paulに生徒みんなが駆け寄り，筆者は「倒された」
問6　筆者の授業のあり方と，それに対する自分の考えを明確に書くこと。このような英作文では初めに自分の立場を明記し，それを支持する理由を付加する形で書くと非常に良い。

【高等学校】

【1】問1　(解答例)　・少女から大人の女性へと成長していくこと。
・他の生徒からいじめをうけていること　　問2　(解答例)　・何回質問をしても「わからない。」という返事だけで，話をしようという気がないから。　問3　a…shocked　　b…hurt　　c…calm
問4　(解答例)・私がナンシーに，彼女の中にいる神様に彼女のかわりに話をさせなさいと提案したから。　　問5　a…difficult (hard)
b…similar (comparable)　　c…accept (encourage)
問6　(解答例)　・I would try to be patient and tolerant enough for my students to start talking about their own problems. They may be able to find what their problems really are through expressing themselves like Nancy realizing her own mission.　(39語)

〈解説〉問1　Nancyの抱える問題を２つ答える問題。第1段落の最終文を参照。　問2　「私」が途方にくれた理由を記述する。第2段落後半，質問に対しNancyが何度も同じ答えを繰り返したことが書かれている。
問3　問題文の空所補充問題。第3段落，Nancyを傷つける言葉を発した後の「私」の動揺と平穏を読み取る。　　問4　内容記述問題。第4段落，「私」はNancy自身ではなく，彼女の中に住む「神様」に話させる

ことを提案する。　問5　問題文の空所補充問題。第5段落，神様の力を借りたNancyの言葉を読み取る。　問6　自由記述問題。解答例のようにNancyが心を開くのを気長に待つことも1つの方法である。または「私」のように機転を利かせた方法を用いてもよい。

2010年度　実施問題

【中高共通】

【１】聞き取りテスト

これから１〜10の英語を１回ずつ放送します。それぞれの英語のあとに，その内容について質問を一つします。その質問に対する答として最も適当なものをア〜エの中から一つずつ選び，その記号で答えなさい。

1　M: How about watching a movie on TV?

W: Don't bother me, Tom. I have lots of work to finish.

Question (M): What is the woman most likely to do?

ア　Do her work.　　イ　Go to a movie theater.

ウ　Take a nap.　　エ　Watch a movie on TV.

2　M: I've waited for you for nearly an hour. I was worried that you might have had an accident.

W: Well, you know this is rush hour. The streets were very busy.

Question (M): What is this woman doing?

ア　She is asking directions.　　イ　She is introducing herself.

ウ　She is making an excuse.　　エ　She is showing her gratitude.

3　M: Did you go to the festival yesterday?

W: No. I went to the dentist because I had a terrible toothache. How about you?

M: Me neither. I went to the hospital to see my friend. She had surgery.

Question (W): What did the man do yesterday?

ア　He went to the festival with his friend.

イ　He went to the hospital to see his friend.

ウ　He went to the hospital to have surgery.

エ　He went to the dentist to get his teeth fixed.

4　M: What's wrong with you?

W: I feel chilly and have a headache.

M: I recommend you go home and see a doctor.

You don't need to hand in your assignment tomorrow.

W: Thank you.

Question (M) : Who is talking?

ア　A doctor and a patient.　　イ　A teacher and a student.

ウ　A pharmacist and a customer.　エ　A father and a daughter.

5　M: Why is it so crowded here today? Is there a summer sale?

W: No. I've heard a famous actor is coming here soon.

M: Well, why don't we wait and see who it is?

Question (W) : What is the man probably going to do?

ア　Buy a concert ticket.　　イ　Drive to work.

ウ　Stay at the place.　　　　エ　Go to a summer sale.

6　(W) Last night I decided to eat out after work. The restaurant where I often eat was closed when I got there. So I ended up buying sandwiches and a salad at a store. They were good.

Question (M) : What did the woman do for dinner last night?

ア　She bought food at a shop and ate it.

イ　She cooked dinner at home.

ウ　She ate dinner at her favorite restaurant.

エ　She ordered pizza and ate it at home.

7　M: How often do you work at your part-time job?

W: Five times a week.

M: How much do you get a day?

W: 6,000 yen.

Question (M) : How much does the woman earn a week?

ア　6,000 yen.　　イ　12,000 yen.

ウ　20,000 yen.　　エ　30,000 yen.

8　M: It's a pity that not so many people came to the concert.

W: How many people were there in the hall?

M: There were three thousand seats in the hall, but only one third of them were taken.

Question (W) :How many people came to the concert?

ア　About 1,000 people.　イ　About 2,000 people.

ウ　About 3,000 people.　ウ　About 4,000 people.

9　M: Can I have your vegetarian option, please?

W: Certainly. Today we have seaweed soup and salad with cheese.

M: I'm sorry but I don't eat dairy products.

W: We can take it off if you like.

M: Yes, I'd like you to. Thank you.

Question (W) : What will the man have?

ア　Seaweed salad.

イ　Seaweed soup and salad with cheese.

ウ　Seaweed salad without cheese.

エ　Seaweed soup and salad without cheese.

10　M: We are going to sing songs at our school festival. How about your class?

W: We want to do something concerning international cooperation. Children born into poverty are more likely to die in their early years of life because of a lack of vaccinations.

M: Are you going to do a campaign to collect funds?

W: No. On the day of the school festival we will have an exhibition of information in our classroom about actual circumstances of developing countries. To make the exhibition better, we are going to listen to an expert's lecture a few weeks before the school festival.

Question (M) : What is the girl's class most likely to do on the day of the school festival?

ア　Do a campaign to set up funds for children in developing countries.

イ　Listen to an expert's lecture to gain information about poverty.

ウ　Exhibit information in her classroom about developing countries.

エ　Sing songs with her classmates to get money for poor children.

以上で英語の聞き取りテストを終わります。次の問題に進みなさい。

(☆☆○○○)

【2】次の各文の(　　　)に入る最も適当な語(句)をア～エの中から一つ
ずつ選び，その記号で答えよ。

1　Mr. Barack Obama's (　　　) address, first speech as president, interested
many people all over the world.

　　ア　illegible　　イ　inaugural　　ウ　inherent　　エ　irrelevant

2　It's important to (　　　) your metabolism if you would like to lose your
weight.

　　ア　decrease　　イ　lower　　ウ　pile　　エ　raise

3　PISA stands for "Programme for International Student (　　　)."

　　ア　Agreement　　イ　Alliance　　ウ　Aptitude　　エ　Assessment

4　Please tell her to wait until I come back (　　　) she come while I am
away.

　　ア　could　　イ　might　　ウ　should　　エ　would

5　The new Course of Study says "a zest for living" is (　　　) needed in
what we call a knowledge-based society than before.

　　ア　any less　　イ　any more　　ウ　no less　　エ　no more

(☆☆○○○)

【3】次のテーマについて，賛成か反対の立場を明確にしてあなたの意見
を90語程度の英語で述べよ。

なお，使用した語数を記入すること。

国際社会に生きる日本人として，生徒に英語によるコミュニケーシ
ョン能力を身に付けさせることは重要である。

(☆☆☆○○○)

【4】 次の英文を読んで，後の各問に答えよ。

One of the major themes in current research on teacher development is a constructivist approach to development that highlights the active and responsible role of teachers to forge their own personal frameworks within their respective situated contexts. Teachers are trained and continue their training in "①communities of practice" in which teachers of varying degrees of experience carry out their roles as practicing technicians who learn from each other. We best fulfill the goal of professional development not through a "transmission" model of education in which knowledge is simply deposited into the brains of teachers, but through a process model in which teachers learn and continue to develop their skill in dialogue with a professional community.

Are you doing the best you can do? Or are you satisfied with getting by? In the stressful (but rewarding) world of teaching, it's easier than you might imagine to slip into ②a pattern of just keeping a step ahead of your students as you struggle through long working hours and cope with large classes. This pattern is the beginning of a downward spiral that you should avoid at all costs. How do you do that? In part by practicing the behaviors of peak performers, people who are reaching their fullest potential and therefore who, in turn, reap success. Consider the following five maxims among many peak performers that you might apply to yourself, even at this early stage in your career:

1. [　　③　　]

Teaching is no easy profession. It requires deep dedication, a willingness to work long hours, a genuine desire to help other people, cognizance of a professional core of knowledge, an ability to be "on tap" in front of students many hours in a day, and more. Are you up to the (possibly) daunting prospect of being a teacher? Almost every "formula" for success begins with the importance of believing that you are fully capable of undertaking the tasks at hand. So, at the outset, you need to be convinced that you can indeed be a teacher and be an excellent one!

2. Set realistic goals.

Peak performers know their limitations and strengths and their feelings and needs, and then set goals that will be realistic within this framework. They set their own goals and don't let the world around them dictate goals to them. If you have a sense of overall purpose in your career as a mission, then this mission will unfold in the form of daily, weekly, monthly, or annual goals. It's always a good idea to write down some short-term and long-term goals. Be realistic in terms of what you can accomplish. Be specific in your statements.

3. Set priorities.

It's crucial that you have a sense of what is most important, what is least important, and everything in between in your professional goals and tasks. If you don't, you can end up spending too much time on low-priority tasks that rob you of the time you should be spending on higher priorities.

4. Take risks.

Peak performers don't play it safe all the time. They are not afraid to try new things. Nor are they put off by limiting circumstances: what cannot be done, or "the way" things are done. They don't linger in the safety of a "comfort zone"; instead, they reach out for new challenges. The key to risk taking as a peak performance strategy, however, is not simply in taking the risks. It is in learning from your "failures." When you risk a new technique in the classroom, try a new approach to a difficult student, or make a frank comment to a supervisor, you must be willing to accept possible "failure" in your attempt. Then you evaluate all the facets of that failure and turn it into an experience that teaches you something about how to anticipate the next risk.

5. Reduce and manage stress factors.

Teaching is a career with all the makings for high-stress conditions. Think of some of the sources of stress in this business: pressure to "perform" in the classroom, high student expectations, pressure to keep up with a rapidly changing field, and so on. Managing those potential stress factors is an important key to keeping yourself fresh, creative, bright, and happy.

(出典：H.Douglas Brown 2007. *Teaching by Principles,An Interactive Approach to Language Pedagogy*－一部改作)

問1　筆者は下線部①を具体的にどのようなものであるととらえているか。本文に即して30字程度の日本語で書け。

問2　筆者は下線部②のような状況をどうすべきだと考えているか。理由も含めて，35字程度の日本語で書け。

問3　本文の趣旨に合うように，本文中の[　　③　　]に適当なタイトルを3語以内の英語で書け。

問4　筆者はなぜ「危険を冒す」ことを推奨しているのか。その理由を本文に即して80字以内の日本語で書け。

問5　the second maximの内容を踏まえて，あなたの英語教師としての目標を30語程度の英語で書け。なお，使用した語数を記入すること。

(☆☆☆☆◎◎◎)

【5】次の英文を読んで，後の各問に答えよ。

　　Growing up, I had an older sister and brother, Mary and John. Each day, we walked down the block to attend St. Joseph's Grammar School in a little country town on Long Island called Lake Ronkonkoma. Mary was smart, worked very hard, and did extremely well in school. John was just as smart and worked as hard, but did poorly. It would be decades before we discovered that my brother had a form of dyslexia that caused him to perceive each word on a page as floating, which required him to strain his eyes to settle it down. While he reads quite well today, throughout his younger years ①it was a traumatic experience, since no one in those days were trained to diagnose or treat dyslexia.

　　Most of the Catholic nuns who taught us were dedicated teachers. Since we were seated each semester according to our grade average in class, John was always assigned the last seats of the back row. The nuns were often particularly harsh to those in the last row — especially Sister Smith. Those kids were generally labeled "poorly motivated."

Years passed. The three of us siblings moved away from our town to the far corners of the country and made our way. Although I reside in California, visits to the home of John on Long Island are always wonderful. On one such trip a few years ago, John said to me, "[A]" I replied to him, "Well, I'd like to very much, but I'm quite surprised you want to go." We hopped in his car and off we went to "The Lake." We drove by our old house, and John suggested to me, "Diane, this is a good chance. Don't you think we should visit our old grammar school?" I was surprised and said, "Do you really want to return there? I'm afraid many of your memories in the school are still painful."

We entered the school yard, and John made another suggestion that absolutely shocked me: "②Let's go over to the convent where the nuns live." I said, "John, I'm certain that all the nuns we knew have retired. [B]" John said, "It may sound crazy, but if Sister Smith is still there, I have something to tell her..." I interrupted him impatiently, "What would you like to say to her?" He didn't answer my question, but John strongly insisted that we needed to go. I followed his lead and approached the convent. We noticed that in the small garden was someone with her back to us dressed in a black habit. We walked up behind the person, and as she turned around, my heart skipped a beat. It couldn't be, but it was: Sister Smith, now some 90-plus years of age.

Startled, she asked who was there, saying her eyes had failed her long ago. I said, "Sister Smith, I don't know if you remember me — I'm Diane Grand." Her face lit up, and she replied, "Praise God, Diane, of course I remember you. Tell me, please, how is your brother, John?" I replied, "Well, Sister, he's very well, and in fact he's right here with me." I looked quickly at his face, which once again was filled with the childhood nervousness. When he spoke, I could hardly hold back the tears as he began to talk to her: "Sister, I'm so sorry I gave you a bad time." She stopped him, and said, "No, John, no. It is I who must apologize to you and thank God I've lived long enough to do so. I don't live here anymore and was just visiting this one week. [　C　] John, we just didn't know in those years what we know today about the different ways children learn. Please forgive me for ③what I've done to you." My brother's eyes were now filled with tears as he said, "Sister, there's nothing to forgive. It's not your fault that you had no idea about my disorder. I always knew that you really cared about me. Thank you, Siste－-thank you."

Clearly this was beyond chance or coincidence, and finally we spoke with gratitude for the healing of a painful chapter in life, recognizing it as a tremendous blessing. Four decades would pass before justice would have its due and a (　④　) wrong would be made right. A few months later, we heard that at the end of a long life of service, Sister Smith had died peacefully in her sleep.

(出典：Gerald G.Jampolsky and Diane V.Cirincione 2008. *Finding Our Way Home*－一部改作)

問1　下線部①が指す内容を50字程度の日本語で書け。

問2　次の英文が下線部②で述べられたJohnの理由となるように，（　a　），（　b　)に最も適当な英語を1語ずつ書け。

John would like to (　a　) to Sister Smith for causing her much (　b　).

問3　下線部③の具体的な内容を50字程度の日本語で書け。

問4　本文中の(　④　)に入る最も適当なものを次のア～エから一つ選び，その記号で答えよ。

ア　fully malicious　　イ　over-optimistic
ウ　totally indifferent　エ　well-meaning

問5　次の質問の答を本文の内容に即して65字程度の日本語で書け。

Why didn't John blame Sister Smith for what she had done to him in St. Joseph's Grammer School?

問6　本文中の[　A　]～[　C　]に入る最も適当なものを次のア～カから一つずつ選び，その記号で答えよ。

ア　It's a miracle that you're here.

イ　Surely no one would know us there.

ウ　There must be someone who knows us.

エ　Wouldn't you like to stay here for a couple of days?

オ　It's just a coincidence that I saw you again.

カ　Why don't we take a drive back to the old neighborhood?

(☆☆☆☆◎◎)

【6】次の英文を読んで，後の各問に答えよ。

　During his life, my father, a college professor, taught me many things — an appreciation of beauty, of the natural universe, and especially of plants. But it is learning from his dying that for me remains most profound.

　It was winter when the journey began. Gray skies thudded into the roofs of buildings; without a moment's notice, the word went out that he would no longer be teaching. I watched as his students, stunned by the news of ①his imminent departure, came in solitude, in clumps, in streams to visit him. They were always bringing him gifts, a plant, some flowers, a box of candy, poems, a raft of beautiful cards. His room was filled with these testaments to his love — the love that he had always given and that now, day by day in these homely gifts, was being returned to him.

　One afternoon as I sat in my father's hospital room, one of his favorite students showed up. The young man had been like a son to my father, so dear that he'd often joined us at our family's dinner table. My father had been like a father to him, had loved him with an intelligence of the heart that his own father had always been unable to give him. This young man was torn to pieces to learn that my father was dying.

　The young man greeted my father; then, suddenly realizing he had forgotten the gift he had meant to bring, he went over to my father's bed and, suddenly in anguish, tears flying down his cheeks, said, "I wanted to bring you a gift, but I forgot it! I haven't brought you anything!" He was beside himself with disappointment. I knew he'd wanted to please my father, to bring some delight to the afternoon; but I realized, too, from his wailing, that he had wanted also to bring the charm that could keep my father from dying, the antidote, whatever it was, to my father's imminent death, the hex that could trick the gods and stay the execution. My father looked up at the tearful young man and said in a solid voice of steady grace, a voice filled with love and conviction: "You have brought yourself. [　②　]."

I watched then as the young man, amazed at first by the simple statement, was gradually moved, from shame about his carelessness in having forgotten the gift, to finally having arrived at the tranquil and beautiful state of knowing that he himself was the gift. From where I sat in the hospital room, I realized that I myself had finally arrived in my father's (　③　)－not the rooms where he taught Camus and Shakespeare and Hellenistic culture, but the real (　③　), the cathedral of life, the temple of wisdom.

"④<u>You have brought yourself</u>," my father said. Yes. Yes, of course. "You have brought your self." How perfect. What a beautiful thing to say. How real. How true. What better gift could anyone bring? And if we are the gift, then it behooves us to craft that gift as fine and true as we can, to make ourselves as deep and real, as filled with light, as beating with love, as grand and generous of spirit as our own struggles will allow.

It has been an exquisite, and ⑤<u>at times intensely painful, journey in my own life</u> to know, to believe, and to feel that indeed, the one real gift I can bring is myself. That learning has been a work of the soul; and it continues still; for the lesson of that afternoon was stilettoed into my heart with a sharpness I choose to never forget. Ever since then, in one form or another I keep asking myself, "Who is the self I am bringing? What is the finest, the most loving self I can bring when I show up as myself?"

My father told his student that he had brought himself, that he was the gift. In so doing, he proclaimed the news about the infinite value of a single human being, the preciousness of a single person who authentically present himself.

In so saying, he soothed a young man's heart, and rescued an afternoon. He told this young man, in effect, that although there may be no talisman, no way of staying the execution, the moments in which we stand exactly and only as ourselves in the presence of one another are far stronger than death.

I learned that day the power of simply being myself, of being real, whatever that means in any given moment. I learned that when you are real, there is room for real love; that when you are real, the souls of your brothers and sisters rejoice; when you are real, the consciousness of the world expands. And when you bring your true self, the self you have worked with, you become the vessel in which all other selves can find room and home.

(出典：Andrea Joy Cohen 2008. *A BLESSING IN DISGUISE*－一部改作)

問1　下線部①は具体的に何を意味するか，20字以内の日本語で書け。

問2　本文中の[　②　]に入る最も適当な英文を5語以内で書け。

問3　本文中の2か所の(　③　)に共通して入る最も適当な英語を1語書け。

問4　下線部④のことばにより，父親が生徒に実際に伝えたことはどのようなことだと筆者は述べているか。70字程度の日本語で書け。

問5　次の英文は下線部⑤のように筆者が述べる理由を表している。英文中の(　a　), (　b　)に最も適当な英語を1語ずつ書け。

　　The author has always been asking herself what her real (　a　) should be like and if she has been trying to make (　b　) to be the finest person.

問6　筆者が父親から学んだことを本文に即して90字程度の日本語で書け。

(☆☆☆☆◎◎◎)

解答・解説

【中高共通】

【1】1　ア　　2　ウ　　3　イ　　4　イ　　5　ウ　　6　ア　　7　エ
　　　8　ア　　9　エ　　10　ウ
〈解説〉リスニング問題。男性と女性の会話を聞き取り英語の質問に対し
　　選択肢から正しいものを選ぶオーソドックスな形式。内容も比較的容
　　易。

【2】1　イ　　2　エ　　3　エ　　4　ウ　　5　ウ
〈解説〉語彙に関する空欄補充。　　[inaugural]＝「就任式の」
　　[assessment]＝「評価」

【3】I think it's important to develop students' communication abilities in
English. Globalization has been accelerating international competition and
increasing the necessity of coexistence and cooperation with different cultures
and civilizations. Students who are destined to survive such a world will have
to have discussions with people from other countries on many occasions.
They will be expected to maintain world peace by living in harmony with
people from many nations and cultural backgrounds. This will be carried out
by using English, which is used in most international conferences as an
official language. (90語)
〈解説〉英文エッセイの問題。条件は①賛成か反対かをはっきり述べるこ
　　と，②90語程度で書くことの2点。採点基準として，内容の適切さが
　　10点，論の展開及び分量が10点，語彙・文法の適切さが10点とされて
　　いる。特に論の展開が重要と考えるべき。

【4】1　経験の異なる教師たちが日頃の活動の中でお互いから学び合う
　　場。　　2　教師としての成長を妨げることにつながるので是非とも避

300

けるべきである。　3　Believe in yourself.　　4　危険を冒すことによって起こりうる「失敗」を前向きに受け入れれば，その「失敗」をあらゆる角度から評価でき，次の挑戦に活かせる貴重な体験に変えられるから。　　5　I would like to acquire a better command of English. In order to accomplish this goal, I'm determined to attend at least five professional workshops a year. (27語)

〈解説〉「教員養成」をテーマとする文章についての読解・記述問題。5の英作文では，採点基準として，内容(5点)，分量(5点)，文法・語法(5点)とされている。内容は①長期的目標と短期的目標がリンクしているか，②現実的・具体的目標であるか，の2点から採点される。

【5】1　ページに書かれた各単語が浮き出て見えるので，目を凝らさなければきちんと読むことができなかったこと。　2　(a)　apologize　(b)　trouble　　3　成績が悪かったので，教室の一番後ろの席に座らせて厳しく接したり，学習意欲が低いとみなしたりしたこと。　4　エ　　5　当時自分の障害についてスミス先生が知らなかったのは先生の責任ではないうえに，先生が自分のことをいつも気にかけていたのを知っていたから。　6　A　カ　　B　イ　　C　ア

〈解説〉「失読症(dyslexia)」をテーマとする文章についての読解問題。dyslexiaについての一定の知識を持っていると解答が非常にスムーズになる。日頃から教育関連の知識の増強が求められる。

【6】1　筆者の父親が間もなく亡くなること。　2　You are the gift　3　classroom　4　一人の人間には無限の価値があり，かけがえのないものであるため，誰かが目の前にいてくれることが，どんなものよりも死の恐怖に打ち勝つ力になること。　5　(a)　self　(b)　efforts　6　自分が自分であり，本物であることはどんな状況でも力を持つ。本物であれば，真の愛情を持つことができ，周りの人々を幸せにし，配慮できるような，他のよりどころとなる人間になれること。

〈解説〉「息子が父親から学んだこと」をテーマとする文章についての読

解問題。父親の見舞いに来た教え子が，贈り物を持ってくるのを忘れて悲嘆にくれていたときに，父親が言った言葉。"You brought yourself."「君は君を持ってきたじゃないか」というセリフで息子が何を学んだのかが問われている。

2009年度　実施問題

【中高共通】

【1】聞き取りテスト

　これから1〜10の英語を1回ずつ放送します。それぞれの英語のあとに，その内容について質問を一つします。その質問に対する答として最も適当なものをア〜エの中から一つずつ選び，その記号で答えなさい。

1　M : Look at my cell phone. I can even use it to take photos.

　　W : You must be kidding! That model is out of date already.

　　Question(M) : What does the woman mean?

　　　ア　The cell phone is ahead of the times.

　　　イ　The camera is ahead of the times.

　　　ウ　The cell phone is behind the times.

　　　エ　The camera is behind the times.

2　W : The pasta was delicious, wasn't it? I'd like to have some dessert. I'm going to order a piece of chocolate cake. Would you like one?

　　M : No, I'm fine, thanks. I'll have a cup of coffee, instead.

　　Question(W) : What does the man want to have?

　　　ア　Coffee.　　　　　　　　　　イ　Chocolate cake.

　　　ウ　Coffee and chocolate cake.　　エ　Nothing.

3　W : I hear you went to that recently released movie. How did you like it?

　　M : Well, some people say the story is boring or even trash, but I found it appealing. You should go.

　　Question(W) : What does the man mean?

　　　ア　The movie theater was dirty.

　　　イ　The movie was interesting to him.

　　　ウ　The story was pure fiction.

　　　エ　The story was really boring.

4　M : Excuse me. Would you mind changing places with me so I can sit next to my son?

　　W : No, not at all.

　　Question(M) : What is the woman probably going to do next?

　　　ア　Find a seat for the man.

　　　イ　Stay seated between the man and his son.

　　　ウ　Get a seat next to the man's son.

　　　エ　Move to where the man was seated.

5　W : Now would you briefly explain your job?

　　M : OK. My job is to represent my country in a foreign country. I usually work for an embassy. I always try my best to create a better understanding with the country where I work.

　　Question(W) : What is most likely the man's occupation?

　　　ア　Astronaut.　　イ　Correspondent.　　ウ　Diplomat.

　　　エ　Trader.

6　W : What time does the train for Oxford leave in the morning?

　　M : Well, there's one at 8:00 and another at 10:00.

　　W : I see. Could you tell me how long it takes to get there?

　　M : About three hours.

　　Question(W) : What is the earliest time the woman can arrive in Oxford?

　　　ア　At 10:00 a.m.　　イ　At 11:00 a.m.　　ウ　At 1:00 p.m.

　　　エ　At 2:00 p.m.

7　W : Can I help you?

　　M : Yes, I want this tiepin and that blue tie. How much are they?

　　W : The tiepin is 10 dollars, and the tie is 20 dollars. But if you buy two ties, you get 10 percent off.

　　M : I don't really need more than one for now.

　　Question(W) : How much will the man probably pay?

　　　ア　28 dollars.　　イ　30 dollars.　　ウ　46 dollars.

　　　エ　50 dollars.

8   W : How's your business going?

   M : Pretty well. I'm thinking of opening a new restaurant in our town. What do you think of that?

   W : Well, recently, restaurants have closed their doors one after another. When you start a new business, you need to consider the possible consequences or dangers. I mean ...

   Question(M) : What is the woman most likely to say next?

    ア   you should do as the Romans do.

    イ   you shouldn't cry over spilt milk.

    ウ   you should look before you leap.

    エ   you shouldn't teach an old dog new tricks.

9   (W)For the most part, things are going pretty smoothly right now. One trouble, however, is a two-car accident on the eastbound side of Lane 37, which is causing long delays. Motorists are advised to use alternate routes.

   Question(M) : What is the purpose of this announcement?

    ア   To give traffic conditions.

    イ   To call an ambulance.

    ウ   To inform the police of the accident.

    エ   To provide driver training.

10   (W)On Christmas Day five years ago, Ms. Wilson was really tired of teaching. Some of her difficult students were too much for her to handle. She felt she didn't want to do the job anymore. That day, she got a phone call from one of her former students.

   (M) "Ms. Wilson! I just called to say, 'Thank you.' I'm sorry I gave you such a hard time in class last year. My parents had just gotten divorced, and I was sad. You helped me a lot. I just wanted you to know that."

   (W)Ms. Wilson almost cried. The phone call erased her doubts about teaching. She is enjoying her job now.

   Question(M) : What happened to Ms. Wilson on Christmas Day five

years ago?
- ア　She ignored her difficult students.
- イ　She got divorced and felt miserable.
- ウ　She had to quit her job.
- エ　She was encouraged by her former student.

(☆☆☆◎◎)

【２】次の各文の(　　)に入る最も適当な語(句)をア～エの中から一つず
つ選び，その記号で答えよ。

1　A (　　) is a large collection of written or spoken texts that is used for language research.
- ア　corpus　　イ　doctrine　　ウ　hypothesis　　エ　mythology

2　The old man (　　) as an excellent heart surgeon when he was young.
- ア　is said to be known　　　　イ　is said to have known
- ウ　is said to have been known　　エ　was said to know

3　"The Catcher in the Rye" was written by the author of "(　　)."
- ア　The Great Gatsby　　イ　The Scarlet Letter
- ウ　Franny and Zooey　　エ　Adventures of Huckleberry Finn

4　(　　) is a technique you often use when looking up a word in the encyclopedia or the dictionary.
- ア　Overlapping　　イ　Scanning　　ウ　Shadowing
- エ　Skimming

5　MEXT determines the (　　) as the standard guidelines for all schools, from kindergarten through upper secondary schools, in order to ensure a fixed standard of education throughout the country.
- ア　National Curriculum
- イ　Courses of Study
- ウ　Basic Act on Education
- エ　National Assessment of Academic Ability

(☆☆☆◎◎◎◎)

【3】あなたは，来日したばかりのALTに学校行事について説明する予定である。次の三つのテーマから一つ選び，あなたが話す内容を80語程度の英語で書け。

なお，選んだテーマと使用した語数を記入すること。

○　文化祭

○　始業式

○　クラスマッチ

(☆☆☆◎◎◎)

【4】次の英文を読んで，後の各問に答えよ。

　　Some years ago, I recorded interviews with a large number of teachers and students. I asked them 'What makes a good teacher?' and was interested in their instant responses. A number of the people answered by talking about the teacher's character. As one of them told me, 'I like the teacher who has his own personality and doesn't hide it from the students so he is not only a teacher but a person as well ― and it comes through in the lesson.'

　　Discussing teacher personality is difficult for ①two reasons: in the first place there is no one ideal teacher personality. Some teachers are effective because they are 'larger than life', while others persuade through their quiet authority. But the other problem is that students want not only to see a professional who has come to teach them, but also to glimpse the 'person as well'.

　　Effective teacher personality is a blend between who we really are, and who we are as teachers. In other words, ②teaching is much more than just 'being ourselves'. We have to be able to present a professional face to the students which they find both interesting and effective. When we walk into the classroom, we want them to see someone who looks like a teacher. This does not mean conforming to some kind of teacher stereotype, but rather finding a persona that we adopt when we cross the threshold. We need to ask ourselves what kind of personality we want our students to encounter, and the decisions we take before and during lessons should help to demonstrate that personality. This is not to suggest that we are in any way dishonest about who we are, but we do need to think carefully about how we appear.

Good teachers are able to absorb the unexpected and to use it to their and the students' advantage. This is especially important when the learning outcomes we had planned for look as if they may not succeed because of what is happening. We have to be flexible enough to work with this and change our destination accordingly or find some other way to get there. Or perhaps we have to take a decision to continue what we are doing despite the interruption to the way we imagined things were going to proceed. When students see that their teachers can do ③this, their confidence in their teachers is greatly enhanced.

Part of a good teacher's art is the ability to adopt a number of different roles in the class, depending on what the students are doing. If, for example, teachers always act as (A), standing at the front of the class, dictating everything that happens and being the focus of attention, there will be little chance for students to take much responsibility for their own learning. Being (A) may work for grammar explanations and other information presentation, for instance, but it is less effective for activities where students are working together cooperatively on a project, for example. In such situations we may need to be (B), encouraging students, pushing them to achieve more, feeding in a bit of information or language to help them proceed. At other times, we may need to act as feedback providers: helping students to evaluate their performance, or as (C): telling students how well they have done or giving them grades, etc. We also need to be able to function as a resource: for language information, etc, when students need to consult us and, at times, as a language tutor: that is, an advisor who responds to what the student is doing and advises them on what to do next.

The way we act when we are controlling a class is very different from the listening and advising behavior we will exhibit when we are tutoring students or responding to a presentation or a piece of writing (something that is different, again, from the way we assess a piece of work). Part of our teacher personality, therefore, is our ability to [④   ], but with the same care and ease whichever role we are involved with. This flexibility will help us to facilitate the many different stages and facets of learning.

問1　下線部①の具体的な内容をそれぞれ簡潔な日本語で書け。

問2　下線部②の具体的な内容を50字程度の日本語で書け。

問3　下線部③の具体的な内容を50字程度の日本語で書け。

問4　本文中の(　A　)～(　C　)に入る最も適当な語を次のア～エから選び，その記号で答えよ。

　　ア　assessors　　イ　controllers　　ウ　counselors　　エ　prompters

問5　本文中の[　④　]に5語以上の英語を補い，本文の趣旨に合うように英文を完成させよ。

(☆☆☆◎◎◎)

【中学校】

【1】次の英文を読んで，後の各問に答えよ。

　Recently, we moved into a really old and ugly house. It needs repair really, really badly. I'm embarrassed to say — but it's true — that I was ashamed of it to the point of being envious of other kids who live in nicer houses. My parents say this house is a "good investment" and that in time we'll get everything fixed up. Right now, we have a big monthly mortgage and so we can't afford to give the house, as they call it, "a facelift."

　The only thing nice about the house is the orchard — it has many fruit trees and flowers. When they're in bloom, the whole neighborhood smells wonderful. Still, the orchard doesn't make up for the tattered appearance of the house, ①which is why I've never had any of my friends over.

　One day when my dad was remarking how pretty the fruit trees and roses looked in bloom, I couldn't resist remarking, "Well, no amount of great aroma from the orchard is going to help me become Karen Park's new best friend!" Karen Parks is the most popular girl at school and the coolest. I'd like to be in her circle. I hoped she never saw my house — or I'd definitely never get invited to hang out with her. Karen is what you might say very "status" conscious. If someone isn't really cool according to her standards, well, then Karen Parks isn't much interested in gracing that person with her presence.

②The remark hurt my dad's feeling. Then he asked me if that's why I'd never invited anyone over. "I think I'll wait until the house gets its facelift, Dad," I replied. My dad was quiet for a moment and then in his usual thoughtful demeanor said, "It's all about people. If you create an atmosphere where everyone enjoys themselves, then that's going to be more important to them than the appearance of the house. They'll understand that we just moved in and haven't as yet started repairs." Then he suggested I have a little party in the orchard and to do that in the coming weeks since everything was in full bloom and looked and smelled so nice. He also told me how we could have electricity for music, lights and a hotplate for food, Furthermore he suggested to me how I could earn money I could use to buy anything I needed for the party. His laying out the possible party plans made me feel (　③　) for making the remark I had.

It was a great party and it was obvious that everyone else thought so. Because the house sits on nearly a full acre, we didn't have to be concerned about disturbing the neighbors, so we cranked the music up and played it at full blast. It was great! Everybody danced the entire time. We danced under the stars, amid beautiful blooms that filled the air with an incredible fragrance. It was magical.

I considered the party a huge success! Still, Dad had been right — it's all about people. That night, all of us dancing under the stars in the orchard could have been at the best prom in the world, but ④it wouldn't have topped the mood we created in the orchard. And you know, no one mentioned the appearance of the house, but everyone did comment on what a cool family I had. And of course, everyone said that we should party again very soon —

and in the orchard.

Word got around at school that everyone had missed the "party of the century." I don't know if it was my imagination, but it seemed to me that after that, I'd become pretty popular. Even Karen Parks came up to me and said how sorry she was to have missed the party (she wasn't invited!), ⑤even suggesting that "we" have another one very soon.

And maybe I will. One thing is for sure: I won't be waiting until the house gets its facelift — not for the party, or to have Karen Parks over.

問1　下線部①のwhichが指す内容を日本語で書け。

問2　下線部②のThe remarkが指す内容を日本語で書け。

問3　本文中の(　③　)に入る最も適当な語を次のア〜エから選び，その記号で答えよ。

　　　ア　ashamed　　イ　amazed　　ウ　excited　　エ　relieved

問4　下線部④をitが指す内容を明らかにして和訳せよ。

問5　次の英文は下線部⑤における筆者の心情を表している。この英文の(　　)に入る1語を本文中から選んで書け。

　　　"I wanted to be Karen's best friend before, but now Karen wants to be in my (　　)."

問6　この話の中で，筆者は父親からどのようなことを学んだか，40字程度の日本語で書け。

(☆☆☆◎◎◎)

【高等学校】

【1】次の英文を読んで，後の各問に答えよ。

　　As Larry Morris, a 39-year-old security guard and father of six, folded his six-foot frame into a desk made for 14-year-olds, his knees knocked against the desk rim and his back crouched stiffly in his seat. It had been 22 years since he last sat in a classroom and carried a book bag. He dropped out of high school at 17 and in those 22 years, he had six sons and two wives. He held minimum-wage jobs but was rejected for better-paying work because he had no (　①　). He decided he would never get anywhere unless he finished high school. So now he is a high school sophomore again, taking notes in geometry or physical science, walking the same halls where he hung out as a teenager, attending the same school as his 17-year-old son Jermaine.

Mr. Morris and six other older dropouts have returned to DuSable High School, the only school in the country with a program that allows parents to enroll with their children and get the diplomas they regretted not earning. As a condition of their enrollment, the parents must follow the rules like any other student.

The parents are easy to spot. They are the ones huffing and puffing up the stairs while teenagers bounce past them. They were like these teenagers 20 years ago, sneaking a smoke in the restroom, and primping and flirting at their lockers before the bell. Now, that is all behind them. ②They are all business. They sit rapt, front and center, copying down assignments as if their rent check depended on it, sometimes bored because they already did next month's homework.

The parents turned out to be model students. "When you ask for a report of a page, they do 10 pages," an English teacher said. They bring calm and wisdom to the building, and students are less likely to misbehave when the parents are around. "I don't want to be cursing and acting silly around them," said Alex Lee, a 17-year-old senior.

The parents try hard not ③to play teacher's pet. After all, they were hardly that the first time. But sometimes they can't help themselves. In his work-study class, Mr. Morris could not resist raising his hand when a student angrily complained that he's had to wait an hour for a job interview. Mr. Morris told the student that those things happen sometimes and that people should not let it stop them from trying. Then, Mr. Morris started talking about the times he got the runaround looking for work, and another parent in the class shook her head in agreement. "Here they go again," a couple of students said, elbowing each other. Since then, the parents have learned not to say things like, "I have a son your age," or, "When I was a teenager...."

The school has tried to prevent some teenage angst by not permitting parents and their children in the same classroom. But it still can put a cramp on a teenager's social life. When the parents first arrived, some students made fun of them, pointing and demanding an explanation. They asked, "What are you doing here?" or, "Aren't you a little too old to be in school?" "It's as if the kids were saying: [④   ]" said Mrs. Wills, the work-study teacher.

At times the resentment has turned ugly. The other day, Ms. Fulton, who never learned to read well before and is now struggling to learn, stumbled over some words when reading aloud in class. "She can't read," shouted a boy in the back. "That's the reason I'm here," Ms. Fulton said. "If you were a kind person, you wouldn't sit and criticize me. You would help me." The tears welled in her eyes. Mr. Morris, sitting beside her, put his arm around her and said: "It's going to be all right. You know you have to expect that here."

The parents are (⑤) that dropping out is not glamorous. Like reformed smokers, they step in when they see students making the same mistakes they did. When a parent saw a classmate sneaking out of class to be with her boyfriend, the parent told her: "You don't need to do that. I did that. That's why I'm still here."

The current class passed its first milestone last week when report card came out. All the parents did far better than they did the first time around.

問1　本文中の(　①　)に入れるのに最も適当な語を本文中より1語抜き出し，適切な形で書け。

問2　下線部②の内容を具体的に30字程度の日本語で書け。

問3　下線部③は具体的にどのような行動を指すか，Mr.Morrisの例を参考に日本語で書け。

問4　本文中の[　④　]に入る最も適当な文を次のア～エから選び，その記号で答えよ。

　　ア　'They are cool. We want to be like them.'

イ　'This is our domain. Can't we have anything to ourselves?'

ウ　'Our school has altered. Should we change?'

エ　'Welcome to our school. We can do something good with you!'

問5　本文中の(　⑤　)に入れるのに最も適当な語句を次のア～エから選び，その記号で答えよ。

ア walking dictionaries　　イ critical information　　ウ suspicious facts

エ living proof

問6　あなたが本文中に出てくるような学校の教師ならば，どのような工夫をするか。本文に出てくる事例を参考にして40語程度の英語で書け。なお，使用した語数も書くこと。

(☆☆☆◎◎◎)

解答・解説

【中高共通】

【1】1　ウ　　2　ア　　3　イ　　4　エ　　5　ウ　　6　イ　　7　イ

8　ウ　　9　ア　　10　エ

〈解説〉1　女性の発言にThat model is out of date already. とある。behind the timesはout of dateの言い換えである。　2　男性の発言にI'll have a cup of coffee, insteadとある。Insteadの後にof a piece of chocolate cakeが省略されている。　3　男性の発言にbut I found it appealing. とある。interestingはappealingを言い換えである。　4　Do you mind + ～ing ?「～していただけますか。」No, not at all.「いいですよ。」　5　男性の発言にMy job is to represent my country in a foreign country. とあり，embassy「大使館」からも外交官だと分かる。　6　男性の発言にthere's one at 8:00やAbout three hoursとある。　7　女性の発言にThe tiepin is 10 dollars, and the tie is 20 dollars. とあり，男性がI don't really need more than one for nowと女性の提案を断っている。　8　女性の発言にWhen you

start a new business, you need to consider the possible consequences or dangers. とあり，注意を促していると分かる。leap「飛躍する」
9　英文は道路が混雑している状況を伝えている。　10　女性の発言にThe phone call erased her doubts about teaching.とあり，教職への熱意を取り戻したと分かる。

【2】1　ア　　2　ウ　　3　ウ　　4　イ　　5　イ
〈解説〉1　corpus「全集」　　2　be known as ～「～として知られている」
過去を表す副詞節(when he was young)より，過去の出来事について現在，述べていると分かる。　3　"Catcher in the Rye"と"Franny and Zooey"は共にサリンジャーの著書である。　4　scanning「本のページを走り読みし，目的の語句を探すこと」　　5　MEXT＝The Ministry of Education, Culture, Sports, Science, and Technology「文部科学省」
Course of Study「学習指導要領」

【3】選んだテーマ　文化祭　　This is one of the students' favorite school events. Some clubs such as brass band or the tea ceremony club present what they have been practicing. Also, the second year students sell things they make by themselves, and the third graders do some performances on the stage. Last year a famous Japanese period play was performed in English by the third year students, and many people enjoyed it. I hope you will join the students and enjoy the festival.

【4】1　一つの理想的な教師像というものがないということ。　生徒たちは教師にただ教える専門家ではなく人間らしさも垣間見たいと思っていること。　2　自分らしさを維持しながらも，生徒に見せる教師像ということも考えて演ずることも必要であるということ。(49字)
3　突発的な事態に対して，柔軟に対応し，所期の目的あるいはそこで変更した目的に向かって生徒を導いていくこと。(52字)
4　A　イ　　B　エ　　C　ア　　5　perform all these roles at different

times

〈解説〉1　：「つまり，」は同格の役割があるので，two reasons＝in the first place以下の文となる。in the first place「第一に，」the other problem is「他方の問題は」とあり，理由が順次，述べられている。　2　第三段落の下線②以降に詳しく述べられている。　3　第四段落の下線③以前に述べられている。　4　A　空欄以降に，standing at 〜 of attention, とあり，教師が授業を一方的に進める様子がteachers always act as controllersの具体例として述べられている。　B　空欄以降に，encouraging students,〜 them proceed.とあり，教師が生徒の学習を支援することがbe promotersの具体例として述べられている。　C　空欄以降に，: telling students 〜 grades, etc.とあり，教師が生徒の学習を評価することがassessorsの役割として述べられている。　5　第六段落にThe way 〜 of writingとあり，指導の目的に応じて生徒へ指導の仕方も違うことが分かる。述べられた様々な指導の仕方が，空欄以降でwhichever roleと表現されている。

【中学校】

【1】1　果樹園が素晴らしくても，家自体が古くて見栄えを良くないことはどうしようもないこと。　2　「果樹園からどんなによい香りがしても，カレンと仲良くなれるわけではない。」という私の言葉。
3　ア　　4　世界最高のパーティーでも，私達が果樹園の中に作り出した楽しい不雰囲気にはかなわなかったでしょう。　5　circle
6　何事も心構えが大切であり，見かけは悪くても工夫次第でみんなが楽しめる雰囲気を作れること。

〈解説〉1　, which は非制限用法，関係代名詞の主格。先行詞は前文Still, the 〜 the house,である。　2　The remark hurt my dad's feeling.とあり，The remarkとは父の耳に入った私の意見だと分かる。第三段落 "Well, no 〜 best friend!" はその意見である。　3　His laying out the possible party plansとは同段落中盤のhe suggested 以降に述べられ内容である。暮らしを悲観している娘とは対照的に父は精一杯，娘のために働きか

けていることがわかる。　4　前文にall of 〜 the world, とあり，果樹園
の星空の下でのダンスパーティーそのものが最高に楽しかったと分か
る。　5　下線のweとはカレンと主人公が同じ仲間であること表す。
6　主人公は父の提案により，夢にも思わなかった楽しい時間を過ご
すことができ，感激した。

【高等学校】

【1】1　diploma　　2　真剣な態度で授業に臨み，課題などへの取り組
みも熱心である。　　3　不平を言う十代の生徒に対して，自分の経験
談を持ち出し，説教めいたことを言ってたしなめること。　4　イ

5　エ　　6　I want to encourage adult students to make speeches about
their experiences or their social knowledge at every opportunity. This not
only enables younger students to learn a lot about people and society but also
helps adult students to keep their pride. (42語)

〈解説〉　第1段落に，He dropped 〜 two wives. He held 〜 no (　①　).と
あり，モリス氏は17歳で高校を中退し，あるものが欠けている理由か
ら良い仕事に就けないと分かる。第2段落にa program 〜 not earning.と
あり，モリス氏が参加している過程は親が子供達と共に通学し，取得
せず後悔した卒業資格を得るためのものだと分かる。　2　同段落の下
線②以降に述べられている。　3　第5段落にMr. Morris 〜 from trying.
Then Mr. Morris 〜 in agreement.とあり，モリス氏の具体的な振る舞い
が分かる。　4　子ども達の言葉 "What are 〜 in school?" より，学校は
子ども達だけの場所であると主張していると分かる。　5　喫煙行為や
授業離脱をやめさせる際に親達が I did that. That's why I'm still here.と述
べたことから分かる。　6　私は，親たちに自らの経験や社会的な知識
を子ども達に伝えるよう促したい。これは，子ども達自身が学ぶだけ
でなく，親たちが誇りを持ち続けることを応援する態度に繋がるだろ
う。

2008年度　実施問題

【中高共通】

【１】聞き取りテスト

　　これから１〜10の英語(うち１〜７は対話文)を１回ずつ放送します。そ
れぞれの英語のあとに，その内容について質問を一つします。その質
問に対する答として最も適当なものをア〜エの中から〜つずつ選び，
その記号で答えなさい。

1　ア　He doesn't want to talk about it anymore.
　　イ　He thinks the same way.
　　ウ　He wanted to eat a piece of cake.
　　エ　He found it very easy.

2　ア　Help his grandmother.　　　　イ　Have his birthday party.
　　ウ　Buy another DVD player.　　　エ　Look for a present.

3　ア　He caught a bad cold.　　　　　イ　He had urgent business.
　　ウ　He couldn't stand the weather.　エ　He didn't have any money.

4　ア　He has nothing to do with the report.
　　イ　He could have helped the woman.
　　ウ　He thought that the woman was sick.
　　エ　He is happy not to be asked.

5　ア　Leave the hotel for a while.　　イ　Fix the air conditioner himself.
　　ウ　Read a book.　　　　　　　　エ　Change hotel rooms.

6　ア　At 10:45.　　　　　　　　　　イ　At 10:55.
　　ウ　At 11:15.　　　　　　　　　　エ　At 11:25.

7　ア　A carpenter.　　　　　　　　　イ　A dentist.
　　ウ　A mechanic.　　　　　　　　　エ　A psychologist.

8　ア　12 dollars.　　　　　　　　　　イ　17 dollars.
　　ウ　19 dollars.　　　　　　　　　エ　21 dollars.

9 ア　Because he was addicted to them.

　イ　Because his father liked to watch movies.

　ウ　Because he didn't like them.

　エ　Because his father didn't let him watch them.

10 ア　Go to college to study architecture.

　イ　Start working as an architect.

　ウ　Study art at his high school.

　エ　Travel to Spain to study Spanish.

(☆☆☆○○○)

【2】次の各文の(　　)に入れるのに最も適当なものを，ア〜エの中から一つずつ選び，その記号で答えよ。

1　Any letter of the English alphabet except a, e, i, o and u is called a (　　).

　ア　consonant　　イ　pronoun　　ウ　syllable　　エ　vowel

2　A (　　) is a story aired several times a week on television or radio about the lives and problems of a group of people.

　ア　fairy tale　　イ　prime time　　ウ　soap opera

　エ　television bug

3　The author of *Dr.Jekyll and Mr.Hyde* also wrote (　　).

　ア　Paradise Lost　　イ　Treasure Island　　ウ　A Christmas Carol

　エ　East of Eden

4　The use of a computer in teaching and learning a second or foreign language is called (　　).

　ア　CLT　　イ　CALL　　ウ　TPR　　エ　TEFL

5　The old man felt so dizzy that he (　　) down on a sofa.

　ア　lie　　イ　lied　　ウ　laid　　エ　lay

(☆☆○○○)

【3】あなたは，授業で自分の好きな絵や写真，大切にしている身の回りのものなどを見せて，それについて英語で語る"Show and Tell"の活動

を行わせる予定である。生徒にモデルを示すとしたら，どのような原稿を作成するか。生徒に見せるものを英語で記入し，80語程度の英語で具体的に書け。ただし，使用した語数も書くこと。

(☆☆○○○)

【４】次の英文を読んで，後の各問に答えよ。

　Teachers often talk about a particular class being difficult, but it is most likely that the problems are caused by a small number of children whose influence is gradually becoming pervasive. It is generally only when we do nothing to address this problem that the whole class becomes involved. Most children want the security that comes from effective teacher control, but do not have enough experience in life to know how to avoid confrontation when things start to move in a (　①　) direction, and do not know how to positively influence the behavior of other children. As adults, we have much more experience in life, and, if we use this experience well, we can avoid individual problems becoming class problems.

　Once a whole-class problem has developed, we need to develop strategies and set goals to work towards solutions. The answer, if there is one, usually involves dealing with the individual problems of the children who were the initial cause of the class problem, making real human contact with children who are charismatic or respected by the other children, and getting the class refocused on learning English.

　I remember taking over a class that was complete chaos. Almost all of the children were badly behaved, and they were not focused on learning English at all. One or two children spent most of the time running around the room, others would jump on the tables, and some would sit silently. It was (　②　).

　I had tried every means to have the control over the class, but I still could not make enough progress. I could not find the catalyst that would refocus the class. There is usually some activity that sparks a change in the attitude of the class, but I could not find it.

Then one day, the class was having a party with some other classes. All of the classes were in a large room, and they were all playing different games. My class was playing the Fish Race game. In this game, each of the children draws a fish on a piece of paper, cuts out the fish and puts it on the floor behind a starting line. Each child then flaps behind her fish with a magazine or a notebook, and tries to move her fish forwards. This was the first time I had seen the class working (③) on an activity.

Just before the next lesson, I sat at a table in the classroom and had pieces of paper, scissors, and colored pencils in front of me. When the children entered the room and started running around and jumping up and down, I ignored them. I just smiled happily and concentrated on making a fish. After a little while, one or two of the children came over to see what I was doing. They were curious. They soon realized I was drawing a fish, and got excited because of their memories of the party. They were soon all excitedly asking to play the fish race game, and finally, when I said, "OK." They were very pleased.

Each of them made a fish. I then looked around the room and scratched my head, wondering how we were going to play with all the desks and chairs in the way. They saw the problem, and quickly realized they needed to clear them. It was the first time I had seen them cooperate and tidy the room! I then looked worried, pointing at the number of children, and the width of the room. They realized they could not all flap their fish at one time, and suggested teams.

At this point, they were (④), and pleased with me enough, for me to be able to introduce an extra rule.

[⑤   ]

They came to realize in this game that learning English and having fun could be one and the same thing, and the new words actually made the game more interesting. Their behavior did not change overnight. It took time, but I had found the catalyst.

321

1　本文中の(　①　)～(　④　)に入る最も適当な語を次のア～カから選び，その記号で答えよ。
ア　anarchy　イ　democracy　ウ　negative　エ　positive
オ　together　カ　reluctantly

2　クラス全体が手に負えなくなったとき，一般的にどう対処すればよいか，本文に即して60字程度の日本語で書け。

3　筆者のクラスの生徒が，自分のクラスで下線部the Fish Race gameを行ったときに気付いたことを三つ，本文に即してそれぞれ30字程度の日本語で書け。

4　次の英文は[　⑤　]の内容である。下線部the Fish Race gameに筆者が追加したルールとなるよう，本文に即して〔　A　〕,〔　B　〕に10語程度の英語を入れて完成させよ。

　　This game is a relay race. One of your teammates stands at a distance from the rest of your team with a pile of flash cards and shows you one of the cards that has a new word on it. You can flap your fish once if 〔　A　〕. If you cannot answer, you can ask your teammates or the teacher and then flap your fish once. After you come to the goal by doing so, other members on your team do the same one by one. The team 〔　B　〕 wins.

(☆☆☆◎◎◎)

【中学校】

【1】次の英文を読んで，後の各問に答えよ。

　　When I was fifteen, my mother suggested that I think about going to boarding school. At that time she was searching for a new husband, and I wasn't cooperating. She felt so guilty about leaving me home alone that she kept inviting me to join in all the fun.

　　Then one day she asked me if I'd like to go away to school. "I've heard of a boarding school, the Scarborough School. It's near home. It's supposed to be very progressive. You'd come home on weekends. Perhaps you'd be happier there." [　①　], but decided that it wasn't a bad idea.

The morning I arrived I was assigned to share a room with four other girls. I'd expected to have my own room. I just sat on my bed and listened to them gab. They were old timers.

The first night in boarding school was one of the loneliest in my life. That evening, we all walked to the school cafeteria for dinner. Students were given assigned seats, and one of the teaching staff was at each table. When I came back with my tray, I sat down next to Mrs. Edith Robinson. I remember her curly gray hair, her plaid skirt, her hazel eyes that seemed inquisitive in a nice way. I played with my food. "Where is your home?" Mrs. Robinson asked. "Manhattan," I said. I could hardly get the word out. "Oh, that's fortunate. You'll be able to go home on weekends." I nodded. My dessert was in front of me, but I couldn't eat it. I was convinced that 〔   ②   〕. Tears dripped down my face. The more I tried to wipe them away, the faster they flowed.

"I teach third grade," Mrs. Robinson said as she handed me a tissue. "There's a little girl in my class whose name is Elizabeth and who's always had a hard time reading. I wonder if you'd consider tutoring her. I think she's scared of grownups. Do you have free time, say at three o'clock, to come to my room and help her?" "I can try." Three o'clock! That was the hour I dreaded. Classes would be over. ③Who should I talk to? What else did I have to do?

The next day and every afternoon after that, I rushed to Mrs. Robinson's third-grade room. There, Elizabeth and I sat on a blue couch in the back of the room while Mrs. Robinson worked at her desk and occasionally chatted with us. Often I stayed even later, chatting with Mrs. Robinson, confiding my thoughts and worries as I erased the board and straightened the desks. Within a month, Elizabeth had started to read. That gave me new confidence. One afternoon, ④I realized I'd made three new girlfriends.

Right before summer vacation, my mother called with a big surprise. She was going to sign me up for Elizabeth Arden's Charm School. They'd teach me about things like good grooming and posture, and I'd make lots of friends.

"I have lots of friends," I argued. "And I don't want to be charming." "That's just the reason you need to go." My mother was (A) with my attitude; I hadn't appreciated her great idea. "I won't go and you can't make me!"

In the days that followed, my mother backed off and let me stay. ⑤It wasn't until years later that I learned that Mrs. Robinson had written to my mother and explained how much I had matured. I was a beautiful girl now, she said, and had good friends. Perhaps my mother hadn't realized that I'd changed during my sophomore year at Scarborough.

My mother complained to the principal, but he managed to calm her down. I never knew what words passed between him and Mrs. Robinson, but I realized that ⑥my mentor had put her job on the line.

After I graduated from Scarborough School, I attended the University of Colorado, and Mrs. Robinson and I corresponded for many years. After college, I got my degree in special education, working with emotionally disturbed children. I lost track of Mrs. Robinson after I married and had children of my own. My attempts to find her were fruitless. The school had changed hands many times and had no records of her whereabouts. But my good (B) of her remain with me.

1　次の英文が[①]の内容になるよう，次の(a)～(d)に入る最も適当な語(句)を下から一つずつ選び，記号で答えよ。

I worried about (a) (b) and (c) (d) in

ア　not　　イ　my friends　　ウ　fitting　　エ　missing

オ　living

2　〔 ② 〕に入る最も適当な表現を次のア～ウの中から一つ選び，記号で答えよ。

ア　I had a terrible stomachache

イ　I had made the wrong decision

ウ　I was reminded of my new father

3　次の英文は下線部③と④における筆者の心情の変化を表している。(a)～(c)に入る最も適当な語を1語ずつ書け。

I felt lonely at first because I couldn't (　a　) myself to the new environment. But thanks to Mrs.Robinson's offer to tutor Elizabeth, I became (　b　) in myself. Finally I made some friends and was (　c　) from loneliness.

4　下線部⑤を和訳せよ。

5　下線部⑥の意味を表すのに最も適当なものを次のア～ウの中から一つ選び，記号で答えよ。

　ア　My principal had made Mrs.Robinson quit her job.

　イ　Mrs.Robinson had taken a risk and she might have lost her job.

　ウ　My mother had tried complaining to the principal in order to protect me.

6　(　A　)，(　B　)に入る最も適当な語を1語ずつ書け。

7　あなたはこの話を通して生徒にどのようなことを伝えたいか，50字程度の日本語で書け。

(☆☆☆◎◎◎)

【高等学校】

【1】次の英文を読んで，後の各問に答えよ。

　A red-headed boy was struggling with tests in my sophomore woodworking class. Pat was one of my most enthusiastic students, and I wondered why he was having so much trouble. I discovered the cause of his problems one day when I asked him to check a posted message in the attendance office and to report the information back to me. He walked slowly out of the room and came back in a few minutes. With tears in his eyes, he said, "Mr. Malsam, I will do anything for you, but don't ask me to read anything." Pat lowered his head and confessed that ①he was illiterate.

　I could hardly believe that he had progressed to the sophomore year of high school and not learned to read. Apparently, he had managed to get through school by (　②　) the teachers' words in the classroom and verbally repeating them back. I don't know how he was able to complete the written work and tests necessary to pass his academic classes, but I suspect he was simply "passed on." After I discovered he could not read, I had my student assistant read the multiple-choice test questions to him at test time and circle the answers he gave. If I had the time, I sometimes pulled him aside and read the test questions to him, scoring his test answers on the spot.

Over the next two years, I learned more about Pat as he continued to take my industrial arts classes. He told me his father had been an electrician and that he'd seen his father accidentally electrocuted and killed. Pat was only five years old at the time. I wondered whether the trauma of seeing his father die and the difficult years that followed, at a time when most kids are learning to read, might have caused or at least contributed to Pat's reading deficiency. I tried harder to teach Pat more about woodworking. He was an eager learner and earned As in my classes and in other industrial arts classes, but he continued to receive poor grades in his academic classes.

One summer, I took Pat and my son on a fishing trip in the mountains. Another time he went with us on an overnight trip to gather wood in the mountains. We became friends, and I think I became somewhat of a substitute (③) for him.

At the end of his senior year, Pat had managed to earn enough credits to graduate from high school. Every year before graduation, teachers in each department select an outstanding student in their academic area. These students, along with scholarship winners and outstanding athletes, are recognized at a special senior awards night. The teachers in our industrial arts department agreed that Pat should receive the outstanding industrial arts student award, because he had demonstrated remarkable improvement and proficiency in all his industrial arts classes. Not only was Pat adept in these classes, he was also very good at assisting other students and helping them set up machines safely. Some of the school's counselors, having earmarked Pat as a slow student, objected to giving him the industrial arts achievement award. ④We insisted that his name be retained on the list for our award, and it was.

At the ceremony, after all the students had received their awards, Pat suddenly stood up. "I can't sit here any longer. There is something I have to say. I haven't gotten any scholarships, but I have earned a high school diploma like everyone else. I never would have gotten this far if it hadn't been for one teacher who took extra time to work with me and who encouraged me when I became discouraged in other classes." He paused. "That teacher is Mr. Malsam." Teachers, parents, and students applauded his impromptu speech. I was stunned at receiving the unexpected public recognition and surprised that this shy young man had the courage to speak so eloquently. It was one of the most (⑤) moments in my twenty-seven-year teaching career.

It has been nearly twenty years since Pat stood up to praise me at the senior awards ceremony. I'm retired now from teaching, but he still occasionally calls or stops by my home to see me. [⑥] but I suspect he learned minimal reading skills on the job. I do know that he continues to work enthusiastically and capably as the school district's head carpenter.

1 下線部①について，その原因として筆者が考えていることを40字程度の日本語で書け。
2 本文中の(②)，(⑤)に入る最も適当な語(句)をそれぞれア〜エの中から一つずつ選び，その記号で答えよ。
 (②): ア deleting イ memorizing ウ looking for
 エ noting down
 (⑤): ア boring イ disgusting ウ promising
 エ rewarding
3 本文中の(③)に入る最も適当な語を1語書け。
4 下線部④の理由を40字程度の日本語で書け。
5 次の英文が[⑥]に入るようにア〜キを並べかえよ。ただし，答えは(a)，(b)に入る語(句)の記号で書け。
I don't know how well he learned to read ( )(a)( )( )( )(b)( )
after graduating from high school

327

ア　better than　　イ　expected　　ウ　had　　エ　I　　オ　if he
カ　learned　　キ　to read

6　Patのように学業上の問題を抱えている生徒に対して，あなたは教
師としてどのような手だてを講じるか，40語程度の英語で書け。た
だし，使用した語数も書くこと。

(☆☆☆◎◎◎)

解答・解説

【中高共通】

【1】1　エ　　2　ア　　3　ウ　　4　イ　　5　ア　　6　イ　　7　イ
8　ウ　9　エ　　10　ア
〈解説〉択一形式なので，質問を良く聞き取ること。特に数字は聞き間違
いが多いので注意する。

【2】1　ア　　2　ウ　　3　イ　　4　イ　　5　エ
〈解説〉1　a，e，i，o，u以外の文字の名前を聞いているので，「子音」
が正解。　2　「テレビやラジオで1週間に数回放送される，人々の生活
や問題についての話」とは，「連続ドラマ」のことである。　3　「ジキ
ル博士とハイド氏」を書いた作者はイギリス人のスティーブンソン。
他の著書に，「宝島」がある。　4　computer assisted language learningの
頭文字をとったもの。「コンピュータ利用の外国語学習」のこと。
5　「その老人はあまりにめまいがしたので，ソファーの上に横たわっ
た」という意味。ここでは自動詞のlieの過去形を入れる。他動詞layは
「横たえる」という意味で，過去形はlaidとなることに注意する。

【3】(見せるもの)　My baseball bat　(原稿)　This baseball bat belonged to
my brother. He used it when he first started playing baseball. He became a

famous player and many people know who he is. He gave this bat when I was twelve years old. He told me never to give up my dream. When I look at this bat, I am inspired by my brother. I want to work hard in the future so that I can realize my dream like my brother.　(77語)

〈解説〉見せるものが自分にとってどのような価値のものなのかを，具体的に説明する。それにまつわる出来事や思い出なども含めると，話の内容に厚みが出てくる。

【4】1　①　ウ　　②　ア　　③　オ　　④　エ　　2　他の生徒からの信望が厚く，また尊敬されている生徒と信頼関係を築き，根本的な原因となっている子どもたちの個人的な悩み等に対処する。

3　・机やイスがゲームの邪魔になるので，隅に片づける必要がある。・部屋の大きさの割に人数が多く，同時に遊べないので，チームで競う。　・楽しみながら英語を学ぶことができ，新出語がゲームをより面白くする。　4　A　you give the correct meaning of the word shown

B　that gets all of its members to the goal fastest

〈解説〉1　①　後ろが名詞であることから，形容詞が入る。「対立」という語が同じ文章にあるので，「否定的な」方向であることがわかる。②　子どもたちが好き勝手に行動しているのは，「無秩序」状態である。　③　1つの行動にクラスが「一緒に」動いている様子がわかる。④　ゲームをやろうとする子どもたちは「前向き」であった。

2　第2段落の最初で「問題が起きたら」と質問を投げかけ，2行目で「その答えは」と書き始めている。　3　第7段落目以降は，子どもたちがゲームをするために動く様子と，それによって私が気づいた点が書かれている。　4　A　新出単語がカードに書いてあることから，その意味を言わせるルールにする。　B　チームが勝つには，メンバー全員が早く作業をすることが条件である。

【中学校】

【1】1 a エ　　b イ　　c ア　　d ウ　　2 イ　　3 a adjust
b confident　　c free　　4 数年経って初めて，私は，ロビンソン
先生が私の母に手紙を書き，私がどれくらい成長してきたかを説明し
ていたことが分かった。　　5 イ　　6 A angry　　B memories
7 私たちは生きている限り様々な困難に必ず直面するが，それから
逃げず，乗り越えなければならないということ。

〈解説〉1 「私は，友だちがいなくて寂しいし，なじめないと心配した」
という意味になる。動名詞を否定するときは直前にnotを置く。fit in
「なじむ」　　2 直後に，「涙がポタポタたれた」という文章がある
ことから，「学校選択を間違ったと悟った」のだとわかる。　　3 最初
は新しい環境に順応できなかったが，ロビンソン先生のおかげで，自
分に自信がついた。そしてとうとう友だちもできて孤独から解放され
た。adjust oneself to ～「～に順応する」　confident in oneself「自信が
ある」　free from ～「～から解放する」　　4 It wasn't until … that～
「…になって初めて～した」mature「十分に成長した」　　5 直訳は
「私の師は仕事を危険にさらされていた」で，仕事を失いかけてはい
たが，やめさせられたわけではなかった。　　6 A 思い通りにならな
かったので，母は私の態度に「怒った」。　　B 音信不通になってしま
ったが，先生とのいい「思い出」は私の中に残っている。思い出がい
くつかあるので，複数形になる点に注意する。　　7 筆者の体験を通
して，考えさせられることをまとめる。

【高等学校】

【1】1 読むことを覚える時期に，父親が事故で亡くなるのを目撃し，
その後つらい年月を過ごしたため。　　2 ② イ　　⑤ エ　　3 father
4 工芸の授業において，技術面はもちろんのこと，人間性も非常に
優れていたから。　　5 a カ　　b ウ　　6 I would try to bring out
the best points in my students. When they faced difficulties, I would give easy
and interesting explanations of the material they find confusing. When they

understood, I would praise them so they would have confidence in themselves. (43語)

〈解説〉1　第3段落で，筆者がパットについてもっと知るようになって，彼の父の死が原因ではないかと考えた。　2　②　note down「書き留める」では，書いたものをその後で読み返すという作業ができないので，不適切。　⑤　思いもかけなかったパットのスピーチのおかげで，教師生活で最も「報われる」瞬間を経験したのである。disgusting「実に嫌な」promising「見込みのある」　3　パットとあちこちに出かけるなど，ちょっとした「父親」代わりだった。somewhat of ～「ちょっとした～」substitute「代わりの」　4　前の部分に書かれている。パットは他の生徒達をよく手伝っていた。そこで，何人かのカウンセラーは反対したが，筆者達は固執したのである。　5　if he learned to read better than I had expectedの語順になる。　6　どんな生徒でも，得意な分野があるはずだから，それを見つけて，そこを突破口にして，興味の対象を広げていく。生徒とじっくり向き合うことが大切である。褒めて伸ばすことも重要である。

●書籍内容の訂正等について

　弊社では教員採用試験対策シリーズ（参考書，過去問，全国まるごと過去問題集），公務員試験対策シリーズ，公立幼稚園・保育士試験対策シリーズ，会社別就職試験対策シリーズについて，正誤表をホームページ（https://www.kyodo-s.jp）に掲載いたします。内容に訂正等，疑問点がございましたら，まずホームページをご確認ください。もし，正誤表に掲載されていない訂正等，疑問点がございましたら，下記項目をご記入の上，以下の送付先までお送りいただくようお願いいたします。

> ① **書籍名，都道府県（学校）名，年度**
> 　（例：教員採用試験過去問シリーズ　小学校教諭 過去問　2025年度版）
> ② **ページ数**（書籍に記載されているページ数をご記入ください。）
> ③ **訂正等，疑問点**（内容は具体的にご記入ください。）
> 　（例：問題文では"ア～オの中から選べ"とあるが，選択肢はエまでしかない）

〔ご注意〕
○ 電話での質問や相談等につきましては，受付けておりません。ご注意ください。
○ 正誤表の更新は適宜行います。
○ いただいた疑問点につきましては，当社編集制作部で検討の上，正誤表への反映を決定させていただきます（個別回答は，原則行いませんのであしからずご了承ください）。

●情報提供のお願い

　協同教育研究会では，これから教員採用試験を受験される方々に，より正確な問題を，より多くご提供できるよう情報の収集を行っております。つきましては，教員採用試験に関する次の項目の情報を，以下の送付先までお送りいただけますと幸いでございます。お送りいただきました方には謝礼を差し上げます。
（情報量があまりに少ない場合は，謝礼をご用意できかねる場合があります）。

◆あなたの受験された面接試験，論作文試験の実施方法や質問内容
◆教員採用試験の受験体験記

送付先	○電子メール：edit@kyodo-s.jp
	○FAX：03-3233-1233（協同出版株式会社　編集制作部 行）
	○郵送：〒101-0054　東京都千代田区神田錦町2-5
	協同出版株式会社　編集制作部 行
	○HP：https://kyodo-s.jp/provision（右記のQRコードからもアクセスできます）

　※謝礼をお送りする関係から，いずれの方法でお送りいただく際にも，「お名前」「ご住所」は，必ず明記いただきますよう，よろしくお願い申し上げます。

教員採用試験「過去問」シリーズ

鹿児島県の
英語科 過去問

編　集　Ⓒ 協同教育研究会
発　行　令和5年11月10日
発行者　小貫　輝雄
発行所　協同出版株式会社
　　　　〒101-0054　東京都千代田区神田錦町2‐5
　　　　電話　03－3295－1341
　　　　振替　東京00190－4－94061
印刷所　協同出版・POD工場

落丁・乱丁はお取り替えいたします。